Understanding Philanthropy

Philanthropy and Nonprofit Studies

Dwight F. Burlingame and David C. Hammack, editors

Understanding Philanthropy

Its Meaning and Mission

Robert L. Payton and Michael P. Moody

Indiana University Press
Bloomington and Indianapolis

This book is a publication of

Indiana University Press
Office of Scholarly Publishing
Herman B Wells Library 350
1320 East 10th Street
Bloomington, Indiana 47405 USA

The paper used in this publication meets the minimum
requirements of American National Standard for
Information Sciences—Permanence of Paper for
Printed Library Materials, ANSI Z39.48-1984.

Manufactured in the United States of America

Library of Congress Cataloging-in-Publication Data

Payton, Robert L.
  Understanding philanthropy : its meaning and mission /
Robert L. Payton and Michael P. Moody.
      p. cm. -- (Philanthropy and nonprofit studies)
  Includes bibliographical references and index.
  ISBN-13: 978-0-253-35049-7 (cloth : alk. paper) 1. Charity.
2. Charities. 3. Charitable giving. 4. Humanitarianism. I.
Moody, Michael P. II. Title.
  BJ1533.P5P39 2008
  177'.7--dc22
                              2007036766

      5 15

TO POLLY AND KAREN

Contents

Preface and Acknowledgments

Unlike the rest of the book, where the voices of the two authors mix as one, in this preface we each contribute separately. This allows us to give a sense of how we each came to this book from our own perspective, background, and biases.

From Robert L. Payton

I've been writing professionally—that is, for publication—for more than fifty years. The book that follows focuses on philanthropy, one of the persistent themes that I've explored in that writing. A second fact of my professional life is that I've been a practitioner as well as a student and teacher of philanthropy. In my old age I've reflected on "experience" in every aspect of my life; I put a high value on experience as a test of my ideas and values. What I write about philanthropy is tested against my own personal experience as a practitioner of philanthropy and in light of the experience of others: employers, colleagues, students, volunteers, and my wife, who practices what I preach and tells me when practice and preaching conflict.

In addition to experience, my way of looking at philanthropy has been profoundly influenced by another fact of my professional life: I have spent several decades in colleges and universities, as administrator, editor, speechwriter, fund-raiser, teacher, and "scholar"—that is, lifelong student, not only of philanthropy but of many other things, with special interest in and emphasis on the humanities and liberal arts. Some years ago I discovered the idea of "the between," where the gods reach down to touch humanity and humanity reaches upward to touch divinity. "The gods" is a metaphor for knowledge; "humanity" is a claim of special status in human affairs for the search for truth, that search being the best of what makes us human.

Or so it seems to me. When I was younger there were periods when I thought a particular approach to knowledge was superior to others. I'm almost embarrassed to admit that I once had that view of what were called the behavioral sciences. As a manager I studied management and organizational behavior until I concluded that too much of that science was shallow and manipulative.

I found that I continually returned to my academic experience at the University of Chicago, where I was ostensibly a student of history but—in good Chicago fashion—explored ancient philosophy and eastern religion and the medieval universities and literature, and other things, with the help of my neighbor across the hall who was studying Orwell and the "ten-minute hate," and with the help of the neighbor who lived immediately below us who was studying educational administration, and with the other neighbor downstairs and across the hall who was still traumatized by his experience as a prisoner of the Japanese in the Philippines and didn't know *what* to study to cope with that.

Most of us living in graduate student housing at the University of Chicago in the early 1950s were veterans of World War II. I've written elsewhere about my military experience. (That word *experience* again.) I mention it because I volunteered rather than wait to be drafted, I volunteered to go in the Army (rather than, say, the Coast Guard or the Signal Corps, which were thought to be safer), I volunteered for the infantry, and I volunteered to become a paratrooper. When I reached the Philippines I volunteered to join the Eleventh Airborne Division, which meant that I saw combat, albeit nothing to do more than write home about. When the war ended, I spent a year in "occupation duty" in Japan, seeing an "alien" culture up close for the first time.

Although I didn't know it at the time, it was my military service that transformed my life by making me eligible for the GI Bill. As a beneficiary of the GI Bill (which, along with the civil rights movement, defined modern America), I was eligible for a college education. Almost all of us were first-generation college students, many of us (including me) having never thought of going to college at all until the government told us it would pay for it in appreciation of our military service (and as an investment in the nation's economic future). We were eager, hard-working, enthusiastic students and several years older, on average, than the typical college generation.

Between my military service and my academic experience at Chicago, I was editor of a weekly newspaper for almost two years in a small Iowa town that also had a daily newspaper. I was able to write about whatever interested me, from the rise of Tito in Yugoslavia to movie reviews or the city council debate over the development of the riverfront. My young wife sold subscriptions on the telephone and raved about the brilliant young editor.

That editorial experience led me into trade magazine publishing, which soon persuaded me that "making a living" wasn't sufficient inspiration. Through the help of several friends—and elsewhere I've written at length about my indebtedness to friends and acquaintances who have helped me along the way—I found myself working as an editor in a university.

My only earned degree is a master's degree from the University of Chicago—no bachelor's degree, no PhD. This is another reason not to describe myself as a scholar. I'm a generalist in a world dominated by specialists, a "public teacher" whose task it is to help the public understand and reflect on and debate public issues, a hanger-on to institutions and organizations doing what I consider to be important things, such as thinking critically and disinterestedly about controversial subjects. Not enough of us think critically and disinterestedly about controversial subjects, but the number per capita is probably higher than in most fields.

It can be exhilarating. I've retired two or three times but can't make it stick. For a couple of years, I've worked with three colleagues in team-teaching the ethics course required of PhD candidates in philanthropic studies. One of my colleagues already has a PhD in comparative literature but is working on a second PhD in philanthropic studies. Another is a retired professor of philosophy, a decade younger than me, a gentle but persistent voice who keeps us from falling victim to our enthusiasms. A third member of the group, the one who is formally charged with teaching the course, is a professor of pediatric radiology in the medical school *and* professor of philanthropic studies in the school of liberal arts. Our students are nine midcareer professionals who want to enrich their intellectual experience as well as advance their professional lives.

The subject we teach—the ethics of philanthropy—borrows extensively from life experience. Each of us has a "philanthropic autobiography" to share, a window on how and why we find philanthropy intellectually as well as morally compelling. I can feel the sap rising in my old bones as I think about my half-century love affair with philanthropy as (to quote myself) voluntary action for the public good. The words *voluntary* and *volunteer* grow richer and deeper as I get (even) older.

I will turn again to the essay I've been working on for several years: my "ethical will," the document, parallel to the will in which I indicate what I hope will happen to my material wealth and possessions—especially the very large library I will leave behind—and to the boxes and boxes of documents and correspondence and other ephemera of a long and active life. . . . Where was I? (I'm eighty years old, remember, and I do blather on at times.) Oh, yes: in my ethical will I shall try to acknowledge some of those (too many to list here) who have helped me along the way, including many who are no longer with us. I will also try to reflect on "the values I most want to live on," as two authorities on that ancient Jewish tradition put it. I will pay special tribute to the liberal arts. I will even suggest wording for my headstone:

Books   Ideas   Talk

Tomorrow (as I write this) my wife and I will quietly observe our fifty-eighth wedding anniversary. In two or three days I will send off this text (with an apology for being late) to my coauthor and to our editor at Indiana University Press.

This book is dedicated to my wife. But it could also be dedicated "To My Young People," the young people I have taught and learned from over the years. Michael Moody was the first.

From Michael P. Moody

This book started as a labor of love, but it became a labor of a different kind. Now that it is done, I cannot imagine *not* having done it. Few things are more professionally and personally fulfilling than writing a book about a subject you think is among the most important in the world, with the person you respect most in the world. It is a piece of work that I will treasure forever.

When I originally proposed to Mr. Payton that I come on as a coauthor for a book like this, my intention was to make sure that his writing and thinking about philanthropy would finally make it out into the public and scholarly domain and be available for future generations. People had been asking him for "the book" for years, and I thought such a book was absolutely necessary for both practitioners and scholars in this field. His writing and perspective on philanthropy had inspired me as a recent college graduate in 1989, as it has so many others since. And as more and more writing emerged out of the basement library on Spruce Drive, spreading like *samizdat* among a lucky few, the desire grew to make sure this work was captured in a book accessible to a wider audience.

But as I got into the hard work of taking this voluminous amount of writing and organizing it into such a book, especially one suitable for an academic audience as we wanted this to be, I realized that my task would have to transcend merely editing and reorganizing. There was a great deal of new writing to be done, along with some rewriting and elaborating and updating and connecting. Of course, by this point I had also become a scholar myself. And I realized that in my training as a social scientist I had developed my own, somewhat different (though complementary) way of thinking about this subject that was so dear to us both. So while the finished product here benefits, I hope, from my contributions as well as from Mr. Payton's, this new, fully coauthored path for the book meant it took much more work to get to this point than we had planned. And I am grateful for the leeway shown over these past couple years by my patient coauthor.

This is certainly not the book that either of us would have produced on his own, but again, I think that adds to its appeal. It is neither all social science nor all practical philosophy and ethics, but borrows insights from both. It has both bold statements about universal truths and principles and nuanced qualifications about cultural differences and open empirical questions. It is not as normative as the philosopher might want, and it is more normative than the social scientist is usually comfortable with. It has the timeless wisdom that has been so inspiring to Mr. Payton's students, colleagues, and others who have read his essays or heard his speeches, but it also has the analytical structure, scholarly connections, additional explanations, and recent examples that I brought to the work. While the core conceptual framework for studying philanthropy here is essentially what I learned from Mr. Payton starting back in 1989, this book presents that framework in a new way that I hope will make it as appealing to scholars as it has been for so many years to nonprofit executives, foundation leaders, fund-raising professionals, volunteers, and so many others.

My first and most grateful acknowledgment goes, of course, to my mentor of eighteen years, whom I will always respectfully refer to as "Mr. Payton," even now that I am well past the age at which you switch from being a mentee to becoming a mentor in your own right. I owe Mr. Payton, and Mrs. Payton, more than I can ever repay, even in a "serial reciprocity" manner of repaying by doing similar things for young people who now come into my life as I came into the Paytons'. My life is fundamentally better because of them both.

I also extend my appreciation to Indiana University and the Lilly Endowment, which supported this field of philanthropic studies and, along the way, supported both Mr. Payton and me. My other mentors at Princeton University—Robert Wuthnow, Paul DiMaggio, and Michèle Lamont—helped me develop the understanding of philanthropy that I incorporated as my contribution to this work. Colleagues at the School of Policy, Planning, and Development at the University of Southern California—especially Jim Ferris and the support of the Center on Philanthropy and Public Policy—made my labor on this book possible over the past few years. A special thanks goes to Gene Wilson, who read the manuscript at a crucial stage, Elaine Otto, who improved our prose, and Patricia Dean, whose earlier editorial work was indispensable. And thanks to the editors and reviewers at Indiana University Press—especially to Bob Sloan and to the book's primary advocate, Dwight Burlingame—for their interest. Dwight and David Hammack helped shape this project during a special summer seminar on philanthropy and liberal education in Indianapolis, which reminds me also to thank Gene Tempel and everyone at the Center on Philanthropy at Indiana University.

Last, but not least, I want to thank my family for teaching me, both as a child and as an adult, what philanthropy means when it connects one person to another. And to my wife, Karen—to whom the book is dedicated—thanks for your abiding faith and inerrant support . . . and for biting your tongue when you knew I was wallowing in a bog of perfectionism.

Understanding Philanthropy

1

Introduction: Why This Book?

*O*seola McCarty worked for most of her life as a paid-by-the-bundle washerwoman, and yet she managed to build up substantial savings through frugal living—she never owned a car—and slow, steady accumulation. She saved enough so that in 1995, when she was eighty-seven, Ms. McCarty was able to make a gift of $150,000 to the University of Southern Mississippi for an endowment that would provide scholarships for needy African American students.

Although her gift made her famous, Ms. McCarty could hardly have expected the attention she received. On the first anniversary of the gift, she was the subject of a feature story on the front page of the *New York Times*.[1] Her gift was seen as an extraordinary act of generosity, both because she denied herself in order to save the money and because she was giving an opportunity to others that she had been denied herself. The *Times* reported that famous people had come to kneel at her feet, to sing to her, to praise her as a saint. President Clinton awarded her the Presidential Citizens Medal, and Harvard gave her an honorary doctorate.

The story of Oseola McCarty's generosity raises key questions about philanthropy: Why did she make such a gift? Why did she decide that philanthropy was the ultimate purpose of her hard-earned savings? How was she connected to the young people she would help? Why do we celebrate and admire her so much more because she gave the money away in this manner, rather than simply because she saved it or worked hard to earn it?

Oseola McCarty's story is about her, about her gift, about the young people who will benefit, about the people who admire her, about their praise for her, and about the media's celebration of her story. Most significantly, though, it is about American philanthropy and American values. In fact, every once in a while we hear similar stories of otherwise "ordinary" people making surprising, extraordinary donations to the causes they care about. Since 1981, Albert Lexie has been shining shoes at the Children's Hospital of Pittsburgh a couple days a week. But he has never kept a cent of the tips he earns. Instead, he donates those tips to the hospital's Free Care Fund—more than $100,000 from a man who earns about $10,000 annually.[2] Do such things happen in other countries? Is there something unique about American philanthropy? What has America done to the philanthropic tradition that it inherited from other places, other times, other cultures?

Another example, from the other side of the world: The terrible civil war that destroyed the former Yugoslavia in the 1990s, and the genocidal "ethnic cleansing" that killed tens of thousands and displaced millions, brought the suffering of displaced persons to the world's attention. Some of the more fortunate were able to flee the war and go abroad to find refuge with relatives or friends. The great majority—hundreds of thousands of them—had no such choice. During the worst part of the fighting they often huddled in basements, fearful for their lives if they went out to seek help or to find water to drink or wood to burn for heat. For years, despite the efforts of relief agencies, many people in Bosnia, Kosovo, and elsewhere lived without transport, without a place to sleep or enough food to eat, without medicine or blankets or adequate clothes. The journal of one of those victims, *Zlata's Diary*, is a latter-day *Diary of Anne Frank*.[3]

The story of the former Yugoslavia—and similar stories of the human consequences of civil war, from Rwanda to Guatemala to Israel to the Sudan—also raises some fundamental questions about philanthropy. The first question is one that will recur throughout this book: What business is it of ours? How do we justify intervening philanthropically in another's country affairs to provide philanthropic assistance?

Aid organizations and even individual philanthropists like George Soros found humanitarian grounds for making the plight of these refugees *their* business, which was enough justification for their philanthropic response. But others who intervened did so for political or economic reasons. Once we intervene for any reason, we face further questions: Are food and blankets and medicine enough? Should philanthropy help families like Zlata's not only find a new home but also make a living? When should we scale back our charitable relief and encourage the new nations to build their own philanthropic institutions so they can "help themselves" and maintain free, open, and democratic societies? And when should we divert our resources to help new refugees in other parts of the globe?

Soros's actions in the Yugoslavian region during and after the war demonstrate one set of responses to these questions. He established one of his "Open Society Funds" there—like he did during the 1990s in most of the emerging democracies in the region—and hired local people to help decide how the money would be used. Grants were initially focused on basic relief and on restoring core infrastructure for necessities like water and electricity. This was a particularly dangerous sort of philanthropic venture in wartime, but this was what the people in places like Sarajevo needed, as they faced daily threats like snipers targeting people at the few places where they could fill their jugs with water. Over the years, the Fund's grantmaking shifted to other priorities such as establishing cultural and educational institutions. These new priorities would be classified more as "development" than "relief," but they are essential for the long-term stability and self-sufficiency of this new society.

These examples of what happens in the name of philanthropy raise questions about the definition of philanthropy, but they also make more concrete the meaning of abstractions associated with that concept—abstractions such as charity, good works, compassion, and community. Ultimately, they lead us to think about the most fundamental questions of the human condition: What should we do when things go wrong in the world? What responsibility do we have for helping others or helping to make the world better? How does philanthropy or "good works" relate to the good life and the good society? These are some of the questions we will reflect on throughout this book. We hope both the questions and our discussion stimulate readers to develop their own answers, for there could hardly be more important questions.

This first chapter will introduce broadly what is to come in the rest of the book, but its main purpose is to explain why this book—and this *sort* of book—is necessary and valuable. We take the position here that philanthropy is an interesting and important subject that deserves to be better understood and to be taken seriously, and in this chapter we introduce how we will do that by focusing on fundamental questions about philanthropy's meaning and mission. We also review some of the details, facts, and figures of what is going on in this field.

Understanding the Meaning and Mission of Philanthropy

What and Why, Not How To

Our approach to improving the understanding of philanthropy in this book will be somewhat different than most other work in this emerging field of philanthropic studies. Simply put, we will be more concerned with the fundamental "Why" than with the "How" questions. And to get at "Why"—such as "Why does philanthropy exist?"—we need to address a range of related, also fundamental "What" questions—such as "What is distinctive about philanthropic action?" and "What, in essence, is this activity we call philanthropy?"

In this way, our intention is to engage the reader in a joint search for the meaning and mission of philanthropy. We get at meaning by asking, "What is philanthropy?" We get at mission by asking, "Why does philanthropy exist?" We should note that this way of thinking about mission is borrowed from the late Henry Rosso, founder of The Fund Raising School, who argued that the "mission" of any organization seeking to raise funds is not that organization's answer to the question "What do we do?" but rather their answer to the question "Why do we exist?" In this book, we ask that latter question about philanthropy itself.

Doing philanthropy involves acts as diverse as consoling or cavorting with a child who has cancer, taking tickets at an art exhibit, writing a check for a relief agency, investing in the endowment of a private liberal arts college, and raising the funds that make the endowment possible. There are skills involved, sometimes highly specialized and demanding technical skills. But there are also motivations involved, values, a purpose, and an implied justification for voluntary action as the mode of action. We know a lot more about the skills than we do about the motivations or the justifications. We understand finance and management technique better than we understand values or purposes. We understand how to claim a tax deduction better than we understand why we can claim it.

Philanthropy is about ideas and values as well as about action, about doing things. Philanthropy is always an effort to blend the ideal and the practical. If you lose a grip on either perspective, you will have put on blinders.

The most common failing in attempting good works is to be too busy to reflect on things like ideas and values, too busy to talk or read. The surface is often misleading; we have to scrape away the layers of our own experience that prevent us from understanding why we did what we did. The most common fault among most of those who are professionally engaged in philanthropy is that they are preoccupied with the "How" and neglectful, even ignorant of the "Why." They are not "reflective practitioners" in the way Donald Schön argues they should be.[4] Philanthropy, when taken seriously, calls for emotion constrained by reason, action guided by thought.

Much of the scholarly work in the field of philanthropic studies suffers from a similar failing. The dominant focus is on the study of and training for "nonprofit management," which, while serving an essential purpose of teaching the important skills, tends to gloss over the more fundamental questions we want to address here. Management studies rarely attempt to think critically about the assumptions underlying their organizations and practices. This is as true in business schools as in programs teaching nonprofit management. As a consequence, most students of business and nonprofits are rarely prepared to deal with foundational critiques of their practices when they arise.

Similarly, much of the scholarship on philanthropy and the nonprofit sector is more focused on questions of how this activity or sector works or how it works best.[5] And while some scholars have offered explanations for why this phenomenon exists—e.g., because of the "failure" of other sectors—and what is different about it, the theory of philanthropy we set out in this book is distinctive in both its terminology and its perspective.[6] We believe it adds some ways of understanding philanthropy that have been missing from standard explanations. Overall, then, this book tries to facilitate more reflective practice and more informed scholarship by asking somewhat different questions and shining a somewhat different light on the subject.

What Is Philanthropy? An Initial Summary

A book by two contemporary French intellectuals, one a philosopher and the other a psychoanalyst, has the straightforward title *What Is Philosophy?* Their answer—"philosophy is the art of forming, inventing, and fabricating concepts"—is deceptively straightforward as well, especially given the obvious complexity of their subject matter. They prefaced their answer to their question with the following declaration: "We had never stopped asking this question previously, and we already had the answer, which has not changed."[7]

In writing this book, and in our experiences thinking about and doing philanthropy in some professional capacity—over the course of about fifty years for one of us, a mere twenty years for the other—we have never stopped asking, "What is philanthropy?" Our simple answer, too, has not changed. It is the same answer proposed by the senior one of us many years ago in a previous book: philanthropy is *"voluntary action for the public good."*[8]

The authors of *What Is Philosophy?* also provide a useful insight into the form of a second question, "What is a concept?" They begin by asserting, "There are no simple concepts. Every concept has components and is defined by them." A concept, therefore, is a "multiplicity."[9]

The concept of philanthropy is a multiplicity. As we explain in the next chapter, our definition itself encompasses many things. Of course it includes *voluntary giving*, when we give our money, either in cash or in property, often on the spot but more often by check—or even by deferred bequests, so-called planned giving, that will come out of our estates one day. But our definition also includes *voluntary service*, when we give our time and sometimes our talent; and our definition includes *voluntary association*, the organized activity without which most voluntary giving and service would be ineffective or even impossible.

Philanthropy is a multiplicity in other ways as well. While our definition of philanthropy is one answer to the question "What is philanthropy?" we will explore many other dimensions of the answer to that question. Philanthropy is moral action in response to the "human problematic." Philanthropy over time represents the "social history of the moral imagination." Philanthropy is essential to a free, open, democratic, civil society. And philanthropy is a tradition in jeopardy, one that needs our stewardship to thrive in the future as it has in the past.

Our conception of philanthropy is an affirmative one; we do not define the field primarily by what it is not, as the term *nonprofit* does (although we do use that term often to refer to the sector or organizations in it). "Good works" is another affirmative way to define our subject matter. The philanthropic tradition includes individual "random acts of kindness," as the bumper stickers and t-shirts proclaim, as well as the more visible, organized, and systematic efforts that must necessarily get most of our attention in this book. Some philanthropic good works seek to reduce suffering and misery, and some seek to improve the quality of life. Philanthropy is diverse and widespread, but we try to capture it in a useful conceptual framework in this book.

The Need to Clarify Philanthropy's Mission

Addressing the "What" questions throughout this book will then help us address the even tougher "Why" questions. But it is essential that we try to deal with those "Why" issues, because foundational questions about the very purpose and essence of philanthropy are arising more frequently and urgently than ever before, especially in the United States. These are arising at the same time that the field is experiencing considerable growth.[10] Both scholars and practitioners are being forced to think harder about the basis for the legitimacy of philanthropy, and to justify the existence of this field they need to present a more sophisticated explanation of the unique contributions philanthropy makes or should make.

We've all seen the media coverage of ethical scandals at the United Way—the most visible, local face of philanthropic giving for millions of Americans—and of the misuse of nonprofit organizations as money launderers and shills by people like the disgraced lobbyist Jack Abramoff. Reports have also questioned the ethical conduct and decisions of the Red Cross and other charitable organizations in the wake of both the 9/11 attacks and Hurricane Katrina—for example, decisions about how much of the millions of donated dollars should go directly to victims. Although these stories and others—such as those about the pay packages of some nonprofit CEOs—are not representative of the vast majority of philanthropic activity, they do force us to confront some tough questions, like what really is different about this sector and why we should hold those who work in philanthropic organizations to a higher standard.

At the same time, philanthropy is in the midst of a growth spurt, both in the United States and around the globe. In the United States, the number of nonprofit organizations continues to increase, and there has been a surge in the number of private foundations. Giving by the wealthy has garnered particular attention lately, as a new crop of millionaires like those flush with "dot com" fortunes turn their attention to being strategic about donating their money, and as Bill Gates and Warren Buffett, the two wealthiest men in the world, have now combined resources to create the largest philanthropic foundation in the history of the world.[11] At the same time, scholars are forecasting a massive intergenerational transfer of wealth in the coming decades—$41 trillion is one estimate—that could usher in a "golden age of philanthropy."[12] This growth and top-end concentration of philanthropy—alongside the scandals, of course—has also led to heightened scrutiny of philanthropic institutions by policymakers and regulators at the highest levels. Surely this discussion over how to regulate philanthropy deserves a better understanding of the core rationale behind the activity, as well as a better understanding of the justifications—in principle, at least—for special considerations like tax exemption.

Another development raising fundamental questions about philanthropy is the increased blurring of the boundaries between the nonprofit and other sectors, as philanthropic institutions have developed new (and highly visible) methods for raising funds through profit-making enterprises.[13] Among these are so-called social enterprises that have taken the ideas pioneered by Goodwill Industries and other revenue-generating philanthropic agencies to the next level. For example, Rubicon Bakery in the San Francisco Bay Area employs and trains individuals with various disadvantages—from homelessness to addiction to mental disability—in good jobs making high-quality desserts, and then funnels all profits into related programs of a community agency that also operates under the Rubicon umbrella. These new social enterprises—which are also increasingly popular in Great Britain and other countries—are nonprofits that make a profit, but their profit-making enterprises meet the organizations' philanthropic goals in two ways: by providing funding for programs serving those in need, and by providing jobs and job training for them as well. Social enterprises are one of an array of recent innovations that blur sectoral boundaries by borrowing and adapting business methods, logics, and concepts for nonprofit purposes. Some of the most creative and committed leaders in the philanthropic world now prefer to call themselves "social entrepreneurs," and social entrepreneurship has become a popular way of describing a variety of new approaches to social change.[14] Social enterprises and social entrepreneurs are the preferred targets for funding from a new class of grantmakers called "venture philanthropists." Venture philanthropists approach their giving with the same mindset and language as venture capitalists making a business investment.[15] Philanthropic entrepreneurs of this sort, while sometimes very effective, force us to reconsider the boundary between what is "nonprofit" philanthropy and what isn't, or how we can view philanthropy as a concept that can encompass its many diverse expressions. These are questions that most people in this field are conceptually unprepared to answer in any depth.

Finally, more broadly, overwhelming recent disasters such as the attacks of 9/11, the Indian Ocean tsunami, or Hurricane Katrina have captured global attention and challenged the global human community with meeting massive humanitarian needs. The astonishing philanthropic outpouring—in money, time, and organization—in response to these disasters has reminded millions of people around the world that they too can play a philanthropic role in the world. But these disasters have also left us struggling for a way to think about the proper role of groups like the Red Cross or Doctors Without Borders versus the proper role of governments. When government is clearly overwhelmed or even harshly criticized for failing to provide adequate relief, should the Salvation Army be held equally accountable for adequately meeting needs? Nonprofit groups cannot be the sole or even the primary source of relief in such cases, but what can or should their role be? What can they contribute that government and business cannot? And should they be allowed to make choices about whom they help and whom they don't help? These sorts of questions confront us even more in times when we consider the role of the growing cadre of NGOs (Non-Governmental Organizations) in both relief and development efforts around the globe.[16]

Lester Salamon is right to argue that the nonprofit sector has been "resilient" in the face of these and other challenges and questions, but surviving in the short term is not the same as thriving in the long term. For philanthropy to survive and thrive, it needs a better understanding of its distinctive meaning and mission. If we want to help the sector respond to what Salamon labels the "distinctiveness imperative," we should discuss and clarify a renewed vision of philanthropy's rationale and role, one that can be used to answer questions about the legitimacy of this activity.[17] The need for this has never been greater.

In exploring the meaning and distinctive mission of philanthropy in a way that responds to these current challenges, we must be sure to consider philanthropy "warts and all," as the old saying goes. We must confront honestly and fairly the bad as well as the good, the failures as well as the successes, the betrayals as well as the great moral victories. This book will attempt to make philanthropy more real and more relevant by writing about virtue and vice among philanthropic practitioners, the underside of philanthropy, the pathologies of voluntary association as faction, and other variations on error, failure, and weakness of will, personal as well as organizational.

Taking Philanthropy Seriously

The current challenges forcing a clarification of the mission of philanthropy have revealed just how deficient our general understanding of philanthropy is. It is about time we took the subject of philanthropy more seriously and stopped taking it for granted. It is an ancient tradition, but a tradition in some jeopardy.

Everyone should know something about the tradition of voluntary action for the public good. We should know about how philanthropy works in some general way that is comparable to our understanding of how government works and how the marketplace works. That is the core reason for writing this book.

Philanthropy, in the broad sense in which we define it, permeates our lives, whether we are conscious of it or not. There are few things that affect as many aspects of our lives as philanthropy, and yet there are few that are less understood. Philanthropy is as important in our lives as are law and medicine, subjects about which we know much more than we know about philanthropy. Philanthropy is an essential tool in our collective attempts to solve public problems, yet there is too little—or only ill-informed—consideration of philanthropy in our public conversation. Unlike business, philanthropy does not have its own regular section in the daily newspaper; unlike politics, philanthropy rarely makes the front page. Yet in the United States alone there are millions of volunteers at work as you read this. Thousands of checks totaling millions of dollars are in the mail today to thousands of philanthropic organizations and institutions, some better known to you than rock groups, college football teams, or breakfast cereals.

To "take something seriously" means to *think about it*. To think about philanthropy means to reflect on it, critically and inquisitively, with an open mind, open to both its limits and its possibilities, its achievements and its disappointments. We try to do that in this book.

To "take something seriously" also means to *take it personally*. Everyone who reads this book, for whatever purpose, brings both knowledge and experience of philanthropy to the reading. Regardless of where we live, most of us have been participants in some form of voluntary action for the public good, either through voluntary giving, voluntary service, or membership in a voluntary organization. But this does not mean we understand that activity very well. For instance, many Americans will say with some pride that "Americans are generous people" or that "giving back" is something we should all do. But the odds are that most of these proud Americans have no handy way to think about the philanthropic sector or familiar words to use when they talk about it. They probably aren't sure they should count as "philanthropy" the time they volunteer for Little League baseball coaching or in their role as secretary of their alumnae club. They are likely to have some idea of what is deductible from their taxes, but they may not know what "501(c)(3)" stands for or whether there is a limit to how much they can deduct for charitable contributions in a given tax year.

Despite its prevalence in the culture, few Americans have thought very carefully about philanthropy—what it is, how it works, its motivations, its results, what part it plays in our society and in the world, the arguments for and against it. Because philanthropy is commonplace, most people have opinions about it in this broad sense, but these opinions are often uninformed. For example, many Americans think that most philanthropic giving comes from large foundations like the Ford Foundation and from large corporations like Microsoft. In fact, a whopping 83 percent of all dollars given philanthropically in the United States are given by individuals, not by corporations or foundations.[18] Similarly, many people assume that most if not all of the funds received and distributed by nonprofit organizations in the United States come from philanthropic contributions. In fact, only a small percentage of the revenues of the nonprofit sector—only one dollar out of every eight received, by one measurement—comes from private giving. As a whole, American nonprofit groups receive less from private giving than from government, and their largest source of revenue by far is neither private giving nor government grants but fees for the services and goods they sell.[19]

Americans also do not have a widely shared understanding of why we do so much of our public work through philanthropy. Political and policy debates that reference philanthropy often reveal an alarming ignorance about the tradition and the sector. Relying on "charities" to deal with public problems becomes an election-year rhetorical prop or a way to shift responsibility; philanthropy is often spoken of as if it were infinitely expandable in scale and conveniently malleable in scope. The media has a hard time explaining the reason for tax exemption or the crucial differences in types of tax-exempt organizations.

Our opinions about philanthropy are uninformed largely because philanthropy is something we have learned about only informally and often haphazardly, from family, church, and tradition. We have not studied it the way we have studied our economic life, our political life, or even our spiritual life. We give less attention to it than we do to golf and tennis, movies and television, clothes and cosmetics, diet and exercise.

Unlike the two other great sectors of public life, business and politics (or the other great sector of private life, the family), philanthropy has only recently become an educational subject. Very few people have learned about philanthropy in formal schooling. Scholars have only recently been studying it systematically. It is unlikely that even the readers of this book have ever taken a course in philanthropy at any level. Philanthropy has been learned by experience, by a precept or maxim taught by one's parents, by imitation or example. Our knowledge of philanthropy is tacit, experiential, tentative.

Finally, an important caveat as we begin this book: when we say philanthropy permeates "our lives" and that "everyone" should understand it better, we mean to include people around the globe, in different cultures and nations, each with their own distinctive philanthropic tradition. In this book, many of our examples come from the United States, and even some aspects of our theoretical perspective are surely influenced by the American philanthropic context that we know best; we are cultural beings like everyone else. But ultimately we believe the understanding of philanthropy we present here will allow people immersed in other traditions and people practicing philanthropy in other societies—especially in other democratic nations—to take philanthropy seriously in their own neck of the global woods. The activities that we call philanthropy look somewhat different in different societies: the relative size of this sector and its relationship with government and government funding vary, the cultural traditions of giving and service vary, the types of institutional structures and labels vary, and so on.[20] This book reflects our attempts to conceptualize how humans everywhere engage the world, why they turn to philanthropy as a response to what they see in the world, and what is distinctive about this response. We hope this book stimulates similar reflections (and perhaps refinements) on the part of each reader. We hope it helps you better understand philanthropy's place in the world, in your specific world, and in your own worldview. However, we should also not forget that philanthropy is increasingly *crossing* global boundaries. *Time* magazine reminded us of that by naming three international philanthropists the "Persons of the Year" for 2005: Bill Gates, Melinda Gates, and the rock star Bono.[21]

Philanthropy Is Important and Interesting

Philanthropy deserves greater attention because it is more important and interesting than most people realize. Anything involving as many as half of all adult Americans, on a regular basis, voluntarily giving away their time and money would seem to be important. Anything that is at the center of current public debates about social welfare (e.g., what role should faith-based charities play in feeding the hungry?), human rights, the environment, and a hundred other issues, including our personal character and virtue and sense of social responsibility, would seem to be important. Philanthropy is a mode of action that shapes our individual lives and the world around us in extensive ways. And philanthropy is important because we often measure others, and sometimes we measure ourselves, by the way we help others in need, by the way we help our neighborhoods and communities, by the money and time we donate to causes we believe in.

A final reason why philanthropy is important is perhaps the most dramatic and compelling: philanthropy is essential to the survival of democratic societies, our own or others just getting started. When crafting our plans and policies to solve social problems, people in democracies often turn to private giving and the nonprofit sector as the chosen alternative, especially when the other two sectors are ineffective. And voluntary associations are a time-honored vehicle that we use to join together with those of like mind and make our voices heard in the public sphere—to advocate, to celebrate, and, yes, sometimes to protest.

Many say this role for voluntary action is even more apparent in the United States than elsewhere, because no nation in the history of the world has relied so extensively on voluntary action to do the public's business. Some go so far as to say that American's reliance on philanthropy is unique. But this is another less-than-accurate assumption that could use some clarification in a book like this one. While not unique per se, America's reliance on voluntary action certainly is distinctive; if philanthropy is a virtue, it could very well be America's most distinctive virtue.[22] Americans turn to philanthropy to advance their vision of the public good more than other cultures do; we use philanthropy to try to do good things, which is why it is a virtue and not a vice. The point is that if you don't understand how the United States works as a three-sector society, as a society heavily reliant on philanthropic action in the third sector, you don't understand the United States. Americans cannot run the risk of remaining largely ignorant of this important—even necessary—element of our democratic life. The same could be said for other democracies around the world as well, including emerging ones.

We are also convinced that philanthropy is interesting. One reason is that it helps to explain how society works; another is that it sheds light on every subject it touches. You can understand art history better when you understand philanthropic patronage of artists. You can understand the civil rights movement better when you understand how organizers motivated volunteers, who could go home whenever they wanted, to stick around despite the very real possibility of being beaten for it. We hope the study of philanthropy is interesting enough that it will someday permeate the intellectual life of the university, helping us to think more effectively about justice and welfare and truth.

Philanthropy Is an Ancient, Universal, and Diverse Tradition

Most of the activities we label "philanthropy" have been going on for a very long time. Organized charity is older than democracy and capitalism, older than Christianity and Buddhism, older than societies and many other traditions that no longer exist. Charity in its less organized, spontaneous form, as ad hoc individual expression, is as old as humanity itself; we can safely consider it universal.

Similarly, the practice of some form of organized philanthropy is common to all of the great religions and civilizations of the world. But this universality does not mean there is not great diversity in philanthropy across the world and over time. The tradition takes a distinctive form in each culture. The fact that organized philanthropy is so ancient and widespread means that cultures have many different philanthropic traditions, and philanthropy has taken many forms. People have tried numerous things in the name of philanthropy: from saving children to saving trees, from saving refugees to saving old buildings, from saving symphony orchestras to saving stray dogs. People have used many words and labels for the activities, the values, and the purposes of philanthropy: charity, reform, liberation, voluntary action, eleemosynary, altruism, nonprofit, benevolence, generosity, good works, and many more. People have also justified and practiced philanthropy in many ways (not all admirable, we might point out): from giving alms because it is required by God to organizing a males-only benevolent society to preserve the status quo in a village, from making annoying fund-raising telephone calls during the dinner hour to making more subtle appeals offhandedly over drinks among friends.

This book argues that "tradition" is important as the record and awareness of the values that are transmitted across time from one generation to another. This does not mean all elements of any tradition are worthy of praise; in fact, the tradition of philanthropy includes within in the value of, and means for, the reform of tradition itself. But this requires paying attention to tradition, and perhaps working to improve it, so that you can pass it on proudly to the next generation. Traditions that are neglected or even actively abused can lose energy and meaning. We do not want to risk neglecting the philanthropic tradition.

Everyone Has a Connection to Philanthropy

As we noted earlier, philanthropy deserves more attention because everyone has some experience with it. Not all the experience is positive, nor is everyone actively engaged in philanthropy, but the experience of giving and receiving assistance is for all practical purposes universal. This is true for Albanians and for Alabamans.

Despite our limited formal knowledge of philanthropy, almost everyone can share some draft version of their "philanthropic autobiography" if the occasion arises. Our connection to philanthropy may go back to a childhood experience of donating money or food items at school or church, or of going door to door soliciting donations for UNICEF or the Red Cross. We have probably continued to give money—some of us sporadically, some regularly. We may have responded to letters requesting a donation. We may have given money to people who asked us for it on the street. We may have made similar token gifts to organizations simply because we were asked. We may have made regular contributions to our favorite charities. We may have attended social or cultural events where at least some of the proceeds from ticket sales went to a charity. Chances are good that we have also volunteered our services at some time, whether for our church, our children's school, or the local soup kitchen on Thanksgiving.

Many if not most of the readers of a book like this have also been on the receiving end of philanthropy—not necessarily direct charity, but philanthropy. The good works of others, past and present, make our lives possible. One of the most troubling inadequacies of the definition of philanthropy as voluntary giving or helping is that it focuses too much attention on the giver. This belies the fact that philanthropy is about receiving as much as about giving.[23] And for most of us, benefiting from philanthropy is not about our own hunger or homelessness but about benefiting from social change, stewardship, or the advancement of knowledge. All Americans are recipients, in a way, of philanthropic acts such as Andrew Carnegie's gifts to start public libraries across the United States. Even if you've never used a public library personally, you've benefited indirectly (if only through lower taxes) from the higher literacy rates and afterschool child care that public libraries provide. People around the globe are the beneficiaries of scientific or medical discoveries funded by philanthropic research grants and endowments.

More generally, there is no such thing as being wealthy beyond the need of the voluntary assistance of others. If helping others is universal, being helped is equally so. In such relations we are close to an existential understanding of the human condition. We are all vulnerable. We have all benefited from philanthropy in some form. We were all infants once.

Most of us don't consider ourselves among "the vulnerable." Until, that is, we realize that someone close to us is but a wayward cell or two from a life-threatening disease. Or until we realize that some of those in dire need of charitable aid following a disaster are wealthy western tourists. At that point the things we value most highly may rest on someone else's philanthropy, perhaps the forgotten donation of a total stranger of an earlier generation, perhaps the voluntary commitment of the stranger we meet in the emergency aid tent.

This is an important and interesting subject, one we must take seriously.

What Is Going On?

It is helpful, before we get too much further, to answer what we consider to be, following the theologian H. Richard Niebuhr, the first ethical question: "What is going on?"[24] We should take the time to appreciate the scale, scope, diversity, and significance of philanthropy in our society and for our individual lives. This is the first, most obvious step in addressing complicated questions like "Why does philanthropy exist?" or "What is philanthropy?" And this step will also provide convincing evidence that philanthropy should be taken seriously.

The Scale of Philanthropy

Although philanthropy claims only a relatively small fraction of our resources—our time as well as our money—its statistical profile is still very impressive. Despite our notorious preoccupation with amusing ourselves and decorating ourselves, we consistently give a share of our valuable resources of time and money voluntarily for the benefit of other individuals or that amorphous entity called "the community." And we give of ourselves in many ways, both formal and informal, even though most of our measurements of this activity—such as those reported below—omit the countless small or person-to-person gestures of helping others.[25]

Philanthropy is a force of major significance in the United States when we consider its scale. American philanthropy, as we define it, encompasses two million organizations, tens of millions of donors and volunteers, millions of full-time jobs, and trillions of dollars in revenues, trillions in expenditures, and trillions in assets. It is much bigger than most people think.[26]

Tens of millions of Americans give money philanthropically, sometimes because that is easier than giving our precious time and our modest talent. According to a survey sponsored by the national nonprofit umbrella group Independent Sector, in 2000 an astonishing 89 percent of American households said they made charitable contributions, and 44 percent of the adult population (and 59 percent of teenagers) said they volunteered. Most of those volunteers (42 percent of adults) said they also contributed money or property.[27] On average, those giving households contribute over 2 percent of their household income (not counting informal giving), and Americans on the whole give about 2 percent of our nation's GDP every year.[28] The wealthiest households contribute the lion's share of total donated funds. By one estimate, the top 27 percent of households give about 65 percent of the total, and the top 0.4 percent (in terms of wealth) give over 20 percent of the total.[29] This is largely because of the economic stratification in the United States, in which these wealthiest households own the lion's share of the wealth and make over half the income in America. And while this inequality of wealth and income is increasing in America, leading to an even higher percentage of total giving coming from the wealthy in the future, when we look at philanthropy in terms of number of households that give some part of whatever income and wealth they have, we see that philanthropy is remarkably widespread and that families at all levels give nearly the same percentage of their income.[30] Sometimes millions of us even give to the same cause: over half of Americans said they had donated to the relief funds for 9/11 victims within a few weeks of the disaster, and even more than this said they gave blood or volunteered their time.[31]

The total amount of money given is also impressive. According to the annual *Giving USA* report, Americans donated $260.3 billion in 2005. Perhaps most surprising to many is that *83.2 percent came from individuals*— 76.5 percent from living individuals, and another 6.7 percent through bequests. In sheer size this individual giving is considerably larger than the amount given by foundations (11.5 percent) and by corporations (5.3 percent). Individuals added to their impressive giving totals by giving time as well. The Independent Sector survey reported that 83.9 million American adults volunteered approximately 15.5 billion hours in 2000. This total is the equivalent of a workforce of over 9 million full-time employees; and if we attach a per hour value to this volunteer work, the total value of donated time is estimated at $239 billion, nearly equivalent to the amount of dollars given in money or property.[32] And all these totals would be even higher if we included the many hours of "informal" volunteering—the prototype for this is the Boy Scout helping the elderly woman across the street—that most of us do as well.

Giving also implies receiving, and the percentage of contributions that were given for various purposes is also different than what many observers would expect. For instance, more than a third (35.8 percent) of all philanthropic dollars went to religious organizations. By contrast, the next highest category of recipient organizations—education—received only 14.8 percent of donations, and no other categories—e.g., health; human services; arts, culture, and humanities; environment—received more than 10 percent.[33] However, the relative role of individuals versus foundations and corporations as primary donors varies across the different fields.

According to the National Center for Charitable Statistics (NCCS) at the Urban Institute, there were 1.4 million nonprofit organizations registered with the IRS as of 2004. This figure does not include those religious congregations who chose not to register and many other community groups, clubs, self-help groups, civic partnerships, and other voluntary associations who are not registered because of their small size or informality. The actual count of voluntary associations in the United States is likely somewhere closer to 2 million.[34] This number has risen considerably in the past couple decades, and the number of private foundations has seen the most precipitous growth.[35] Again, philanthropy is a big and growing part of our lives and our society.

While many of these 2 million voluntary associations are very small—with modest budgets and sustained by volunteers—there are also some very large organizations, such as private universities with massive endowments and nonprofit hospitals with huge annual budgets. Considering just the nearly 500,000 U.S. nonprofit organizations (including foundations) that are large enough to have to register their finances with the IRS, we get a good sense of the impressive financial scale of this sector. In 2004, these reporting groups took in $1.36 trillion in revenues and reported $2.97 trillion in assets. This means *the nonprofit economy in the United States is larger than all but a few national economies around the world.*[36] However, a very large portion of this revenue and assets (and expenses also) is accounted for by the education and (especially) health care subsectors.[37]

As mentioned earlier, many people are surprised to learn that private charitable donations (from individuals, foundations, or corporations) are not the primary source of revenue for nonprofit organizations, that the philanthropic sector as a whole receives more money from government than from private giving, and that dues or fees-for-services (e.g., tuition paid to private universities) are by far the largest source of revenue.[38] There is also some evidence that the share of funding coming from private giving is declining.[39]

However, the picture is more complicated when we look at specific types or fields of nonprofit groups. Religious groups look more like the common perception of nonprofit groups in that they *do* receive the majority of their funding from private donations, whereas health care organizations—which make up such a huge chunk of the financial tally of the sector—get a significant majority of their funding from fees.[40] This variation should be seen as evidence of the tremendous diversity and scope (see below) of philanthropic organizations. These organizations make up a significant portion of our social and economic life, but taken together they are very difficult to capture with simple definitions or shorthand assumptions.

Philanthropic organizations employed—as paid employees, not counting volunteers—12.5 million people in 2001, accounting for 9.5 percent of total employment in the United States.[41] This means *the nonprofit sector employs more people than the federal government and all fifty state governments combined* and more than many major industries.[42] And this impressive employment figure does not include the volunteer workforce, which we described earlier as the equivalent of another 9 million full-time employees. Moreover, employment in the nonprofit sector is growing at a faster rate than either business or government employment. The number of Americans working in the nonprofit sector has more than doubled in the past 25 years. Again, health services organizations account for the largest share of employees (41.9 percent), while only 0.3 percent work for foundations.[43]

At least some of those millions of people, especially those employed full time, think of themselves as being part of "a field," sometimes called philanthropy, sometimes the nonprofit sector, sometimes the "voluntary" or "independent" or "third" sector. They have a tenuous sense of being part of something bigger and distinctive, of being part of a sector that deserves a place alongside business and government, making the United States a three-sector society. This loose categorization is there for them even though their first identification is likely with a cause—for example, "human rights" for people who work for Amnesty International, "the arts" for people who work for the Phoenix Symphony. Often their primary identification is even more specific to an institution than to a cause—to the University of Chicago instead of "education," to the American Academy of Pediatrics instead of "health," and so on.

The Scope of Philanthropy

The scale of philanthropy is only one dimension for assessing its importance. Its diverse and extraordinary scope is another. As we noted earlier, philanthropy deals with the most important social and moral issues affecting society as well as our individual lives. In fact, these crucial issues confronting society—moral issues like social welfare, human rights, the environment—often arise as salient issues first in this "third sector," this public space where the voluntary work of society is carried out. Our moral and political agenda is often set by voluntary associations who advocate for something to be put on that agenda, like women's rights or laws against gay marriage.

Philanthropy has been a significant influence in social, political, religious, moral, economic, scientific, and technological affairs. The spectrum of causes advocated by philanthropic organizations extends from efforts to limit air pollution to efforts to define the rights of children, from providing exhibition opportunities for artists to providing hospice care for the terminally ill. Philanthropy has been influential in shaping the outcome of issues in religion, education, health, social welfare and human services (including family, children, and youth), the arts and humanities, cultural preservation, community service, sports and recreation, international relief and development, and the environment.

The practices of philanthropy are as various as the needs they serve. The list of human needs in the New Testament that begins "I was hungry and you gave me food" is part of the cultural and philanthropic literacy of the West. Food and drink, companionship and compassion, medicine, liberation, work, education, worship, music—all are needs to which philanthropy responds with voluntary gifts of money or service. The strategies that are available are dictated by the needs. In the case of refugees, for instance, those strategies would include relief and rescue, rehabilitation, return, and economic development.

However, when assessing the scope of philanthropy, we must again remind ourselves that there is a vast and largely uncharted ocean of informal, spontaneous, interpersonal philanthropy. We make a mistake in measuring the scale and scope of philanthropy if we neglect or forget about the pervasive, character-shaping good works that are immediate, direct, or personal—the domain of traditional benevolence, love of neighbor, civility, and tolerance, the "ordinary virtues" if you will. As we noted earlier, we do not have adequate ways to measure the impact of all this sort of work on people, on the communities in which they live and work, and on the nation and the world. But this informal philanthropy clearly matters, especially to those receiving the help, whether they are our closest friends or a stranger. We must think of philanthropy as encompassing both the spontaneous, individual acts of kindness and the planned, organized efforts that ensure acts of kindness are not ineffective or short-lived.

Finally, we must remember that philanthropy, as voluntary action for the public good, appears in every civilized society. What makes American philanthropy distinctive is that we rely more extensively on philanthropy than any other society in history. But other cultures and other nations have their own philanthropic traditions, and so "what is going on" in philanthropy, in all its forms around the globe, is even more diverse than we experience in the United States.

Everybody's Philanthropic Autobiography

Finally, to understand "what is going on" in philanthropy, we cannot forget the individual dimension, the fact that philanthropy is very often intensely personal. As we said, everyone has a connection to philanthropy. And an individual's personal, particular connection is how he or she understands the meaning and mission of philanthropy. Most readers of this book will make sense of the definition of philanthropy as voluntary action for the public good through the filter of their own lived experience.

A starting point for reflection is one's own "philanthropic autobiography." The readers of this book are likely people who have some interest in the idea of philanthropy, so it seems reasonable to ask where that interest might have come from. Where do you develop your interest in philanthropy? What are the origins of the values that bring you into philanthropy? Where do you get your sentiments and attitudes and ways of thinking about relationships to others? What are the stories you have to tell about your philanthropic life? Your answers to these questions can also tell us something about the philanthropic world in which you live. Just as Gertrude Stein's story of her life and travels, in *Everybody's Autobiography*, told us something about America, every American's philanthropic autobiography tells us—and that person—something about American philanthropy.[44]

Philanthropic autobiographies usually center around family, school, church, mentors, and sometimes even life-shaping experiences. The occasional newspaper story suggests there are genetic influences at work; some of us may be wired to be philanthropic, just as some of us may be wired to be optimistic. For those not yet ready to leap to that conclusion, there are memorable experiences from childhood, influential mentors and peers, and the moral catechisms we once memorized and may still retain. Most people who are philanthropic seem to have been socialized into giving and serving, either by being explicitly taught or, more commonly, by following the example of family members or others. Some philanthropic mentors have offered a lifetime of help and advice, others a single penetrating observation. But many philanthropic autobiographies include a story of being inspired by another's generosity and perhaps one's gratitude and desire to "go and do likewise." Again, Andrew Carnegie provides a good illustration. Carnegie is one of the best known figures in American philanthropy, and he became so partly because of the generosity of a man named Colonel Anderson, who allowed Andrew as a young boy to use his private library. The impact of Colonel Anderson's generosity was not manifest until decades later, but it affected the lives of the millions of people who have used "Carnegie libraries" since. Later in this book we will label this sort of philanthropic sequence of continual giving back as "serial reciprocity."

For some people, the lived experience with philanthropy even includes being on the receiving end of charitable gifts meant to help the poor. But most readers of this book have not had this experience, though many will have a memory of the other side of this philanthropic exchange, of bringing cans of food to school or church to "feed the hungry." So we must remember that some aspects of philanthropic experience are, like L. P. Hartley said about the past, a foreign country.[45] Few of us can do more than imagine what it means to be an artist in search of the subsidy that will give the freedom to create, the opportunity to perform or exhibit. Only a few of us will have picketed on behalf of civil rights or against abortion or stood in a vigil protesting an execution. Fewer still will have accepted physical risk and hardship to protect forests or to counsel families in a high-crime neighborhood. It requires imagination and empathy—important attributes for philanthropy—to put oneself in the place of someone at the bedside of a patient dying of cancer or AIDS or Alzheimer's Disease, much less in the place of the sufferer. On the other hand, many of us have visited museums often enough to have a notion of what it would be like to work in one; we've taken flowers and gifts to the bedridden who had no family to bring flowers or comfort or even silent companionship, and someone has probably brought flowers to us. We may have served as a volunteer usher in a theater to see the play without buying a ticket. We may have helped to organize the large dinner to raise funds for the hospital and even sat on the dais to be recognized and applauded for our tireless service.

When people talk about philanthropy, it becomes clear that philanthropy raises their values to the surface. To talk about one's philanthropic autobiography is to define oneself, sometimes to reveal a different identity from the one others might have known or expected.

Philanthropic autobiographies, like all other autobiographies, are continuing narratives. Many people, as they reflect on their values, begin to realize that their values have changed as they have matured and become acquainted with their own vulnerability. Many people speak of their understanding of philanthropy being reshaped and transformed by tragedy. We also learn by experience what we're good at and what we don't do very well. We begin to recognize that we are neither candidates for sainthood nor hopeless sinners. We begin to develop a worldview, and our worldview has a place for philanthropy within it.

Teaching about Philanthropy, for Philanthropy

Public Teachers

We end this chapter with a final explanation of why we feel this book—and this sort of book—is necessary and valuable. It is always presumptuous to identify oneself as a "public teacher," but this is how we think of our role in writing this book. Public teachers are leaders who help others think about and understand difficult social issues and public problems.[46] We see this book as a guide to thinking seriously about an activity that helps to shape and define us as humans and a tradition that is essential to maintaining the good life and the good society.

The commonest method of learning about philanthropy is through the informal teaching of persons who are experienced in philanthropy. One reason informal teaching is so widespread in philanthropy is philanthropy's emphasis on action: philanthropy is tested, as pragmatic truth is tested, by what it does. Action means experience, and experience in philanthropy is very personal and individual for most people. "This is what I've done and this is what I've learned from it" is usually a more powerful teaching approach than a how-to manual based exclusively on theory or doctrine or a survey course on laws or technique.

A second reason for the tendency to rely only on informal teaching is the emphasis of philanthropy on values: philanthropy is about affirming what one believes is important, not just for oneself but for others. It is one thing to say, "I believe . . ."; it is another to manifest belief in action. To declare that you feel sorry for people who are down on their luck is an assertion of their value in your eyes and of your sensitivity to their plight. To do something about the troubled situation of strangers calls for more than sympathy and empathy; it calls for action based on your values. And for many reasons this can be hard to teach except by example or exhortation.

Our public teaching about philanthropy is not meant to replace this informal teaching, but to complement and enhance it. We seek to help people find their way through the complexity of philanthropy not by teaching them skills or giving them "best practice" guidelines, but by leading an exploratory dialogue on the fundamental purpose and place of their philanthropic action in their lives and their societies. Teaching itself is a philanthropic activity—it is the gift of one generation to another to pass along

what it knows and understands and values about good works, the good society, and the good life. This is our contribution.

The Audience

There are, broadly, three audiences for this book, for our public teaching.

We assume some readers of this book will be *young people*, often undergraduate and graduate students. The young people who might find this
book interesting and helpful are those who think "life is about more than
just making a living"; it is also about making a constructive difference for
others—friends and strangers alike—for the community, writ large and
small, and for oneself. Many of these young people will have been active in
some kind of volunteer or community work and want to do more of it.
Some might even think they want to pursue a career in philanthropy. We
hope these students—of whatever age and circumstance—will themselves
aspire to become public teachers in turn as they discuss with others the rationale for philanthropy. We hope they can use their understanding of philanthropy's meaning and mission to lead the field more effectively in what
will surely be a complicated future.

Another group of readers we have in mind are *practitioners*, laborers in
the vineyard of philanthropy—fund-raisers, board members, nonprofit executives, community leaders, perhaps even people of considerable means
in search of ways to use their wealth constructively and imaginatively.
Some of these readers are employed full-time in philanthropy. Others are
active as volunteers. These practitioners are those we mentioned earlier
who are often frustrated because the immediate demands of their work
cause them to be preoccupied with the how of their work to the neglect of
the why. They complain of "never having time to think about the big issues in what I do." Some may even have lost some of the enthusiasm that
drew them into philanthropy in the first place. Philanthropy calls for a ma-
turity based not only on experience but also on reflection. This book is intended to draw the reader into a more reflective approach, respecting the
complexity and subtlety of philanthropy.

The third group to whom this book is addressed are *scholars*, most of
whom will know more than we do about some specific subject discussed in
this book. We believe that philanthropy, when taken seriously, critically,
and constructively, is both intellectually engaging and illuminating. Scholars who explore the philanthropic dimension of their discipline usually dis-
cover surprising and enlightening connections, and they begin to trans-
form and enrich their approach to their own fields. Studying philanthropy

also helps bridge a growing disconnect, lamented by many scholars, between academic work and the serious problems of society.

Seek Simplicity and Distrust It

Whoever they are, we ask that readers of this book keep in mind Alfred North Whitehead's advice to "seek simplicity and distrust it."[47] He wasn't advising us to abandon the search for useful generalizations; he was simply cautioning us to remember as well that things are always more complex than our generalizations imply. Our generalizations in this book, while we hope they are useful, should be treated with this same skepticism; readers should use this skepticism as an incentive to revise your own ideas. In fact, any time you ask "Why" questions, you should not be satisfied with simple answers. So the reader in search of simple solutions and rules of behavior or social doctrine should look elsewhere.

Still we do suggest several simplifying conceptual frameworks to help make sense of philanthropy. But philanthropy is interesting partly because of its ambiguity and complexity, which we embrace in this book. Philanthropy as we define it is also celebrated as a haven of pluralism and a vehicle for the expression of diverse voices. We embrace that pluralism in our intellectual approach here by being eclectic in our methods, sources, and modes of thought, as befits a book coauthored by one person trained as a historian and philosopher and another person trained as a social scientist. Some of the key ideas discussed here come from sociology and political science, a few from economics, and many from philosophy, history, and religion. Our commingling of social science and humanities perspectives is another way this book introduces a unique perspective in this emerging field of study.

The key ideas about philanthropy that we raise cannot be pursued very far in this book; the intention is to open up ideas rather than to attempt to close them. Whatever this book achieves, it seeks balance, proportion, perspective, reflection, openness, and criticism of a constructive kind. It assumes some bias on the authors' part, but it also assumes that an earnest effort to control for it will stand a better chance of a durable result than cheerleading or cynicism. Having said that, we do take a stand in favor of philanthropy; that is a bias we can live with.

Good Works, the Good Life, and the Good Society

This book has a larger, normative purpose beyond the purely scholarly one. We are convinced that philanthropy is important and necessary and good—indeed, that the good society and the good life are not possible without good works. We want this book to help people take philanthropy seriously, to explore it both as an external social phenomenon and as a personal record of internal experiences and values. This mission is based on the assumption that when voluntary action for the public good is a defining characteristic of the culture, individuals lead better lives—better by their own standards, better as seen by others—and that society is a better place.

We believe deeply in the importance of philanthropy, especially with respect to its influence on the values of our society. Philanthropy speaks for values that constrain and modify, and occasionally domesticate and civilize, the strong values of power and wealth that drive politics and economics.

As we will describe later, we believe in the philanthropic philosophy of "meliorism," which holds that "the world can be made better by rightly directed human effort." So a primary reason to study philanthropy is to do philanthropy, and the contention here is that the odds of doing it better are increased by understanding it better, by noting some of the views that modify or contradict its claims, and by arguing with yourself as well as with others about it.

The challenge of this book for you the reader, then, is to confront the subject in as clear-eyed a way as possible; think hard about it, look at the evidence, accept or at least don't dismiss out of hand critiques you can't answer. If you turn out to be a believer in the social value of philanthropy, as we are, you will be more likely to make a useful contribution than if you simply echo the words and imitate the values of others. The study and practice of philanthropy should help people develop morally and socially. Our conviction is that the study of philanthropy, linked to its practice, will help us find meaning, purpose, and hope in our lives.

We set out here to promote philanthropy, but to do so in a way that transcends cheerleading, advertising, and tax incentives. We believe teaching and learning about philanthropy can change one's worldview; it has for us and for many others engaged in the serious study of philanthropy. Education is the key. Education is *always* the key.

2

Voluntary Action for the Public Good

$\mathcal{M}$ost readers of this book can surely come up with at least a tentative answer to the question "What is philanthropy?" Chances are that these answers will vary widely, from "giving money" to "giving to help others" to the more literal and more general "love of mankind." In fact, the same would be true if we asked scholars of philanthropy for their definitions.

We said in the previous chapter that to get at the "Why" questions about philanthropy, we will explore some of *our* answers to this question, "What is philanthropy?" And we have already given our primary (though not our only) answer: "Philanthropy is voluntary action for the public good." The purpose of this chapter is to unpack that definition. In doing so we will have a chance to discuss many of the features of the broad and diverse subject of philanthropy and to clarify just what is distinctive about philanthropy and what is special about its mission.

A Broad, Affirmative Conception of Philanthropy

We started this book with the assertion that the concept of philanthropy is a multiplicity. In fact, when we dig deeper we see that our basic definition itself embraces this multiplicity. "Voluntary action," as we define it, encompasses both voluntary giving *and* voluntary service, the former usually referring to gifts of money and the latter to gifts of time. But we also include voluntary association as a third form of voluntary action. Voluntary association is the vehicle or instrument for philanthropic giving and service; it organizes gifts of money and time to accomplish public purposes. Philanthropy's impact on society is only possible because of voluntary associations.

Our definition of philanthropy is broader than most, and this is by design.[1] The single word *philanthropy* is used here to encompass many things, as the single word *business* does, and as *politics* does. Philanthropy and business and politics are umbrella terms, even though "circus tent" might be a more useful metaphor. Under the circus tent called philanthropy, one would find a diverse array of topics and terms: gifts and grants, volunteers and trustees, foundations and endowments, special events and fund-raising, advocacy and reform, Alternative Spring Breaks and service learning, scholarships and awards, and many more.

Defining philanthropy as voluntary action for the public good assumes that philanthropy is manifest in action, not simply in purpose or intention. However, the definition also specifies that action, in order to be classified as philanthropic, must have a particular purpose—to achieve some vision of the public good. While this public good purpose might be mixed in with other, even selfish reasons for action, the action should be considered philanthropic, in our view, if it is voluntary and if it is seen by the actor as action to achieve the public good—or at least *a* public good. The point is that, taking all the pieces of our definition together, we argue that *both* the intentions and the actions of philanthropy are important.[2]

Another way to approach this issue is to try to identify the objectives of "voluntary action for the public good." A useful way to classify these objectives is to boil them down to two general types: (1) to relieve the suffering of others for whom one has no formal or legal responsibility, and (2) to improve the quality of life in the community, however one defines that idea. The first objective involves meeting basic needs such as food, shelter, clothing, and medical attention; the second involves enhancing the life— cultural, educational, recreational, etc.—of a community, however big or small. The range of specific philanthropic activities designed to achieve one or the other of these objectives is diverse, from direct service to organizing to fund-raising to advocacy. But both of these objectives have a prominent *moral* dimension; that is, they require intervening in other people's lives presumably for their benefit in some way. As we will argue, in our conception of philanthropy this moral dimension is the most important characteristic of the subject.

The Debate over Terms: Philanthropy as an Essentially Contested Concept

Philanthropy is an example of what the British philosopher W. B. Gallie called "essentially contested concepts." According to Gallie, these are concepts in which "there is no one clearly definable general use . . . which can be set up as the correct or standard use" and that "inevitably involve endless disputes about their proper uses on the part of their users."[3] He offers democracy and art as examples of such concepts. Definitively resolving the disputes among various uses of such concepts is impossible. But Gallie and others say we should examine the contestation over such concepts because we can then gain insight into the arguments and reasoning behind competing uses, including our own. It helps us understand the complexity of the activities or ideas denoted by the concept.

Philanthropy is an essentially contested concept; it is an idea that is bent and distorted by attempts to contain within it a diversity of human phenomena that resist generalization and categorization. And different users of the term *philanthropy* endlessly dispute its meaning. In fact, the dispute goes beyond the meaning of this one term, as many people are dissatisfied with the use of a single term to encompass such disparate activities and values.

Philanthropy is just one among several circus tent terms in common use; others are *voluntary sector, nonprofit sector, third sector,* and *independent sector.* Philanthropic organizations are sometimes called *nonprofit,* or *not-for-profit,* or *nongovernmental* (NGOs). The ancient term *charity* is sometimes used instead of the ancient term *philanthropy,* and others like *benevolence, altruism, humanitarianism,* and *civil society* drift in and out of the conversation as well. *Eleemosynary* never did become popular, although the word *alms* remains from the dregs of it. And in the academic writing on this subject there are even more "tongue-twisting mouthfuls"—QUANGOs, PVOSs, and so on, as Adil Najam found when he tried to make sense of the literature.[4]

For some people who work in this field, this quibbling over terms is distracting, confusing, or unimportant. But it is helpful to engage the terminological debate a bit here, not merely because we need to stake out our place in the academic landscape but also because the issues raised by this debate about an "essentially contested concept" are central substantive issues for understanding the subject itself.

Nonprofit is probably the dominant term in the United States, at least when we are speaking of organizations that make up a sector. Internationally, the preferred term is *nongovernmental organization,* which is used to refer both to organizations that operate in multiple countries, such as Catholic Relief Services, and to domestic groups in individual countries.

One theory that you sometimes hear is that *NGOs* is the preferred term in countries with a traditionally strong governmental sector, while *nonprofits* is preferred in countries with a traditionally strong market sector.[5]

Nonprofit began to dominate in the United States as a new wave of scholars entered the field whose orientation was economic, political, legal, social scientific, and organizational. As a term of social science, *nonprofit* seeks to be value-neutral, to avoid the normative connotations often attached to words like *charity* and *philanthropy*. However, using *nonprofit* as the primary term has some serious downsides, as many observers have pointed out.

One downside to *nonprofit* is that it implies that the most important thing about the field is money, which is a serious mistake. It implies that the most important characteristic of voluntary associations seeking to do the public business is that they don't distribute their surplus if they generate one. Many of the standard, economics-inspired theories of the nonprofit sector identify this "nondistribution constraint" as the source of the sector's distinctiveness.[6] Another downside is that *nonprofit, nongovernmental,* and similar terms define the subject by what it is not, rather than by what it is. As Roger Lohmann put it nicely in a 1989 article, "And Lettuce Is Non-Animal."[7] A negative definition simply isn't a sufficient definition.

There are also specific problems with theories that emphasize the nonprofit-distributing aspect. For one, many business enterprises, despite their owners' best efforts, could technically be labeled nonprofit, at least in lean years; this is why some people prefer the more precise term *not-for-profit*. And, further, many nonprofits actually turn a profit through their fee-generating activities—think of a busy suburban YMCA gym, or a popular museum store full of expensive items—even if they don't give these profits to staff or stockholders at the end of the year.[8] And finally, some critics note that focusing on the nondistribution constraint as the defining feature discounts the significance of small, community, and grassroots associations, many of which have small budgets and so have nothing to distribute even if they could.

This last point suggests the more important, general problem with focusing on nonprofitness as our primary defining term. Philanthropy is about more than money; it is about mission, shared values, organization, and much else before and besides money. The impersonal and economistic term *nonprofit* obscures the sector's charitable roots, its moral dimension, and its often personal meaning; *nonprofit* reveals nothing of the positive values embodied in and promoted by philanthropic giving and serving.

Besides *nonprofit*, there are limitations to the other proposed umbrella terms. While the voluntary or private character of this action is clearly important (and included in our definition), calling the philanthropic sector the *voluntary sector* is problematic because this term would apply equally well to the marketplace. *Independent sector* is now used both as a label for this part of society and as the proper name of the umbrella organization, Independent Sector, representing groups within the sector.[9] And *third sector* is often rejected by scholars who point out that voluntary institutions serving the public good *actually came first*, historically; voluntary associations existed before formal government or business organizations.

Other umbrella terms that are used in different places and in certain circles are *civil society* and *civil society organizations*; these are the preferred terms of the international umbrella group CIVICUS, for instance. *Civil society* is a hotly debated term, recently in vogue in the academy, that unfortunately suffers from being too variously defined—sometimes the family or business is included, sometimes it is meant to describe a quality of society rather than a part of society. We like that *civil society* is an attempt to define the field in a positive way, that it is deliberately broad in scope, and that it emphasizes (in some connotations) the moral and value-laden nature of the work. But we think *philanthropy* is the more appropriate broad and affirmative term, for reasons we describe below.

In Europe, *social economy* has become a popular label, and in the corporate world all things philanthropic or nonprofit are often labeled part of the *social sector*, a term related to the ideas of social entrepreneurship and social enterprise mentioned earlier. In Canada, *voluntary sector* is the norm, while in the United Kingdom the terms *voluntary sector, charity*, and *community organizations* are common.

The issue of how to include less formal, or less publicly oriented, types of organizations also raises problems. It is difficult to find a comprehensive terminology and definition that will encompass the cooperatives, mutual-benefit, or "member-benefit" organizations like the Elks Club or credit unions (which are often defined in opposition to "public-benefit" groups), neighborhood or grassroots associations, and many others that Peter Frumkin describes as "the army of less visible associations, clubs, networks, and groups through which communities come together and act."[10] A few years ago, Lohmann proposed using the umbrella term *the commons* as a way to avoid the term *nonprofit* and to encompass those associations that were producing common goods through uncoerced cooperation.[11] More fundamentally, Lohmann and other scholars such as Jon Van Til also try to move *away* from structural definitions in terms of organizations in a sector and to shift the focus onto definitions derived from the form and purpose of voluntary action.[12]

The Internal Revenue Service's taxonomy of tax-exempt entities is a likely source to turn to for clarity and authority on this issue, but in fact it provides little guidance. The two main categories, 501(c)(3) and 501(c)(4) organizations, carry outdated and cumbersome titles. 501(c)(3)s are described as "Religious, Educational, Charitable, Scientific, Literary . . . Organizations" (the list goes on after "Literary"). These (c)(3)s are further subdivided into "Private Foundations" and "Public Charities." The 501(c)(4)s are labeled "Civic Leagues, Social Welfare Organizations, and Local Associations of Employees" even though most people in the field refer to (c)(4)s as "advocacy organizations" and think of them as the groups that are unrestricted in their lobbying activity.[13] Further complicating matters are the many other categories of organizations in the IRS code, including categories for chambers of commerce and the recently controversial new type of political advocacy groups known (because of their IRS classification) as "527s"—for example, the group Swift Boat Veterans for Truth that ran ads against U.S. presidential contender John Kerry in 2004 was a 527.[14]

As we wade through this terminological debate, we should remember that our terms are always social and cultural constructions; they are context-bound attempts to capture and simplify what is inherently complex. And as we noted, this field is particularly complex. Any umbrella concept for this field must capture phenomena that vary along multiple continua—from informal to formal, from big to small, from relevance to one or two places to relevance across the globe, from huge hospitals to tiny toy train hobby clubs, and so on. Still, we need these umbrella concepts. To help us make sense of this diverse activity as an interconnected part of society, we need to construct categories and terms that are general enough to encompass the diversity but also appealing enough to be used widely—terms comparable to *business* or *government*. Trying to remedy this perception problem and craft useful general concepts is a key purpose of books like this one, and we propose philanthropy as one such concept. But we should also remember that our constructions are inevitably informed by our own traditions and biases. Every country, for instance, has a slightly different set of terms and concepts that reflect their different culture and history and institutional makeup. And we should accept that any such constructions in a plural society will also always be disputed. The debate over this and other essentially contested concepts will go on.

Toward an Affirmative Conception

As we said, in this book we are proposing an affirmative conception of philanthropy. Other recent work has presented some elements of an affirmative view, and this work is helpful to our task here, even if it does not go as far in this direction (or in the same exact direction) as we do.

Lester Salamon, in his well-known primer on the field, offers a summary of six characteristics shared by what he prefers to call "nonprofit organizations." These organizations are

> 1. formally constituted;
> 2. private, as opposed to governmental;
> 3. not profit-distributing;
> 4. self-governing;
> 5. *voluntary, and*
> 6. *of public benefit.*[15]

This is a useful list, first, because it includes more than just the standard "nondistribution" criteria that is listed here as #3. But it is also useful because it ends with the two key general qualities (italicized here) that are highlighted by our basic definition.

However, as noted, Salamon intends this list to describe characteristics of nonprofit organizations, rather than characteristics of all philanthropic action, as our use of #5 and #6 does. In fact, Salamon adopts the usage habit of many people in this field, making a primary distinction between what he calls the "private nonprofit sector"—a sector of society populated by nonprofit organizations—and something separate that he calls "philanthropy"—the private giving that is one source of monetary support for those organizations in that sector.[16] This narrower (than ours) conception of philanthropy—philanthropy as *just* voluntary giving—is perhaps the most common usage of the term, but one we find less satisfactory than our more general meaning of philanthropy.

Still, we clearly agree with that aspect of Salamon's definition which emphasizes voluntary action for the public good. In another book, he defines nonprofit organizations as "entities dedicated to mobilizing private initiative for the common good."[17] By our definition, this means nonprofits are entities dedicated to philanthropy as a broadly conceived type of action. Philanthropy is not to be distinguished from the nonprofit sector; philanthropy as a concept encompasses the nonprofit sector.

Salamon's summaries of the nonprofit sector also detail the range of "roles" played by this sector, which is another significant way to establish an affirmative foundation for why this sort of activity exists. Salamon borrows directly from Ralph Kramer's famous summary of these roles, but both of these scholars owe a debt to Alexis de Tocqueville.[18] Citing Tocqueville is, for good reason, de rigueur in any account of the importance of voluntary action and associations for a democratic society. Tocqueville observed that Americans turned to associations whenever they wished to get some public or communal work done or to express a shared interest. In addition to these roles, Tocqueville saw associations as an antidote to despotism, to the tyranny of the majority, and to the perils of individualism. Tocqueville even saw associations as playing a socialization role, functioning as "great free schools" teaching the civic skills—such as "the general theory of association"—that are necessary to make democracy work.[19] As we will discuss in chapter 6, this makes philanthropy and especially voluntary associations an essential element of a free, open, and democratic society.

Modern scholars, following Tocqueville's lead, identify an even wider range of functions or social roles served by the nonprofit sector. In his book *On Being Nonprofit*, Peter Frumkin has built a conceptual framework for studying nonprofits around the idea that there are "four functions of nonprofit and voluntary action."[20] Two functions of the sector—what Frumkin labels "service delivery" and "social entrepreneurship"—illustrate an "instrumental rationale" for the existence of the sector; the sector exists to do what is needed. The other two functions of the sector—what Frumkin labels "civic and political engagement" and "values and faith"—illustrate an "expressive rationale"; nonprofit and voluntary action exists to express values and ideas.

Other scholars, including Salamon and Kramer, present similar lists of functions or roles. We find it most parsimonious to distill these down into what we can call *five roles for philanthropy:*

---

1. *Service role:* Providing services (especially when the other sectors fail to provide them) and meeting needs.
2. *Advocacy role:* Advocating for reform, for particular interests, for particular populations, or for particular views of the public good.
3. *Cultural role:* Providing a vehicle for expressing and preserving cherished values, traditions, identities, and other aspects of culture.

4. *Civic role:* Building community, generating "social capital," and promoting and increasing civic engagement.[21]
5. *Vanguard role:* Serving as the site for social innovation, experimentation, and entrepreneurial invention. (We borrow the term *vanguard* from Kramer.)

Not all of these roles are viewed positively by all observers, and some have become tools to make political or ideological arguments of various sorts. The advocacy role is particularly controversial. Despite its central importance to the pluralist vision of democratic governance, in which citizens organize into groups to advocate for their shared interests, this advocacy activity has been criticized as blurring the boundaries between government and private interests, as politicizing (and therefore sullying) charitable groups, etc.[22] In fact, as we saw, this advocacy role is singled out for explicit regulation in the IRS tax-exemption statutes. In addition, the crucial service role has been used by some on the political right wing to promote philanthropy and nonprofits (particularly faith-based ones) as an alternative to a bureaucratic welfare state or to champion voluntary associations as "mediating structures" that intervene between individuals and big government and help check the unnecessary growth of government.[23]

But despite these disputes, the main point remains that voluntary action serves essential, positive roles in society. So these summaries of the purposes of nonprofits are crucial steps toward an affirmative answer to the questions "What is philanthropy?" and "Why does philanthropy exist?"

Our theory of philanthropy's mission embraces this range of positive functions. We agree that philanthropy (and the nonprofit sector it encompasses) serves needs—for example, relieving suffering, improving the quality of life—and expresses collective values. However, listing philanthropy's roles is only part of an affirmative rationale for why philanthropy exists. We also think it is necessary to identify shared qualities of all sorts of philanthropic action and to clarify a general purpose for this action, as we do in this book. For example, we present philanthropy as voluntary action that advances a vision of the public good, as moral action that intervenes in the lives of others so as to make the world better through human effort.

Why Philanthropy: An Affirmative Term

The term we wish to propose for this field is *philanthropy*, which we define more broadly than most others do. The term comes from the Greek *phil-*

anthropia, meaning "love of mankind." In some of its modern uses, *philan-thropy* still retains its ancient meaning of general benevolence, of kindness, of generosity toward humanity. The modern English word *philanthropy* today is usually defined by dictionaries both as the sentiment of love and as action conducted in the spirit of this sentiment.[24]

Philanthropy defines the field in a positive way, in terms of what this sort of action does and why. It affirms a value, a concern for the well-being of people beyond oneself, and a concern for the public good. It asserts that the most important aspect of action (formal or informal) in this so-called sector is the public purpose and mission of that action. *Philanthropy* is the best term, in our view, because it highlights this essentially moral nature of voluntary action for the public good. Even if we use the term in neutral, social scientific ways (as we often do), it is a normative term describing normative human activity.

The story of philanthropy in any culture records a moral quest that has shaped the moral agenda of that culture across the generations. As later chapters will argue, the history of philanthropy is the "social history of the moral imagination." Philanthropy is a primary way that humans enact their moral visions of what is good, visions which always differ among people and groups within any single society. Humans use philanthropic action to relieve suffering or meet other pressing needs, to improve the quality of life or civic capacity in our communities, to advocate for or express ideas or values or identities, to experiment with new ideas for social change as well as to preserve traditions in the face of impending change. All of these and more are specific roles for philanthropy that can be encompassed by a broad, affirmative conception of philanthropy.

We prefer to define philanthropy more as a tradition than as a sector (though we use the term *sector* when it is relevant) to emphasize the deep historical roots of philanthropy—that is, some form of philanthropy has existed in all societies from the beginning because it is a basic human response to the human condition. We also want to emphasize the breadth of what is included under "voluntary action"—it is more than just formal organizational action in a bounded social sector. And like all traditions, the philanthropic tradition in any society has culturally specific content. The specific story of how the moral imagination has been enacted through philanthropy in the United States will be different than the story in Mexico or India. Different religious doctrines, different national heroes, different linguistic resources, and different economic and ethnic patterns will all make for different philanthropic traditions.

There are other, related affirmative terms that fit our focus and that we will use occasionally in this book, such as *good works* and *charity*. (And there are others that we find appropriate but don't use much, such as *benevolence* and *beneficence*.) When referring specifically to formal organizations or to "the sector," we occasionally use the terms *third sector* and *voluntary* or *nonprofit*—in addition to calling them *philanthropic organizations* in a *philanthropic sector*, which we would ultimately prefer. This is because terms like *nonprofit sector* are so common and widely used in the United States that readers are comfortable with them, and our purpose in holding up philanthropy as the umbrella term is to highlight and encompass key issues, not force people to change their language all at once.

However, we *do* want to encourage the use of our broader meaning of the term *philanthropy*. As noted earlier, many (perhaps most) people in this field define philanthropy in a narrower way. These narrower connotations include the following:

1. Philanthropy refers to giving (or perhaps giving and service both) and is therefore distinct conceptually from the nonprofit sector. Philanthropy is giving, and nonprofit groups are the entities that receive that giving.
2. Philanthropy refers to large-scale giving by wealthy "philanthropists," a meaning that was cemented a century ago as a way to describe the relatively new phenomenon of massive giving by people such as John D. Rockefeller and Andrew Carnegie.
3. Philanthropy refers solely to giving by private foundations or other institutional grantmakers.

There are surely other commonly held understandings of philanthropy not listed here. We find these narrower meanings to be problematic for a number of reasons. We believe the ancient concept of philanthropy contains more richness and versatility within it than just the notion of giving, or giving money, or giving only by certain people or certain institutions. And the fact is that sustained voluntary giving and serving are impossible without voluntary associations—the three parts of our definition of philanthropy are inextricably linked in practice. Think of the philanthropic response to a disaster like the 9/11 attacks. Gifts of money were an essential part, and so were the Herculean efforts of volunteers, and none of the philanthropic help would have been possible without the coordination provided by voluntary organizations. This is true whether we consider the immediate relief efforts or the much more difficult long-term work of helping the victims and the community recover, mourn, and rebuild their communities and their lives. We deserve a definition of philanthropy that highlights the integration of these elements, *not* just the money part. And all things "nonprofit" are best conceived as *part* of a general conception of "voluntary action for the public good" rather than distinct from it.[25]

The broad, affirmative definition of philanthropy we propose here is, we argue, the best term to capture, unify, and help perpetuate this diverse but vitally important part of our lives. Of course, we realize that usage won't change overnight, and that activity (which is most important after all) will continue whether we have a useful general term or not.

Philanthropy and/versus Charity

Philanthropia was not the only ancient word meaning love or good works toward others, and these other words are also affirmative and focused on the moral dimension. The word *charity* is derived from the Latin word *caritas*, which meant love of others in a way that was distinct from other forms of love (e.g., erotic love, friendship).[26] *Agape* is another Greek word for love that comes from a root verb meaning "to treat with affectionate regard" and that refers to self-giving and selfless, even sacrificial, forms of love. In the Jewish tradition, the Hebrew term *tzedakah*—often translated as "charity" or "righteousness"—is the key. It is a concept that brings mercy and justice together in one idea, contending that it is impossible to have one without the other. Other religious traditions have similar focal terms.

Of these other possible alternatives to the term *philanthropy, charity* is the most common and intriguing, so we should take special care to consider its relationship to philanthropy, as we use these two terms. The common usage of *charity* versus *philanthropy* can be confusing. In this book, *philanthropy* is used primarily as an umbrella term for the entire spectrum of voluntary actions for the public good, while *charity*—which was at one time the umbrella term for the field—is used more narrowly. Occasionally, in popular usage, the two terms are differentiated according to the two broad objectives of voluntary action mentioned earlier: *philanthropy* for acts to improve the quality of life versus *charity* for acts to relieve suffering. Similarly, on an international scale, humanitarian "relief" aid is often referred to as charity, while "development" aid is called philanthropy.[27] In this view, if charity is a matter of bringing blankets and medicine and food to refugees, philanthropy is a matter of getting the refugees back home and putting their society back on the road to social and economic recovery.

This way of distinguishing charity and philanthropy is sometimes handy, but in our usage, while we keep the more restricted connotation of charity (as acts to relieve suffering), we prefer a broader meaning for philanthropy.

Until about 1950, the word *charity* was the most widely used general term, unsatisfactory though many at the time thought it to be. *Charity* was the word in the tax law (it still is), and most people had an idea of what "charitable contributions" meant. The word *charity* was the umbrella term in the 1937 *Encyclopedia of the Social Sciences*, but *philanthropy* had replaced it in the 1967 *International Encyclopedia of the Social Sciences*.

Both philanthropy and charity are *normative* words—both words affirm something of fundamental value and importance. But as we noted earlier, for many people the word *philanthropy* has come to be more associated with money, particularly as philanthropy and fund-raising have become professionalized. In that sense, *philanthropy* appears to have lost its connection with benevolence. As most people use the word, it is about money, perhaps at bottom even about the redistribution of wealth. A similar fate befell the word *charity*. In the sixteenth century, Francis Bacon saw charity as "the bond of Perfection, because it comprehendeth and fasteneth all the virtues together."[28] The King James Version of the Bible refers to "faith, hope, and charity, these three" and says that "the greatest of these is charity" (I Corinthians 13:13). But the divine aspiration of charity became mixed with the mundane practice of almsgiving, and in time charity was also reduced to money. Almsgiving tainted the ideal of charity and made it a symbol of social inferiority and dependency; it connected the idea of charity to the idea of a "handout" and even to begging for handouts. This alteration in the term is revealed in the expression "I'd rather die than accept charity."

As noted, *charity* means love, and because *love* has several meanings, the word is always at risk of being misunderstood. Consider the famous passage about charity in Corinthians: the term in the original Greek New Testament was *agape*, which was translated into the Latin *caritas* and then into the English word *charity*. Today the term is often translated as "love," as in "the greatest of these is love." This is why the Corinthians passage is a favorite in Christian wedding ceremonies, where it can be quoted as "Love is patient; Love is kind," and so on (I Corinthians 13:4), even though the "love" referred to is technically not romantic love. In other cases, we have tended to reduce love even further to erotic love and then to feel awkward and embarrassed when we use the word in connection with friendship, benevolence, or even charity. But we have no acceptable alternatives to charity-as-love. And we are reluctant to give up a term that still carries, at least for some, such powerful emotional and historical freight.

This usage discussion could go on for pages. Our approach will be to focus on developing philanthropy as the core concept, but occasionally make use of charity (despite its baggage) when we want to emphasize the specific aspects of the field that fit with that term—e.g., acts to relieve suffering. Historically, we believe charity and philanthropy represent compatible and complementary rather than exclusive and opposing values. Both terms refer to values that are important parts of the tradition of good works we are concerned with here, and both sorts of values have inspired practices we consider essential.

For example, Jane Addams and Hull House, and the settlement house movement in general, distinguished between the two ideas and sought to provide both charity and philanthropy, moving from one to the other. They began with people who needed immediate charitable help, gave them that help, and then led them to help themselves through such "philanthropic" programs as literacy classes. Similarly, we noted in the previous chapter how the work of Soros's Open Society Fund in the former Yugoslavia in the 1990s moved from meeting the necessity for the charitable relief of immediate suffering (and threat) to the need for long-term development of philanthropic institutions. In sum, while the basic distinction can occasionally be analytically useful, our broad, affirmative conception of philanthropy is meant to encompass charity under the umbrella of philanthropy.

Voluntary Giving, Service, and Association

We can already see how attempts to capture a complex subject like philanthropy in a phrase or sentence or concise definition are always flawed. They break down under close analysis, especially when they are pressed too hard to cover too much. This does not mean we can do without definitions; it simply means we should take the time to examine our working definitions closely. In our definition, "voluntary action" includes voluntary giving, service, and association. By bringing them all together under the umbrella of philanthropy, we want to emphasize their interconnectedness. In the sections that follow, however, we will separate them for a moment and take a closer look at each of these three dimensions of philanthropy in turn.

Voluntary Giving

Voluntary giving, as we usually use the term, is about gifts of money or property. We all know that some people give money rather than time and talent to the work of philanthropy. There are various ways in which these gifts can be made, from buying a box of Girl Scout cookies to developing a sophisticated pattern of planned giving. Sometimes funds are given directly to a voluntary organization; sometimes they are channeled through intermediary agencies such as the United Way or a community foundation. More and more people with the means to do so are even starting their own private foundations. Some donors are dissatisfied with the normal vehicles for giving and come up with new ones, such as special "donor-advised funds" and mutual funds that give a portion of proceeds to charity (and only invest in socially responsible businesses). Recently, groups of donors around the country have started forming "giving circles" in which they pool their funds and collectively decide on joint gifts.[29]

Gifts of property are common, too. The most familiar is the gift of clothing and canned goods for the poor, usually in winter and on the occasion of religious holidays. Companies often donate products; a great many of them did so following Hurricane Katrina. This reminds us that not all giving is from individuals (although the numbers we gave in the previous chapter show how the vast majority of giving *is* from individuals). A great deal of voluntary giving also comes from a variety of philanthropic foundations. Foundation giving is often a particularly visible and carefully determined form of giving; foundations are behind many of our most treasured activities and institutions, as well as many of our most notable efforts at fundamental social reform, and our most innovative efforts at global development.

We often give to strangers, such as refugees halfway around the world. But not all strangers in need are in other countries, and not all are refugees. In fact, only a very small part of our giving goes abroad, and only a very small part goes to help those who are not citizens of our own country. In fact, most of our giving is not only domestic but *local*. The largest part of the taxes we pay goes to national expenditures; that largest part of our voluntary contributions stays in the community. As Jefferson and Emerson and others have said, the wisest giving is to those things we know best; those things often are closest to home.

Giving money, unlike most forms of giving service, can usually be done at a safe distance. But many people give both money and service. As a general rule, service seems more often to lead to giving money than the other way around, but it is clear that the two are mutually reinforcing for a variety of reasons. This is a fact confirmed by many scholars and relied upon by many fund-raisers—fund-raisers know that people who identify with a group and its mission, and who build relationships with other people in the group, will be more likely to give money to that group and to give more generously. One study found that the amount of money donated by volunteering households in the United States was more than double the amount given by nonvolunteers.[30]

Research has also shown that the following factors will tend to increase a person's philanthropic giving: attending religious services regularly, being involved in giving or volunteering as a youth, having generous parents, having a college education, being married, having children, and not being worried about having enough money in the future.[31] And as obvious as it seems, it is important that we remember that people often give because they believe in the mission or cause of an organization.

The more cynical readers will say, though, that giving is at least partly driven by tax considerations, at least in countries that allow such tax deductions. And yes, many Americans keep track of their charitable contributions so they can "write them off," even though many people admit they are not quite clear about how tax deductibility (and tax exemption for nonprofits) works.[32] Most research on the United States has shown that taking a charitable tax deduction does *not* change whether someone gives, but it does affect how *much* they give. Itemizers give at least a third more than people who do not itemize.[33]

However, the most commonly cited reason for giving listed by donors when we survey them is shockingly simple: they gave because they were asked.[34] The asking itself, as we all know, is a very large and by now quite sophisticated business. But asking matters. Many people give money or property only when asked, and although most of us complain about being asked too often, even incessantly, the most common explanation (or excuse) for not giving is not being asked.

Voluntary Service

Voluntary service is an important dimension of American life, important to those who offer it and to those they serve, and important to the society as a whole. Voluntary service covers a vast array of activities. It includes everything from the Candy Striper pushing a refreshment cart down a hospital corridor to an accountant donating time as a tax consultant for a small nonprofit, from a college student volunteer making recordings for the blind to a celebrity making a public service announcement about domestic violence. Volunteers raise money for the United Way, restore hiking trails, develop rural cooperatives in Africa, sort clothing to be sent to tornado victims, and publish Web sites to argue for reforms in education policy.

Because voluntary service depends simply on human resources, on giving your time and yourself, there is no such thing as having nothing to give. Time is said to be more precious than money; the Greek philosopher Theophrastus is often credited with the aphorism "Time is the most valuable thing one can spend."[35] Because of that, the gift of service can be a more generous gift than a gift of money. In fact, in many cases gifts of money are a poor substitute for the intimacy and companionship that are desperately needed. One cannot help but be deeply impressed by—and envious of—those people of infinite compassion and patience who sit by the beds of the dying, particularly those who were not previously their family or friends. They give the voluntary and valuable gift of silent companionship, the gift of human presence. A gift of one's time to philanthropy reduces the time available for other things—family, friends, recreation, relaxation, reflection. Giving service means that people become involved personally in the cause; it often involves personally intervening in the lives of others for their benefit.

The varieties of voluntary service are beyond enumerating but can be roughly categorized under two headings: service to others as individuals, and service to community. Voluntary service to other individuals in need— one individual helping another where the consequences of not helping are evident and serious—is considered by many people to be the most basic form of philanthropy. Service to others in need is the most immediate and personal and self-revealing—therefore the most challenging—form of service. Service to community can focus on alleviating suffering and misery, but it can also be about improving the quality of life. For example, service to community can involve picking up trash at the beach, or it can be devoted to reconciling groups who have been in conflict. We should remember that service to community is seldom a matter for individuals acting alone, which is another reason why voluntary service is so closely connected to voluntary association.

The reasons why people volunteer are similar to the reasons why they give. Being asked is the most commonly cited reason—one study found that 93 percent of young people who were asked to volunteer did, but only 24 percent of those who were *not* asked ended up volunteering anyway.[36] Religious participation and membership in organizations also increase volunteering, as does having volunteer experiences as a youth. Going to college seems to have a particularly significant effect on volunteering. Women volunteer more than men, and married people volunteer more than single people. And despite the stereotype that elderly retirees and other people who "don't have to work" make up most of the volunteer workforce, research shows that employed people are more likely to volunteer than un-employed people.[37]

We should remember, though, that there are troubling criticisms of voluntary service and of volunteerism. For some, the word *service* implies superiority of position rather than mutual respect. "I've come to help you" is resented as elitist, and the self-appointed helpers are said to focus on what they have to give rather than on what people need. This sort of crit-icism is not new, of course. The same denunciations were leveled against the upper-class ladies in the United Kingdom and the United States who practiced "friendly visiting" with poor families in the late nineteenth cen-tury, expecting that their manners and advice would help cure the illness of poverty. A related criticism of voluntary service is that it implies that every-one can afford to give time and money to the causes they care about. And while it is true that poor people do not volunteer in formal organizations as much as those in other income brackets, they do give their time philan-thropically—remember, for many their time is the only thing they have to give.

Voluntary Association

While our definition of philanthropy includes the immense number of in-formal acts of giving and serving, this book is mostly about voluntary ser-vice and voluntary giving that has become organized and systematic. The instrument of voluntary action in that organized form is the voluntary as-sociation, a term which we use in a broad sense to describe the range of groups with a philanthropic purpose, from small grassroots associations to large, bureaucratized nonprofit institutions.[38]

Much of philanthropy couldn't happen at all without organization. Or-ganized philanthropy via voluntary associations gives leverage to the efforts of single individuals who would otherwise lack the strength in some cir-cumstances to ease the burden of suffering or effect the improvement that seems necessary or desirable. It is possible for a single individual to give a few dollars to a homeless person to buy something to eat or a place to spend the night, but it is not possible for a single individual to house and feed and attend to the other needs of dozens of families in a homeless shel-ter for months at a stretch. If a single individual responds with sympathy to the televised picture of a hungry child in a refugee camp orphaned by a tsunami halfway around the world, and that individual wants to give money or personal assistance to that child, action (especially effective action) is possible only via a mediating organization. And giving blood or organs to those who need them most would be impossible without institutions coordinating this giving.[39]

As Tocqueville famously pointed out, Americans seem to be "forever forming associations."[40] And as we noted earlier, Tocqueville argued strongly that associations are necessary for a well-functioning democracy. So associations can be seen as making organized philanthropy possible, but also making democracy possible.

Philanthropic organizations are in many ways like other types of organizations. Organizations require resources. Organizations must have a mission, and organizations must have goals and objectives. Organizations must be managed, and organizations must have measures of success and failure. While the goals and mission of philanthropic organizations may be different, the principles that control or limit or guide the management of such voluntary associations are often indistinguishable from the principles that managers of government agencies or business corporations confront.

Like all organizations, voluntary associations undertake a diverse range of actions. They implement philanthropic programs, they create and maintain their organizational structures and cultures, they reform and adapt to changing environments, and so on. The array of specific forms of voluntary associations carrying out these actions has become even more diverse in recent years, as illustrated particularly by the new hybrid forms of revenue-generating philanthropic organizations.

The secret to a successful voluntary association and perhaps the real test of philanthropy are to be found not in giving or service but in fundraising. The principal philanthropic difference between the United States and the rest of the world may be the extent and the effectiveness of organized fund-raising. Fund-raising on a large scale is more highly developed and more widely practiced in the United States than anywhere in the world. The observers who claim that American philanthropy is unique are probably closest to the mark when we consider the scope and systematization of our fund-raising. Many people throughout the world, as well as many Americans, think of fund-raising as at best a necessary vice, at worst demeaning and crass. They never imagine that fund-raising can be ennobling and empowering, that it can be an affirmation of the mission of a philanthropic organization rather than a cheapening of it.

When we talk about the organized side of philanthropy, we must also confront the fact that over the past century philanthropy—giving, volunteering, fund-raising, etc.—has become much more professionalized. In addition to the people who give money and service and the people who are helped by it, there are a great many people who make their living helping others—or by helping others to help others. And those people—who live *off* philanthropy rather than simply living *for* philanthropy, to modify Max Weber's famous distinction—have honed their craft, built their specialized knowledge, and established their standards of practice just like other professionals.[41] In addition to individuals and companies functioning as fund-raisers, there are associations of fund-raisers and of fund-raising companies; there are private foundations and public foundations and community foundations and family foundations—and associations of foundations. There are specialists who advise the wealthy about their philanthropic giving and about the tax consequences of giving in one way or at one time or another. There are people who design direct mail campaigns and others who call people on the telephone to ask for donations of used clothing. There are groups that specialize in helping people adopt children and other groups that specialize in helping children gain access to health care or to summer camp or to computers. And even some of the people who are professional lobbyists for nonprofits in Washington and in state capitals fall under our definition of people working in the philanthropic sector.

Philanthropy and the Three-Sector Society

The Filer Commission and the Concept of a Three-Sector Society

Having described the key elements of our basic definition and general concept of philanthropy, we can now discuss the relationship of our conception to the more familiar understanding of the "three-sector society." This three-sector image is most prominent in the United States (which is our focus here), although it could be argued that, with some modifications, we could apply this image to other democratic societies.

Philanthropy has had a prominent role in the shaping of American society. Yet it was only thirty years ago that a national commission, noting the magnitude of philanthropy and the significant social issues it deals with, chose to describe the United States as a three-sector society, composed of government (the first sector), the marketplace (the second sector), and philanthropy (the third sector). The Commission on Private Philanthropy and Public Needs (known as the Filer Commission after its chairperson, John Filer) was set up at the instigation of John D. Rockefeller III (grandson of the original philanthropist), who saw a need to recognize public and voluntary activities that fell outside government and the marketplace.

In 1975, the Filer Commission's path-breaking report offered a new description of American society to replace the public-private dualism of the past. The report consisted of a summary volume entitled *Giving in America* and five accompanying volumes of studies and reports.[42] In addition, there was a report prepared by a dissenting group known as the Donee Group, who felt the Commission and its findings neglected minority and other voices and failed to emphasize funding of activism and advocacy.[43]

The specific recommendations of the Commission as well as the dissenting comments undoubtedly had some modest impact on current policies and will surely continue to be of more than historical interest. However, in retrospect there are two enduring contributions of the Commission's work that should not be underestimated. When considered together, these two contributions suggest that the Filer Commission should be considered a watershed in our national development.

First, the Commission began the development of a more extensive knowledge base—about giving, volunteering, and the organizations which mobilize that giving and volunteering—that has now dramatized the extraordinary scale and scope of philanthropy in America. This knowledge has changed our very understanding of what democracy means.

Second, the Commission promoted the image of America as a three-sector society, in which a previously ambiguous and mostly hidden dimension of American society—the public but nongovernmental dimension, the philanthropic dimension—was labeled a "third sector." In this way, the Commission provided a new way of thinking—the concept of a third sector and the beginning of an understanding about how the three sectors differ and how they resemble each other, about how they interact and how they influence each other—that has changed the way we think of ourselves as a society. The Commission made it seem plausible and helpful to bring together under the common rubric of a third sector many philanthropic activities that are diverse and dissimilar. As we suggested before, there is no consensus about usage of the term *third sector*, and there are important limitations to the whole "sector" metaphor.[44] But despite this, we believe the admittedly simplified notion of America (and other democracies) as three-sector societies is useful for two reasons: (1) because it highlights the importance of this neglected third sector, and (2) because it makes it easier for us to conceptualize the many diverse activities of philanthropy under a single category.

Defining Features of the Three Sectors

The third sector concept can be made to fit with the definition of philanthropy we offer in this book if we specify more precisely what sorts of organizations we classify as part of the third sector and what the defining features of each of the three sectors are. In doing so, we will move further toward our goal of identifying the shared characteristics of philanthropic behaviors and organizations.

To start, think about what sorts of organizations we should include in our list of organizations engaged in what we call philanthropy. The Salvation Army, Harvard University, and Amnesty International are all on the list, but the Republican Party, West Point, and AT&T are all not on the list. National Public Radio is on the list, but CBS is not. Catholic Relief Services is on the list, but the Agency for International Development is not, nor is ExxonMobil Corporation or Archer-Daniel-Midlands, "supermarket to the world." The YMCA is on the list, but Hilton Hotels are not.

But what do those organizations on the list have in common, and what similarities are the most important? Is tax-exempt status the key? Is it the nondistribution constraint? Why does it make sense to group the odd bedfellows of the Sierra Club and the Christian Coalition together (under the banner "philanthropy") and to distinguish them both from their seemingly more natural allies, respectively, the Environmental Protection Agency (which is under the banner "government") and the big Christian publishing company Zondervan (under the banner "business")?

Of course, making such distinctions and classifications is always tricky and sometimes unproductive. But we think it is important to try to distinguish the philanthropic sector from the others and to clarify very clearly what makes it distinctive. One reason why is because, when set off by itself, philanthropy is usually thought of as more marginal and less important than business and government, or it is simply absorbed into business and government as a special case of each. We need to counter this view. Philanthropy is certainly like business and government in some important ways. All three need mission and shared values. Each sector involves social organization, each sector needs resources both human and material, and each sector reflects a range of past experience. But the three concepts and sectors are also different in some important ways. Each has its own mission and distinctive values, and the rules constraining organization and resources are somewhat different for each.

In an effort to sharpen the differences among the sectors, it is useful to think of an essential, defining term or idea for each, the idea without which the sector collapses. Here is our attempt to capture the essence of the sectors in this way: *Government*, the first sector, is essentially about *power*. *Business*, the second sector, is essentially about *wealth*. *Philanthropy*, the third sector, is essentially about *morality*.[45] Taking this effort one step further,

Table 2.1. Defining Features of the Three Sectors of Society

Sector	Means	Ends	Defining Idea
Government	Public Actors	Public Good	Power
Business	Private Actors	Private Good	Wealth
Philanthropy	Private Actors	Public Good	Morality

table 2.1 tries to illustrate these distinctive ideas as well as some other similarities and differences among the sectors in terms of their means and their ends.

Politics is defined by power, and what makes the first sector, government, distinctive is the legitimate power to use coercion. Max Weber famously defined the state as the entity with a monopoly on the legitimate use of physical force.[46] This power comes with considerable responsibility and accountability; we require a lot from those to whom we give the power to govern us, to coerce us. This power is eminently public power, not private or personal power. The means for exercising this power are "public" actors (in many senses of the word). And the ostensible purpose of the use of this power is to achieve the public good. The difference between government, defined in this way, and philanthropy is most clearly brought out by the government's power to levee taxes. If a nonprofit soup kitchen were to attempt to dock all workers' wages in their community in order to raise money for a new building, they would get in a lot of trouble. But if a government agency decided to provide food for the hungry, it could tax citizens to create the resources it needed. This does not mean philanthropy (or business, for that matter) never involves power plays or coercion. It is just not the same sort of legitimate power that makes government a distinctive means of action.

Business and the private economic marketplace is defined by the right to acquire, use, and dispose of property or wealth. Action in business is conducted by private actors seeking private goods. The most familiar measure of wealth in the marketplace is profit, often spoken of as the "bottom line," even by people who have never learned to read a balance sheet or an annual financial report. This well-known bottom line of creating wealth through profit is what the second sector is ultimately focused on. When we look at wealth, however, we always encounter reminders of how its distribution is unequal; it accumulates in some places and not in others. The capitalist system is remarkably efficient and effective at creating wealth and sometimes even at creating astonishingly large individual fortunes for people like Henry Ford, J. Paul Getty, and Bill Gates. However, capitalism creates and concentrates wealth more effectively than it distributes it. The other sectors redistribute the wealth—not all, but some of it—and most wealthy individuals who become philanthropists, like those above, prefer that the third sector play more of this redistribution role than the first sector. In sum, as we are often reminded by critics of philanthropy who simplistically claim philanthropy is a rich man's game, money and wealth are certainly one aspect of philanthropy. But wealth is not the defining core of philanthropy as it is for business. Philanthropy depends on the private economic marketplace to provide a notable share of its resources, but on the other hand some of the human needs that philanthropy tries to meet are the unfortunate consequence, the dark side, of this marketplace.

The defining feature of philanthropy, as we have noted, is that it is about morality and moral action. This deserves some initial explanation here, because saying that philanthropy is defined by morality might raise some eyebrows. The discordant word *morality* may call other things to mind—prudery, Puritanism, censorship, or perhaps obligatory actions that seem like the opposite of voluntary action. But we mean to use the term *morality* and moral action a particular way. First, as noted above, we focus on how philanthropy is the primary vehicle people use to shape and advance the moral agenda of our society, the most important issues we face, and the values we espouse. The story of philanthropy is the story, essentially, of people and groups exercising their moral imagination to think about how to make the world a better place and working to make it so.

We also argue that philanthropy is about voluntary interventions in the lives of other people for their benefit. Such interventions are, by our definition, moral actions. They are moral because they are primarily other-directed and because they are voluntarily so. Government often intervenes in the lives of people for their benefit, but the interventions are not voluntary and can be coercive (think of fluoridation in public water systems). This does not mean the intentions of the voluntary intervention are always purely altruistic, only that the act seeks primarily to benefit other people. Of course, philanthropy may also serve the needs and interests of the philanthropist. But the basic moral position—however frequently compromised or ignored in some cases—is that the needs and the interests of the persons served come first. Also, moral actions are voluntary in the sense of being freely chosen, not in the sense of being devoid of any feelings of obligation. We choose to do what we think is right for others, even when we feel (as we often do) that we should act this way. And finally, philanthropy is defined as about morality even if the moral act itself does not achieve moral results. It often does, of course.

These definitions and distinctions of the three sectors are intended to be suggestive rather than neatly and clearly descriptive. John Simon of Yale Law School, one of the first scholars to pay serious scholarly attention to philanthropy, called this attention to the differences among these three sectors "border patrol." In philanthropy as in immigration, of course, it makes a difference which side you're on. The boundaries among the three sectors, as we construct them socially and conceptually, are what sociologist Eviatar Zerubavel calls "fuzzy" boundaries in social life.[47] They are permeable, seem unclear to many, and are constantly shifting, but they are necessary for making sense of the world.

We should note that, despite their distinctiveness, there are many similarities between sectors. Philanthropy is like business in being about private actors acting voluntarily but also because both sectors encourage and thrive on entrepreneurial activity and self-motivated innovation. Philanthropy is like government in being about action to achieve the public good, as well as to provide "public goods" in the economist's sense—goods that everyone has equal access to regardless of how they're paid for. Like business, the third sector offers individual choice; we can "buy" the charity of our choice. Unlike business, there is no market test. A nonprofit can lose money indefinitely. Unlike government, the third sector doesn't have to win majority approval. In fact, these last two points provide the inspiration for a common criticism of the philanthropic sector, that there is no objective basis—like profits or votes—to determine "success" or to use it as a way to hold people accountable.

We should also remember that the three sectors continually interact, cooperate, and even compete. This makes defining philanthropy even trickier. Government relies on philanthropic and business "partners" to provide services. In fact, this government funding is a primary source of income for the philanthropic sector. Nonprofit organizations are seen as good allies for government and business because, on average, nonprofits offer credibility and efficiency; they are close to the people, and they are committed to their mission. Government also funds philanthropic organizations through such things as grants for the arts or for scientific research. In the other direction, business and philanthropy often seek to influence public policy, to change the way government limits or encourages social as well as political and economic action. And we know that philanthropy is also a familiar activity of for-profit business corporations. ExxonMobil Corporation may not be on the list of charitable institutions, but its charitable contributions are tax deductible, including those made to the tax-exempt philanthropic unit known as the ExxonMobil Foundation. The term *corporate philanthropy* itself suggests the permeability of the sector boundaries. The sectors also compete. Nonprofits "sell" services—e.g., Catholic hospitals provide fee-for-service care to people who can pay rather than just serving the indigent, and we have seen that fees are the largest source of revenue for nonprofits. Some nonprofits sell their goods and services in the same markets where businesses and governments are selling.

Many observers believe the boundaries among the sectors are blurring now more than ever, with government "devolving" more and more activities to nonprofits and nonprofits commercializing more and more in an effort to maintain sustainable funding. And we certainly live in a time of often bewildering sectoral confusion. All we have to do is look at hospitals to see how difficult it can be to distinguish what is government, what is for-profit, and what is nonprofit. All of this should prevent us from drawing the boundaries too starkly, but it should not keep us from thinking about what makes philanthropy distinctive.

In conclusion, it is important to remind ourselves of some general qualifications for the three-sector model we have just given:

1. Philanthropic organizations often include ties to government or business.
2. Philanthropic practice often resembles actions usually associated with governments or markets.
3. Government and the market have philanthropic interests.
4. In a three-sector society, philanthropy is complicit with government and the market in shaping the society as a whole.

Philanthropy, the third sector, is not pure and disinterested; it is an integral part of the system. Pity the society that is concerned only with the first two sectors—or the one that thinks the third can stand alone.

Voluntary? Action? For the Public Good?

Each piece of our basic definition of philanthropy can be—and has been—questioned and challenged. As a final step in presenting our definition, we will unpack it and examine it critically, one piece at a time. Isn't doing good works really a moral obligation rather than a voluntary choice? Do impulsive, unplanned, unorganized actions count? Who decides whether something is really seeking or achieving the public good? *When* is voluntary action for the public good? These are questions we should not avoid just to retain our neat and tidy definition.

Voluntary

Technically, by our definition, for an action to be philanthropic it must be voluntary, by which we mean it must be relatively free and uncoerced behavior.[48] Philanthropic action is neither mandated by law nor done in response to threats or other forms of compulsion. People join philanthropic organizations voluntarily and can leave them when they choose. However, the meaning of philanthropic action as "voluntary" in a pure sense can sometimes seem an unreasonable and unnecessary ideal feature of our definition.

The understanding of voluntary here can perhaps best be illustrated by the difference between a gift of money and a tax. One chooses to make a gift; one has no such choice about paying taxes. The failure to meet formal obligations like paying taxes often carries painful consequences. There is an "or else" quality about this sort of formal obligatory action that does not hold for voluntary action.

But this does not mean there is no sense of obligation at all in philanthropic, voluntary action. Voluntary actions can sometimes be viewed as morally obligatory. In many religious traditions, for example, giving to the poor is not considered a voluntary choice but a canonically prescribed duty of all believers. This might be seen as a relatively benign form of coercion that is integral to philanthropy. We know, for instance, that people who go to religious services give more than those who don't. But still, as a form of coercion, it appears to make philanthropy less of a "free choice." However, moral obligations—despite occasional feelings to the contrary—are often perceived to be less binding, or at least less enforceable, than formal obligations like the legal and contractual obligations of law and business. People who feel they "have to do something" to help the victims of war, famine, or natural disasters won't be punished if they don't do something. Even when philanthropic action is done out of a strong, even seemingly inescapable feeling of obligation, we consider this voluntary insofar as we still have to choose, in most cases, to fulfill this felt obligation to do good. There is usually only shame to pay if we don't.

Inevitably there will be other external influences motivating or perhaps obligating philanthropic behavior as well. As described earlier, research finds that commonly cited "reasons for giving" include being involved with the group you donate to, perhaps as a volunteer, and simply being asked to give, which is often the number one reason given. Social pressure and peer pressure to give can become coercive at times. For instance, a familiar complaint against workplace giving has long been that contributions are sometimes the result of something very much like intimidation. Kenneth Boulding wrote of the distinction between gifts and tributes, the latter being something that looks like a gift but is really a required payment to a tyrant or a pirate or the like. He discussed these ideas in a little book originally entitled *The Economy of Love and Fear*, which reminds us that we can turn over money out of fear of what will happen if we don't as well as out of loving concern for someone else's well-being.[49]

Another way in which we might identify the voluntary nature of philanthropy is to say that it is giving without expectation of a tangible return. Generally speaking, "voluntary service" means a gift of time and work without financial or other material compensation. Similarly, giving money (or other valuables "in kind") philanthropically is supposed to be a "one-way transfer of exchangeables," as Boulding puts it. There may be a "return" given back to the philanthropist, but it should be of a different sort than the exchangeable (in a market sense) that they gave; it should be, say, a word of thanks or perhaps access to a special viewing of an art exhibit (a ticket that can't be sold).

In general, the idea of voluntary action contains both a strength because of its appeal to our autonomy and a weakness because of our unreliability. The notion of voluntary is both promise and threat: I am free to act, but to act I must decide. To a free person, a voluntary action is almost always preferable to an obligatory one. If the voluntary quality of philanthropy is lost or seriously compromised, something important is lost—our individual freedom and the degree of our control over it. And in day-to-day life, the same forces that impinge on our freedom in other aspects of our lives appear in philanthropy as well, forces such as the pull of life's other activities ("I can't volunteer right now with all I've got going on at work") or a lack of resources ("I just don't have the money to give to every cause I want to support").

In the end, we are certainly on thin ice when we include "voluntary" so prominently in our definition, but we find the distinction of voluntary actions from obligatory taxes or exchanges of tangibles to be important, especially when highlighting the moral dimension of voluntary actions. But we should still be cognizant of important questions like "Where do we draw the line between coercion and legitimate forms of encouragement?" And we should think carefully about cases that blur the lines of what is voluntary. For example, traditionally we have qualified the definition of "volunteers" to include people who dedicate their lives to service but who receive some basic, subsistence level of support—from a religious institution, from the state as in the case of the Peace Corps, VISTA, or AmericaCorps, etc. But some people object to these volunteers being paid at all for their service. The same sorts of questions have been raised about "mandatory community service" quotas that some high schools and colleges now require for graduation. Is such required service still voluntary service? Is it philanthropic? Is it worth mandating volunteerism of the young if it leads them into a lifetime of volunteering that is not so coerced?

These are tough issues. But for the most part, voluntary philanthropic actions can be defined as relatively free, uncoerced actions that are uncompensated. And felt obligations or external influences can be part of the motivation to act, so long as they have been reflected upon and integrated into the decision to be philanthropic. This seems to fit with our shared expectations.

Action

Philanthropic action takes many forms. In theory, such action can include things we do spontaneously, as a matter of course, or even without thinking. It can include actions as familiar as holding the door open for a stranger carrying packages—common courtesy or informal kindness is a form of philanthropy—or as rare as pulling a stranger from a flooded river. But most of the actions we want to talk about are more organized and formalized.

Whether spontaneous or organized, acts of mercy to alleviate the immediate suffering of others—Good Samaritan sort of acts—are often seen as the most fundamental philanthropic acts. But many other sorts of actions fall under the definition of voluntary action for the public good as well, from writing a check to support the local Girl Scout troop to hitting up your friends for donations to the Planned Parenthood chapter on whose board you serve. Philanthropic action includes both individual and organized action. Individual acts of giving or service bring personal meaning to philanthropy. Organized actions bring meaningful social outcomes and stability.

Philanthropic action is also traditionally divided up into either *service* or *advocacy*, although there are many other types of actions besides these. While service is considered the classic type of philanthropic action, advocacy has grown increasingly prominent in the past few decades and also has a long history.[50] Rather than directly improving the conditions of individuals or communities, advocacy involves efforts to influence others (the neighborhood, the general public, the government) to take action to improve conditions—specifically, to take the action you argue should be taken. One of the best known and most respected leaders of American philanthropy, Brian O'Connell, has argued that advocacy is actually philanthropy's most important function.[51] It is the preferred path of many, on both sides of the political aisle, who want to see significant social change. This form of action, while sometimes engaged in by individuals, is usually done through voluntary associations in order to exert a greater impact. In fact, advocacy often involves representing and promoting the interests of an organized constituency. Advocacy also shows how philanthropy is about ideas as well as practical action in the traditional sense. Promoting ideas is, at times, a form of philanthropic action.

Philanthropic actors are constantly innovating and creating new forms of action—this is part of what we called philanthropy's "vanguard role"— as well as adapting and expanding on traditional or received forms. Social movements are particularly fertile grounds for the invention of new forms of collective action, new means of forcing the social changes they define as for the public good. Take the strategy of nonviolent civil disobedience, for example. This technique of action was pioneered by Gandhi and his followers. Civil rights leaders in the United States then adapted and advanced the technique, borrowing also from Christian teachings on nonviolence and America's own history of civil disobedience by people like Henry David Thoreau. They then passed the technique on to a generation of new activists via formalized trainings that taught them, for example, how to stifle their violent impulses even when there was a crowd dumping food on them at a lunch counter. And now this classic form of philanthropic action is being employed in novel ways by movement activists protesting everything from abortion clinics to World Trade Organization meetings.[52] Modern movement groups are also using technology such as cell-phone text messaging to devise new forms of action, such as the "flash mob." More generally, technological advances from the self-adhesive mailing label to the Internet have changed the way philanthropic groups ask for and spend charitable donations. Again, philanthropic action takes many forms, and technology usually adds to the list.

For the Public Good

Voluntary giving, service, and association—those are proposed as the elements of voluntary action. But voluntary action to what end? We say that the goal of philanthropic organizations is the public good. But what do we mean?

The use of the term *public good* implies, for most people, that there is an absolute good of some kind and that we know for certain what it is. The public good, in this view, is determined by purely objective standards, and while it may not be universal in a pure sense, in any given case or on any issue we should strive to achieve the single "correct" vision of the public good. This understanding of the public good can lead to problems. One of the common criticisms of philanthropic actors is that they are condescending. This can be a criticism, in a sense, of their insistence that they know what the true public good is. Some of those involved in the settlement house movement, for instance, assumed there was such a thing as high culture, known to the educated and privileged, that could and should be shared with those who were "uncultured" as the best way to help them rise out of their difficult circumstances. Modern social workers reject this view as demeaning and paternalistic, despite sharing the underlying concern with helping the disadvantaged. But let's say we all still agree with this underlying concern, that it is good for there to be less poverty and squalor, less hunger and despair. Does this mean there is such a thing as the public good?

The absolutist view of the public good sees it as (by definition) opposed to and exclusive of "self-interest" or "special interests." This harkens back to what Rousseau meant by the "general will," which he saw as applying *only* to what was good for everyone as a unified collectivity and *not* to the mere aggregation or summation of individual wills, which he called the "will of all."[53] But in public life and in the world of voluntary philanthropic action, it is not always so easy to distinguish who or what is pursuing a special interest and who or what is pursuing the public good. Take what some consider the most powerful "interest group" in America, the nonprofit association previously known as the American Association of Retired Persons and now officially just called AARP. When AARP advocates for greater funding for gerontological research, it is seeking a goal that disproportionately benefits its members, yes, but few could argue that such research does not also serve some public good. At the very least, such research will benefit nearly all of us, because nearly all of us will become "senior citizens" at some point. Yet AARP is routinely called a "special interest," and the policy goals it pursues are denounced as self-serving rather than for the public good. How do we make sense of this?

In the famous tenth essay of the *Federalist Papers*, James Madison defines a "faction" as "a number of citizens . . . who are united and actuated by some common impulse of passion, or of interest, adverse to the rights of other citizens, or to the permanent and aggregate interests of the community."[54] The first part of this fits our description of "voluntary associations" very well, but the second part would suggest that factions are voluntary associations working *against* the public good. However, as Martin Marty points out, Madison neglected to consider that some factions— Marty's example is civil rights groups—are *both* collections of people who share a particular passion or interest *and* groups that work for things like peace and justice and "the logic of rights and freedom for the good of the whole."[55]

Economists offer another way of thinking about the public good by giving a formal definition of "public goods" that focuses on the technical qualities of those goods. Public goods are goods that are "indivisible" or "nonrivalrous"—meaning one person's use does not diminish another's—and "nonexcludable"—meaning anyone can benefit from the good regardless of whether or not they helped provide it. Certainly these sorts of goods are the sorts that philanthropy provides, as does government. Some public goods, such as public radio, are jointly provided by philanthropy and government, while other public goods, such as national defense, can only properly be provided by government. This is the basis for the main explanation offered by economists for the existence of this otherwise odd phenomenon of voluntary action for public good—rather than only for private good, which makes more sense in a world populated by *homo economicus*. Put simply, economists explain that voluntary action for the public good exists because, for various and complicated reasons, the market and government fail to provide the optimum amount of certain public goods.[56]

Economists also use this standardized view of public goods to posit what they consider an inherent problem facing a society that must produce adequate public goods. Why would anyone help produce public goods if they could still benefit from the goods whether they helped produce them or not, when they could just get a "free ride." How can you raise money for a community park when the families in the neighborhood will be able to use the park even if they don't contribute to your campaign? Mancur Olson offered a famous summary of this "free rider problem" and argued that the way to overcome it was to offer "selective incentives" to people so they would contribute toward public good provision—like offering glossy magazines or tote bags to entice people to donate to public radio.[57] For economists, the offering of selective incentives can explain the observed fact that, yes, people do indeed consistently give for the public good.

In our view, while tote bags or other incentives surely explain why some people engage in voluntary action for the public good, there is another explanation that should not be discounted, one that relies on the appeal of the public good itself to those who choose not to free ride. Perhaps those people give voluntarily to help provide public goods because they agree with the mission of the group. This again highlights the moral dimension of philanthropic action for the public good. Further, we think a more general view of the public good that goes beyond the mere technical qualities of "goods" will better encompass the diversity of the field.

We find it most useful to think of the public good as a constantly contested and debated ideal. It is an aspiration worth discussing and arguing about as well as pursuing through action, but not a preexisting and fixed standard to be achieved. Philanthropic action is action seeking someone's vision of the public good. It is voluntary action with the purpose of doing, advocating, or providing something that is seen by the actor as somehow for the public good.

This public good mission might be more implicit than explicit, more disputed than we would like, or more limited in scope than some ideal of the universal good for a universal public. It will often be mixed in with other, even "self-interested" intentions for beneficent action like the desire to feel good about yourself, to make a name for yourself in the community, or to get a tax break. And action designed to achieve the public good might not lead to good outcomes in all cases. Even the widely praised and relatively innocuous (despite the insistence of the bell ringers) voluntary action of putting money in a Salvation Army container around holiday time is sometimes criticized as either not serving the public good or doing so in such an inefficient way that, if everyone did things this way, could lead to longer-term "public bad."[58] But the key measure is whether the action is seen by the actor as for the public good, even if there is also some self-interest involved.[59]

This point of view is why we can include corporate philanthropy as philanthropy under our definition even if we accept that corporate giving is partly motivated by "enlightened self-interest"—that is, through giving, the corporation seeks to maintain a good image in the community or to educate future workers. While some critics claim outright that corporate philanthropy is either hypocritical or deliberately deceptive or both, our approach focuses not on whether it is really motivated only by self-interest or whether it is deceptive but on how the business doing the giving considers the giving to somehow serve a beneficial public purpose such as education, even if this education might also serve the corporation's interests.[60] Put another way, acting for the public good is not the same as acting altruistically.[61]

The most important point, however, is that it is through philanthropy that people affirm what they believe is in the public good and what they think contributes to it. This means, more dramatically, that the meaning of the public good in any society is determined partly, even primarily, through philanthropy. It is perhaps too convenient as a turn of phrase, but we say *philanthropy makes the public good.*

Craig Calhoun offers a nice way of thinking about the public good as constructed in this way. He argues that the public good is not something that is to be "found" but something that is "forged" in the course of the public sphere debate among active and vocal groups: "The public good is not objectively or externally ascertainable. It is a social and cultural project of the public sphere. . . . It is created in and through the public process; it does not exist in advance of it."[62] This perpetual contestation and debate is an essential part of public life, even though we act very often as if the contest were over and the meaning of the public good were fixed. But remember, the participants in this public conversation about the public good are often voluntary philanthropic organizations advocating for their vision of the public good and working on projects inspired by their visions.[63] Clearly, then, the advocacy role of philanthropy described earlier is a means of deliberating about the public good, but in a sense the service role is part of the deliberation as well. For instance, when a nonprofit drug counseling center helps someone with their addiction, they are affirming several ideas about what is in the public good: the view that suffering should be relieved, that the community problems caused by drugs should be reduced, and perhaps even that treatment or "harm reduction" is a better solution to the drug problem than prohibition or incarceration.

This last example reminds us that, even though we see the public good as something constantly being constructed, and even though there are many views of the public good—such as the preference for drug treatment—that are *not* shared by all or even by most of us, there remain a great many visions of what is for the public good that *most* of us can agree on. Those visions are often the core missions of philanthropic action. We can return to the summary of the two core objectives of philanthropy that we introduced at the beginning of this chapter: to relieve suffering and to improve the quality of life. While different philanthropists might define these objectives in different ways, it is hard to dispute that they are public good objectives in general. They are certainly "public" in that they extend beyond family and friends and encompass persons for whom the philanthropist is not formally or immediately responsible. They encompass the community at large; they encompass strangers. And they involve the desire to do good for those public "others."

Surely we can agree that philanthropic action seeking to relieve suffering or to improve the quality of life is for the public good and worthy of praise. Philanthropy is more praiseworthy than many of the other things we spend our money and time on. In the rough hierarchy of virtuous behavior, philanthropy ranks well up on the list, at least alongside patriotism and devotion to family and an honest day's work. It is because philanthropy is so praiseworthy that spending time here exploring the definition and meaning of philanthropy has been worth our effort.

3

Because Things Go Wrong: Philanthropy as a Response to the Human Problematic

*P*hilanthropy appears in some form in all cultures and civilizations and through all recorded history. It seems there is something about the world, and about humans in this world, that calls philanthropy into being. Philanthropy is a response. But to what? What is it about the world that causes us to respond philanthropically, that makes philanthropy seem to be a reasonable response?

The purpose of this chapter is to begin to establish the larger context for philanthropy, the general condition of the world—what we will call the human problematic—to which philanthropy is a response. We follow the previous chapter's summary of our broad conception of philanthropy with an exploration of how that conception fits into the larger world and how it relates to some fundamental questions about humans. We believe understanding these issues is essential to understanding why philanthropy exists—why it emerges as a human response to the human condition in the world.

While we will be making some bold claims about elementary features of the human condition and human nature, this chapter is not so much an exercise in presenting universal knowledge as an exercise in conceptual generalization and practical philosophy. Like much of this book, it considers fundamental characteristics and causes of voluntary action for the public good in human societies, but tries not to lose sight of the fact that this philanthropic action is always expressed in ways that are patterned by culture and history. Philanthropy is found everywhere as a response to inevitabilities of the human condition, yes, but what is defined as an appropriate or conventional philanthropic response is different in Elizabethan England than in Maoist China.

The Human Problematic

Like it or not, we humans face difficult problems. This means there are questions that humans everywhere and always must attempt to answer. These fundamental problems and questions are the inevitable reality we call the *human problematic*. The human problematic is defined by two other basic realities: the first is the *human condition;* the second is *human nature.* It is this human problematic that sets the context for why philanthropy exists in the world.

Philanthropy exists because of two truths about the human condition: things often go wrong, and things could always be better.

First, *things often go wrong.* Systems fail. Natural and human, social and political, economic and biological systems fail, and as a consequence humans suffer. As we grow up, we all learn by experience as well as by observation that in many situations individuals and societies are overwhelmed by circumstances either natural or man-made, that we sometimes can't cope without help. It is through no lack of will or desire or moral fiber that Ethiopians die of starvation. It is through no ethnic flaw or cultural decay that people find themselves swept away by a tsunami. We are all vulnerable to suffering, even if some of us are more vulnerable to certain types of suffering than others. Philanthropy is an act of response to this inevitable suffering; we shouldn't forget there are other possible responses. Also, we shouldn't forget that sometimes what is going "wrong" is disputed or that the definition of wrong varies across cultures, groups, and times. Whether husbands routinely beating their wives is an example of something going wrong or not depends on when and where and whom you ask, and this will then influence whether philanthropy or any other intervention is called for. In fact, philanthropic action itself—the exercise of the moral imagination—is often part of the process of declaring which "conditions" are defined as "problems." What we do to make things better reveals what we consider to be going wrong.

Second, *things could always be better.* That is, humans can imagine ways in which life could be more agreeable, comfortable, congenial, pleasant, fruitful, productive, profitable, etc. Philanthropy is an expression of this human moral imagination that seeks to improve the quality of life. (In the next chapter, we will see how this belief that things can be made better through philanthropy fits with a philosophy we call "meliorism.") Of course, "could always be" does not necessarily imply "will always be." Philanthropy is about trying to make things better, sometimes in the face of dauntingly unfavorable odds.

These two features of the human condition set the stage for humans to respond to problems, and *the philanthropic tradition is the history of this response*. In the stream of this tradition usually called "charity," we respond to suffering and distress and acute need. In the stream of this tradition usually called "philanthropy," we respond to our awareness of ways we can improve the quality of life. Both streams mingle in a shifting current with the political forces of order and the economic forces of the market, all adapting to one another and to the natural course of the river of humanity.

What makes the philanthropic response to the human condition difficult is that the human condition is uncertain. Many of the most fundamental threats to human well-being are far beyond human control. The media make it possible for us to observe the incredible power and destructiveness of routine natural phenomena like earthquakes, floods, hurricanes, and volcanic eruptions. But humans themselves are capable of behavior that tests our most generous definition of the human; we often make the human condition worse. We delude ourselves if we forget that barbarism is usually rationalized as necessary and that this usually leads to acts of even worse barbarism. Most wars, civil and otherwise, contain evidence of this. And, of course, the media now makes it possible for us to observe these acts of barbarism, regardless of where they occur.

Human nature—the other reality contributing to the human problematic—sometimes leads us to make things worse. However, it is also human nature, in part, that impels us to respond philanthropically. Yes, it is hard to deny what many people believe, that egoism and self-interest are "just human nature." But we need not deny this in order to accept that the opposite quality, altruism, is also "just human nature." Concern for others is a defining characteristic of humans. We see this illustrated time and again in the philanthropic response to the human condition.

One conclusion to draw from all of this is that life is problematic. Utopia is a useful way of thinking how things might be better; it is not useful to expect that things will ever be perfect or even settled. A problematic life in a problematic universe is apparently inevitable. That humans, both individually and in society, are also problematic seems to be another inevitable reality. The combination of those different kinds of problems often leaves us trying to make sense of evil and misfortune—and of goodness and joy. And we often make sense of these things through our philanthropic response.

Perhaps it is useful to pause and summarize this argument about the context for philanthropy before going into it more deeply.

1. Things often go wrong; things could always be better.
2. Philanthropy is one response to those aspects of the human condition, a response that is essential to our understanding of our human nature.
3. The human condition creates often unpredictable opportunities and challenges.
4. Human nature responds in often unpredictable ways to alleviate suffering and to improve the quality of life.
5. The unpredictable quality of the human condition and human nature constitute the human problematic to which philanthropy responds.

In the sections that follow, we explore more deeply the specific elements of this argument. We discuss the human condition in terms of our life in the natural world and in terms of our "life chances" in the social world, and then we examine what it means to say that concern for others is part of our human nature. Once we have established philanthropy as a human response to the human problematic, though, we will argue that philanthropy is only one possible response. Self-help, mutual aid, and government assistance are others. But philanthropy is distinctive and necessary.

Life in a Natural World

Humans exist in a physical and material world, in turn a habitat in a larger universe, and throughout that universe external forces impinge on human affairs in often unpredictable ways. From a human perspective, the natural world is an uncertain place, often friendly but also often hostile. From a geophysical perspective, earthquakes are perfectly normal phenomena that result from the movement of tectonic plates; from a human point of view, earthquakes are often catastrophes. Like earthquakes, floods, tornadoes, hurricanes, droughts, famines, and plagues are usually seen as "evils" of human existence, some of the consequences of living in a less than perfect world. They cause vast loss of life as well as other, sometimes unbearable costs. For example, the Indian Ocean tsunami in December 2004 was completely understandable—though extremely rare—from a scientific point of view, but utterly devastating in terms of human suffering. Beyond the incalculable cost of perhaps 300,000 or more lives, the economic, environmental, and psychic costs of this natural event are staggering. No more dramatic illustration that the human condition is uncertain need ever be presented for us to understand this truth.

Such "failures" of a natural system are opportunities for philanthropic initiative. Some of our best and most honorable philanthropic work is done under the banner of humanitarian assistance when natural systems malfunction. Our worldview is likely to assume that human reactions to natural disaster and human suffering will be roughly the same wherever disasters occur. We know that people will suffer, will find themselves beyond their ability to cope, and may call for help from anyone, even people half a world away.

Natural disasters are part of the human condition, part of the physical environment in which we must live. But that physical environment also has a remarkable set of chemical and biological characteristics that make what we call human life possible. Disasters exist alongside the fecundity of the soil, the rainfall that nourishes it, and the sunshine that rescues us from winter, both physically and psychologically. Despite the sometimes overwhelming scale of destruction and loss of life, humans generally seem to accept the human condition and to find the struggle for survival worthwhile.

So the human condition involves existence in a world that permits survival, growth, and development, but also a world in which things often go wrong. While Earth sustains human life, it also makes human life difficult. Not everything goes wrong, and things do not always go wrong, but the human condition is one in which many humans find survival difficult, growth inadequate, and development impossible.

We should also remember that humans are expected to survive in the most diverse physical circumstances, and the different natural environments in which people live have something to do with their social and cultural condition. Generally there is enough stability of environmental conditions that most people are able to accommodate to severe environments and live fulfilling lives. Or so we sometimes think, when our empathy is great enough for us to imagine how their lives could be fulfilling under such severe conditions. This raises important questions for philanthropy: Who are we to decide that some people are so miserable in their circumstances that they need help—our help—to improve their condition or to escape from it? Whose definition of what is "going wrong" here should determine the actions taken? And, again, what business is it of ours?

There may be a tendency to think of natural disasters as simply "natural," that is, not mediated by human intervention. But during the famine in Ethiopia in 1984 we became aware of how political and economic action (or inaction) can turn a natural lack of rainfall from a manageable burden into social chaos. And, tragically, most of us watched on television as the delay in human response to Hurricane Katrina multiplied the suffering. The lesson here is that human systems malfunction; all systems do. John Gall even claims that any large system is going to be operating most of the time in "failure mode."[1] In Ethiopia, the political-economic system failed and contributed to famine because of tribal conflict and other problems. Similarly, following the breakup of the Soviet Union, the newly independent republics were faced with a legacy of environmental pollution that was much worse than in Western Europe and in the United States, in part because of decades of governmental neglect and suppression of those few who dared to advocate environmental responsibility in this system. And, of course, humans alone—sometimes intentionally, sometimes not—create disasters that have catastrophic effects akin to natural disasters; they even hijack planes and fly them into crowded buildings.

With those bad examples in mind, we know, too, that although human interventions to reshape or weaken natural forces often fail, they also often succeed. The damage from earthquakes causes immediate suffering but sometimes leads to new building materials and improved architectural and engineering design. The air in Pittsburgh is cleaner, after years of damage to the public health, thanks in part to some citizens who could envision a city with clear skies instead of a city with skies thick with industrial pollution—and because humans developed the technology to remove more of the toxic material before it escaped into the air.

The point is that while humans often can and do make their lives worse than natural conditions alone would impose on them, humans also have the capacity to correct nature, reduce the severity of biological accidents, and eliminate some diseases altogether. Very often, they do this through philanthropy.

In sum, the Earth is a place where humans react to nature in complex ways—political, economic, and moral—sometimes to improve the human condition and sometimes to make it worse. The idea of "progress" assumes that on the whole the human condition has been improved through these human reactions, that the human condition is better now than it was in the past largely because of human interventions. Philanthropic responses to the human condition, in particular, often occur under the assumption that people in extreme circumstances, at home or abroad, would be better off with our help, whether they ask for it or not.

Life Chances

The human condition involves more than humans responding to a natural world. It also involves humans dealing with the reality of widely varying "life chances" in the social and economic world. The concept of life chances comes to us from Ralf Dahrendorf, a German-born sociologist whose long and illustrious career included a stint as the head of the London School of Economics and service on the board of the Ford Foundation. Dahrendorf borrowed the idea of life chances from Max Weber, who used the term in his massive *Economy and Society* as a way to describe someone's class position.[2]

Dahrendorf expanded on Weber's view and claimed that life chances are the social conditions in which individuals realize their potential.[3] Life chances is one way to talk about the varying circumstances in which human beings find themselves. The notion of the human condition grows more problematic when we think, for instance, of the contrasting life chances of an eight-year-old girl in Pyongyang in 2005 and her counterpart in Peoria.

Apart from the qualities of the individual, life chances often seem to be the result of a dice game in which others throw the dice. A child born with spina bifida in the United States in the twenty-first century has a good chance of living; born in an earlier time, the child would have died. In either case, the choice is not the infant's to make. The life chances of most Americans are materially superior to those of most Rwandans, Kurds, or Haitians. Actuarial tables projecting the life expectancy of a white male born in South Bend, Indiana, in 1926 would reveal a longer life expectancy than if that same person had been born in South Bend fifty or a hundred years earlier. Some people are born into situations in which nutrition will be inadequate while others will be born into circumstances in which good food is never a question; for the latter, the more pressing problem may be whether the parents will be able to afford college tuition. The Physical Quality of Life Index developed by the Overseas Development Council once identified Sri Lanka as the most desirable place in the world to live based on measures of literacy rate, infant mortality, and life expectancy. The irony is that Sri Lanka has also been the site of an endless and murderous ethnic civil war.

Dahrendorf explored two aspects of life chances that influence their significance for us: ligatures and options. Ligatures are the ties that bind us to a place, to a culture, and to people. Options are the choices we are free to make. Ligatures are critically important in helping people to know their place in the scheme of things; membership, as Michael Walzer and others have observed, is an important social value because it meets a profound human need.[4] Options are variously available—for example, girls have different options than boys as they grow up.

The life chances presented to Mozart included his exploitation by his father, Leopold, and participation in a rich and productive musical culture in eighteenth-century Europe. The ligatures binding Mozart to his father, like the musical conventions of the time, were strong enough to affect his otherwise boundless creativity. Mozart's life chances also included the lifestyle of the court and the aristocracy, with the problematic assistance of patrons and benefactors. (The problematic of philanthropy as patronage is an important theme in the history of the arts.) An eight-year-old Nigerian boy who was in the secessionist province of Biafra in 1968 may have suffered brain damage as a result of severe malnutrition during the blockade of his country; his modern counterparts in Rwanda and Burundi and the Darfur region of Sudan number in the tens of thousands. Their life chances—the social conditions in which they realize their potential—are as remote from us in the United States as Mozart's.

The movement toward modernity may be seen as the world of options being offered more and more to those bound by a world of ligatures. An essential difference between the premodern world and the modern world is that the former was dominated by ligatures and the latter by options.

The point here is that philanthropy is a response to the human reality of life chances, and philanthropy is usually on the side of options. A familiar principle of philanthropy is to help people help themselves. Very often people want to help themselves by changing their life chances, by improving their options, for example, by escaping prejudice and stereotyping and oppression in all its forms. Philanthropy is often in the middle of these efforts, usually on the side of options and usually seeking to make things better.

Through the exercise of the moral imagination by some, the life chances of others have been dramatically expanded: women can now aspire to be political leaders; minorities can aspire to higher education; children in wheelchairs can attend whichever school they want. Working conditions for women, children, and the disabled have been improved to resemble the circumstances of healthy adult males (that is, the population with, historically, the best life chances in the workplace).

The test of the impact of the moral imagination on life chances is often at the margins. The moral imagination has to expand to include those hitherto excluded, and it has to protect the valid claims of those included originally. In order to enhance the life chances of some individuals, rights readjustments may require a painful reduction of the rights of others.

Taking this analysis further, though, we must acknowledge that, in some cases, philanthropy is about strengthening ligatures rather than expanding options. This is true for those repulsive associations we would rather not have to include under the philanthropic umbrella, such as the Ku Klux Klan. KKK members, unfortunately, believe they are engaging in "voluntary action for the public good" by limiting the options of people with certain ligatures such as membership in any race but white. But in other cases, philanthropy is used in a positive way as a means of celebrating ligatures such as one's racial heritage or hometown. However, when we act philanthropically to celebrate our ties to a people, a place, or a culture—for example, by joining the National Association for the Advancement of Colored People or giving money to our hometown library—we are often simultaneously acting to increase options, to improve either our life chances or those of someone who will soon grow up with ligatures similar to ours.

In sum, we can see that "life is problematic" in another sense: people have different life chances. This, too, is part of the human condition; this, too, is a reality that calls philanthropy into existence. One way we often talk about this part of the human condition is in terms of "fairness" and "justice." Some people are disadvantaged or suffer in ways that seem unfair. The popular way of ducking that harsh fact is to repeat the maxim often attributed to John F. Kennedy: "No one said life has to be fair." The question for us is whether philanthropy would be necessary in a just society. We will never know. Society is not just, and that is one reason why philanthropy exists.

Human Nature

At one point in Plato's *Republic*, Socrates interrupts his dialogue with Adeimantus and his companions to observe:

> I think we have neglected one thing in particular.
>   What?
>   We have not yet given a full accounting of human desires, nor have we sufficiently described their nature. We must consider these matters; otherwise, our inquiry will remain incomplete.[5]

Plato is talking about how the tyrannical man evolves from the democratic man, saying we must understand human nature to understand this evolution. But today he might as well be talking about how someone like Mother Teresa evolves. We say she is an exception just as we say the tyrant is an exception (of the opposite kind, of course), but exceptions to what? Perhaps they seem exceptional because they don't fit our "on the average" notion of human behavior, what we usually have in mind when we use the term *human nature*. Humans have some traits in common, traits that define humans and bring out their differences from other creatures. Understanding philanthropic man requires understanding something of these common human traits.

But how do we decide what these traits are? In a twist on Plato's approach, James Madison in the *Federalist Papers*, Number 51, suggests a method for defining human nature when he asks, "What is government itself but the greatest of all reflections on human nature?"[6] That is, behind the words in the text of a constitution lie assumptions about what people are like, how they will behave, and what their tendencies and preferences are. Sometimes constitutions are useful as guides to human nature, and sometimes they are not. Read the Soviet Constitution of 1936 for evidence of the latter.

We think what Madison says of the ubiquitous human institution of government can also be said of another such institution, philanthropy. Philanthropy, too, is a pretty good reflection on human nature. The philanthropic tradition is built on assumptions about human nature, but more important, it reveals some of our shared human traits.

As many philosophers have argued, it is probably foolish to put too much stock in comprehensive notions of human nature. Human nature is increasingly under attack as a concept. Theories of human nature are quite reasonably thought to be inadequate to capture the essential diversity of humanity. And most scholars—us included—prefer to think about human nature as providing basic capacities and the underlying "hardware" that are then conditioned and directed into thought and action through the "software" of socialization. So the universal "human desires" that Plato identifies are always expressed in culturally specific ways that change over time; we might all feel compassion or sadness naturally, but we must learn how to be compassionate or to express our sadness in ways that others in our world will understand and accept.

Human nature is a useful concept because most people believe there are common traits that can be used to define humans—in fact, what these common traits are is something we are taught by our culture. For instance, most of us think humans are capable of a range of emotions, but we are also blessed with the capacity to reason and reflect on existence, meaning, and life. Humans are clever and at a decisive comparative advantage in most of their relations with other creatures. However, we should remember the idea from the introductory chapter that a concept is a "multiplicity." Human nature is a multiplicity.

Two thoughts about human nature—at least human nature as most of us conceive it most of the time—are particularly important to understanding philanthropy. The first and most important point has already been mentioned: that concern for others is a defining characteristic of humans. The second point is that human nature provides us with a capacity for both good and evil, virtue and vice. (The emphasis on "capacity" here is important, of course, when we remember the diversity of human variation and differences in the expression or fulfillment of our capacity.)

To be human means to be in some way able to respond to the needs of others, to have the ability to get beyond the self. Human nature includes a capacity to love one's neighbor, to follow the Golden Rule, to emulate the Good Samaritan. Humans have the capacity to recognize need in the circumstances of others and to reach out to them, even strangers and enemies, to offer assistance of some sort. If we learn of someone who seems utterly indifferent to the pain or suffering of others, it is common to speak of him as "inhuman."

Whether the capacity of concern for others is the result of millions of years of evolution, or the result of ethical evolution across human culture, or perhaps a gift from God, is a disputed question. We know that what we call "altruism" is practiced in some form in cultures around the globe—it is what anthropologists would call a "cultural universal"—even though the specific forms of showing concern for others vary by culture. For thousands of years, millions have found happiness and meaning through alleviating the suffering of others. Across languages and histories and wars and plagues and triumph and tragedy, there is evidence of human effort to lessen agony and to encourage happiness.[7]

When we think of concern for others as a fundamental human trait, we are not surprised when it shows up in many aspects of human affairs, including some aspects of life that are usually thought of only in nonphilanthropic or even antiphilanthropic terms. For example, the military sometimes engages in humanitarian relief efforts; governments admit refugees because "it is the right thing to do"; business enterprises contribute to local schools, etc. Hospitality to strangers, a form of philanthropy more widely honored in the ancient world than in the modern, appears in societies that are not notably religious as well as those operating under a strict religious edict to "help others."

Most of us make a provisional choice and decide that human nature permits altruistic behavior even though most human behavior seems to be guided by self-interest. Sometimes we will recall sophomoric debates about whether there can be anything other than self-interest. Some will even feel they are being particularly clever in exposing someone else's high-mindedness as simply another form of egoism: "You only help her because it makes you feel good about yourself." But sometimes we encounter examples of human behavior that simply cannot be explained as anything but one human helping another out of concern for their well-being. Wesley Autrey, a New York construction worker, was trying to help a college student at the subway station who was suffering a seizure. The student suddenly fell down onto the subway tracks, and Autrey jumped to his aid and covered him with his body just before the oncoming train screeched to a halt over them. He later explained, "I just saw someone who needed help. I did what I felt was right."[8]

On the whole, we learn from experience that people are capable of wonderful as well as appalling things. That there is abundant evidence of misanthropic kinds of behavior is undeniable, but the presence of evil does not imply the absence of good. This brings us to the second point: human nature endows us with the capacity to behave in ways that are regarded as good as well as ways that are called evil, to exhibit qualities considered virtues as well as vices. If altruism is a humanizing capacity, it competes with our other dehumanizing and inhumane capacities.

In western civilization, we have inherited a useful checklist for thinking about the admirable and despicable qualities that seem to appear in most of us—the seven "theological and cardinal virtues" and the seven "deadly sins." In the nineteenth century, most educated people, religious or not, would have been able to tick those off. The seven virtues are faith, hope, charity, prudence, justice, fortitude, and temperance. The seven vices are pride, envy, wrath, sloth, avarice, gluttony, and lust. The specific items on the two lists have been debated in the West for a couple of thousand years, but lately they seem to have passed from our cultural heritage; few young people or adults can name more than a couple. (Modern Christians do a little better remembering the Ten Commandments, but not much. As a father once shouted after his son, "Obey the Ten Commandments! Any two!") We mock such devices these days, but variations on them are enormously popular. Note the success of William Bennett's *The Book of Virtues* and Stephen Covey's *Seven Habits of Highly Successful People.*[9]

Eastern religious traditions and cultures have comparable lists that may have some specific differences but are largely similar in the qualities identified as either good or bad—and the lists are also similar in considering all the qualities as "human." Hope, justice, envy, avarice—all these characteristics seem to be always within us as humans, struggling to control behavior.

Philanthropy is on the list of virtues under the name of charity, but more broadly, philosophical thinking about virtues and vices can help us understand philanthropy.[10] For example, human nature considered as a tension between virtues and vices helps us to understand why we can know the right thing to do and fail to do it. The Greeks called this "weakness of will." Aristotle discussed the virtues on a scale from excess to deficiency and found true virtue in the middle.[11] Others take exception, of course, because the pattern does not work out as neatly as it should: excessive courage is what we call true heroism, for example. Finding the right place between generosity and avarice requires the ambiguous virtue of prudence. But prudence can be a barrier when risk is called for. Philanthropic foundations are frequently criticized for being unwilling to take risks on new ideas or on people whose social credit ratings are low.

Virtue and vice as traits of human nature help us to understand the problematic quality of philanthropy.[12] We can use the assumptions underlying those lists to anticipate what we will do and what others will do when we come together in some philanthropic enterprise. Pride can stand in the way of charity. Pride can shift the focus from the recipient to the donor, and it can prevent would-be recipients from accepting help from others, because it is difficult to accept a position that implies inferiority. Again, this is all part of the context for the philanthropic response to the human problematic.

The American philosopher Arthur O. Lovejoy, well known and respected in the first half of the twentieth century for his important contribution to the field known as the "history of ideas," wrote a little book entitled *Reflections on Human Nature*.[13] Lovejoy studied the writings of seventeenth- and eighteenth-century theologians and philosophers looking for their understandings of human nature, and he concluded that the most important factor in human motivation was the need for praise. Often praise is all we have to give in return for the good things that people do. However, as Lovejoy noted, while the need for praise motivates people to higher levels of performance and service, if they seem to need praise too much, we deny it to them. They commit the sin of pride, if you will. Praise, like respect and honor, is a gift that must be earned but cannot be commanded or claimed.

We praise Mother Teresa not because we ourselves have needed or felt her healing and compassionate touch but because we admire what she did for the poor and dying. In many ways she symbolizes some of the things we value most, even though we don't—or can't—emulate her behavior. She cultivated her capacity for virtue and suppressed her capacity for vice. Mother Teresa said that her motivation was not to receive praise but to serve God.[14] If she did seek our praise, would we think less of her?

These things are of some consequence in a culture of philanthropy that rarely has financial rewards to offer and is always on the edge of cheapening praise by giving it too readily. History finds ways to offer praise over the centuries to people whose tarnished reputations might have left them in neglected graves. Andrew Carnegie has managed to win a claim on us despite the stories of his acceptance of brutality in conflicts with labor. Much the same has been true of John D. Rockefeller. On the other hand, it seems entirely proper to praise those caring for AIDS victims in Africa, or volunteers at inner-city homeless shelters, as "heroes" or even as "saints." Sometimes we want to find reasons for praise when they aren't really there, but other times praise is both needed and deserved. If heroes need praise, we need heroes.

This discussion of human nature as part of the context for philanthropy leads to a simple conclusion: Philanthropy is a means of getting closer to our own humanness and the humanness of others. Philanthropy is a laboratory of vice and virtue, a laboratory for the study of human nature at its best—and sometimes at its most disappointing.

Responses to the Human Problematic

Our discussion so far has focused on the nature of the human problematic to which philanthropy is a response. Things often go wrong; things could always be better. And philanthropy is often how we go about making things better—or at least making them less bad. But we still need to consider why and when philanthropy is the best response, or at least a preferred or appropriate response.

We shouldn't forget that philanthropy is only one particular sort of response. There are other possible responses, including (although we don't discuss it here) ignoring the problems. To understand what is distinctive about the philanthropic response and what its particular role is, we must

nk about the range of possible responses. In doing so, we will also de-
op a way of thinking about the allocation of responsibility in society
more generally.

We start with the following scenario: Imagine that someone for whom
you have no formal responsibility comes asking for assistance, with no
promise of anything in return. Such a scenario—begging for help, asking
for alms—is as old as recorded history. This would plausibly be considered
a request for a philanthropic response, according to how we've defined
philanthropy. In fact, responding charitably to a direct request for assistance could be considered the most fundamental, primal act of philanthropy. But remember that we want to use this scenario to think about the
range of possible responses, not merely philanthropy. Assume that your
response is up to you, and that if you give something, it will be voluntary,
not coerced, and that you will derive no financial benefit from your response.

If it is helpful, you might make the scenario even more specific. Think
of being solicited by one of the panhandlers who are, sadly, present on the
streets of most every modern city. Few situations trouble our consciences
more directly, especially the consciences of young people, than being asked
for help by a panhandler—and this, in itself, should tell us something about
human nature. When confronted with such an appeal, how should one respond? This familiar confrontation with the panhandler is an experience
that each will deal with according to his or her own moral conviction, but
our response is also influenced by social norms and expectations, cultural
conventions, and even by thoughtful consideration and reasoning using the
facts available to us. This makes the scenario a good one to use as a model.
It is an opportunity to reflect on how philanthropic choices are made by
individuals, but more important for us here, it is a way to think through the
much larger question of the role of philanthropy in society.

In such a situation it is reasonable to ask several questions (whether you
vocalize them or not) about what type of response to the request is called
for, and through this to decide whether to respond philanthropically.
These questions can apply whether the philanthropic request comes from
the proverbial beggar on the street or from an arts organization, a shelter
for battered women, or a liberal arts college raising money for scholarships. The questions apply also to the "thinking" of organizations such as
foundation boards or nonprofit service providers, as well as to individual
reasoning. There are four questions relating to four responses, categorized
according to the source of possible assistance and the locus of control: self-
help, mutual aid, government assistance, or philanthropy.

Self-Help

The first and most fundamental question is about self-help: What is the person doing to help himself or herself? There is a deep and stubborn moral conviction that each of us (allowing for obvious exceptions) must accept some responsibility for our own survival and well-being. One of the great virtues of the philanthropic concern for the dignity of the individual is respect for the ability of the individual to help himself or herself. In some circumstances, the person might be totally helpless, in which case this question is irrelevant. Most of us would agree that it is pointless to ask the question of a two-year-old, for example, or to deny assistance to an Alzheimer's disease victim that we meet on the street because we think they should just be working harder to help themselves. It is when the person appears to be able-bodied that doubts about deception come into play.

The question has to do with the notion of desert: is the person deserving of my help? This is the sort of question people ask of panhandlers who seem to be physically and mentally capable of taking care of themselves. In the nineteenth century, such people were referred to as the "undeserving poor," people who could work but chose not to, presumably preferring to live on the work of others. There are, of course, also the "deserving poor," people who seem incapable of coping with, or are overmatched by, their circumstances. It is possible to be deceived by the panhandler; it is possible to deceive oneself by dismissing the panhandler as undeserving.

The question takes on different nuances as the requests rise in value and complexity. To what extent do we expect college students to pay for their education? Should we subsidize graduate education for rocket scientists? For neurosurgeons? There is also a strong cautionary note: It may even be harmful to help people who don't help themselves. Such assistance may encourage dependency. What may be true of individuals may also be true of organizations: organizations sometimes come to rely too heavily on a single patron. They may become too lazy to make an effort to raise money from other sources. If so, they are likely to give away their moral integrity along with their economic independence.

Another way of thinking about the self-help response is to consider whether it is best to intervene, but to intervene with the goal of "helping them help themselves." Sometimes this is the purpose of other sorts of responses, of course—governments providing training for the unemployed, nonprofit groups offering small "microcredit" loans to poor people operating small businesses, enacting the mission of the classic proverb "Give a man a fish, feed him for a day; teach a man to fish, feed him for a lifetime."

But sometimes as John D. Rockefeller once wrote, "The best philanthropy, the help that does the most good and the least harm, . . . is not what is usually called charity. It is, in my judgment, the investment of effort or time or money, carefully considered with relation to the power of employing people at a remunerative wage. . . . If we can help people to help themselves, then there is a permanent blessed conferred."[15]

Rockefeller echoes exactly the teaching of the twelfth-century Jewish philosopher Maimonides, who ranked eight levels of giving (*tzedakah*) into a hierarchy from the highest (best) to the lowest form. The lowest form is to give with a heavy heart or a negative attitude (so long as you conceal this, Maimonides said, this is still charity). But the "best" form of charity was, as Rockefeller said, to do something so that people needing help can become self-sufficient, such as giving them a loan or giving them a job in your business.[16] Enabling self-help becomes the highest form of philanthropy. One person who believes this is Muhammad Yunus, the Bangladeshi economist who recently won the Nobel Peace Prize for his idea of microcredit financing as a strategy to alleviate poverty.[17]

This point of view, unfortunately, has been lost in the narrow insistence on profit as the justification for pursuing the self-interest of business. It is also lost when we assume that the only way business can help those in need is through the other two sectors—through their taxes or through the reasonable expectations we place on them to "give back" through corporate giving or social responsibility programs. Creating jobs to allow for self-help is a way to help as well.

Mutual Aid

The second question, after addressing the question of self-help, is about mutual aid: What are the people who are considered formally responsible for this person doing to help him or her? For individuals this usually means family, close friends, maybe neighbors; for organizations this usually means those parties who are most directly concerned or connected: the alumni and parents of the college, for example, or the residents of the community that might benefit from the organization. But it is generally agreed that before someone approaches a stranger for assistance, they should call on family, friends, or significant others.

This second question arises because we know that no one is without "significant others," in the sense that we are all part of networks of relationships based on mutual aid. Each of us comes into the world in the midst of what the sociologist Georg Simmel called a "web of group-affiliations."[18]

This web makes claims on others on our behalf. The family is the first and most obvious resource, but mutual aid might come from co-workers, neighbors (think of the classic American example of mutual aid: the barn-raising), fraternity brothers and sorority sisters, members of benevolent societies, trade unions, business clubs, and a vast array of other associations that follow what has been called a "norm of reciprocity."[19] This norm, when generalized, means that we can expect assistance from others in these networks and are also expected to assist others, and if this norm is operating, it helps build trust, which makes society work in many other ways as well.[20]

The importance of mutual aid is revealed most dramatically when we encounter situations where it doesn't exist. Many people are homeless because they have been evicted by their own families; others decided that life on the streets is better than life at home. For whatever reason, they don't have working networks of mutual aid—unless they find a way to partner with others in a similar situation, which we know sometimes happens. When mutual aid fails like this, other responses—from government, from philanthropy—may become the last resort.

Much of self-help and mutual aid have a private interest: we help ourselves in all sorts of ways in which we benefit privately and directly; we associate with family and friends in business and other economic activity. For instance, in some cases, we might well conclude that persons who want to be physicians should pay part of the cost by working and that their families should help if possible. The reason for helping individuals and groups to help themselves goes beyond the benefit to them; if individuals and groups become more capable of helping themselves, the community will benefit. The benefit to the community is what carries assistance from the private domain to the public. For many organizations, self-help and mutual aid are often a matter of ingenuity, working overtime without being paid for it, getting more help from volunteers, even getting clients to help.

Government Assistance

The third question is about government assistance: Is this person asking for help with a need that government should meet? Or is their need one that only government can adequately meet? Some requests reflect needs that far exceed what we might expect of self-help and mutual aid. In some cases it is unreasonable to expect either a panhandler, his relatives, or those of us passing by to solve his problem. These cases are often seen—though hotly debated—as one of the fundamental rationales for government interventions.

Many will argue that each of us has a right to food, shelter, clothing, and other "basic needs," such as health care, that might be far more expensive than an individual person, family, or philanthropist could be expected to provide. If basic needs are a matter of right, then they are a claim on all of us, and they call for government assistance. In such cases we know we must tax one another to generate the resources that are needed. Almsgiving is supplanted by tax revenues; one gives whether one considers the other deserving or not.

This third question, then, has to do with the responsibility of government for the public good. And we can see the question arising in the history and debates about government's responsibility in any major area of public policy. Take the example of public education in the United States. Before the mid-nineteenth century, education of our children—those few who were privileged enough to be educated—was considered the responsibility of private institutions, from the family to churches to elite private schools. That is, it was provided through a mix of self-help, mutual aid, and philanthropy. But then, along with industrialization and democratization, the idea spread that children of all classes and circumstances should come together in "public" schools; only the very rich and the very religious would remain outside the new government system. Government assistance in this case was actually based not on economic need but on the need to create and maintain a democratic polity, to ensure the public good by producing an educated citizenry. Of course, in recent years, we have revisited this question of government's role, and many reformers are claiming that the public good is better served by returning—via vouchers or other policy tools—some responsibility for education to private (non-profit and even for-profit) educators.

Some problems are just too large, like poverty in America or the spread of AIDS in Africa, to be dealt with through self-help or mutual aid. In other cases, solving a problem requires the unique qualities of government intervention, such as its monopoly on the legitimate use of physical force, which might be necessary to protect our lives or our property. And then there are some things that the society needs from individuals that individuals can rarely if ever be expected to pay for completely: advanced education and training in medicine and astrophysics, for example. While many would not hesitate to assert that government assistance is the answer in these cases, and many others would strongly contradict this view, what is certain is that these needs raise fundamental and constantly debated questions in any society: Which things should be paid for not by voluntary gifts, or even private investment, but by taxation? Which things cost so much that it is unreasonable to expect individuals or their families to pay for them by their own efforts? For instance, who should pay for the high cost of medical technology? Daycare? Hospices for the terminally ill who have no family or friends? Art museums? Parks? Philosophy?

Finally, at a broader level, government assistance can take on shades of mutual aid, to the extent that we view helping members of our community—perhaps only taxpaying members, or legal and documented citizens—as taking priority over helping nonmembers. In just about every instance when the United States is called upon to provide humanitarian assistance, and nearly every time international aid is debated, someone offers the argument that instead of sending more money overseas we should spend that money helping Americans in need first. Government certainly has a role in responding to requests for assistance, this argument goes, but not all requests for assistance hold the same weight; the United States government is not as responsible for non-Americans as it is for Americans.

Last but Not Least: Philanthropy

After addressing these previous three questions, and especially when we are dissatisfied with the answers we get and when we feel the initial request is still not being dealt with, we come to the fourth question. Should I give? How much assistance can be provided voluntarily, in gifts of service or money, for the benefit of those in need, even if we have no formal responsibility for them and if we are not promised anything material in return? When is voluntary action the necessary or best path to achieve the public good?

Sometimes philanthropy makes sense because all else has failed or because other responses will take too long or are incomplete. In some cases self-help and mutual aid are insufficient to meet the needs, and governmental resources are either inappropriate or unavailable, and so philanthropy is the human response we turn to. In other cases philanthropy fills a complete void where the other responses are nonexistent. And in some cases we decide that philanthropy is the best, most appropriate response regardless of whether the other responses are failing or not. Often the answers to the previous questions are uncertain, or we have doubts or a lack of information, and we act for fear that otherwise help will fall through the cracks of existing policies or programs. Sometimes we just decide philanthropy is called for because it seems the right thing to do.

So while philanthropy is sometimes a last resort, at other times it is a complement to other forms of help. Sometimes philanthropy provides the

Band-Aid immediate assistance, before family or government (or self-help) takes over to provide long-term care; sometimes philanthropy works to eliminate the cause of the injury, letting friends or government offer the Band-Aid. Requests from strangers so often have a kind of immediacy to them that we feel some sort of action is called for now, and so we act philanthropically without really knowing the full answers to our other questions. Or perhaps the goad to action is a determination to take a different kind of action: to join with others in a public protest against governmental inaction in the face of homelessness. "I won't help this person directly, but I'll set out to help others like him. I'll work to prevent people like him from falling into conditions like these."

Deciding How to Respond

The Meaning of How We Respond

These four questions are central to the way we choose to live our lives as individuals and as a society; how we answer them gives shape to our lives. They are the sort of fundamental questions we confront as an inevitable consequence of the human problematic. As individuals, we must figure out how to respond to the requests for assistance that we know will come because we know that things often go wrong. As a society, considering the different kinds of needs to be met, we have to decide how much weight we want to assign to self-help, to mutual aid, to government assistance, and to philanthropy.

The interaction among these four types of responses makes up the agenda of political and social life in a society like the United States. Self-help, mutual aid, government assistance, and philanthropy provide a checklist for thinking about the ways that responsibility is allocated in our society. Consider health care costs, for example, or debt relief in Africa, or support of the arts, or education reform, or even disaster response. Are families solely responsible for supporting young musicians, or should the government provide scholarships to those children with the most promising talent? Should the United States forgive the debts owed by struggling African nations, or should it focus on encouraging multinational corporations to help these countries nurture their own market economy? If someone in the United States smokes her entire life and gets lung cancer when she is elderly, should Medicare pay for her treatment even if she (or her children) have the means to pay for it themselves?

In a larger sense, every political or policy discussion of large public issues involves a debate over these four possible contributions to the work of society, and our political conflicts are often over whether or not to change the mixture of the four responses. These questions form the background of every American presidential election campaign; they shape every party platform. To what extent is each of us responsible for ourselves? To what extent should we be expected to rely on others with whom we share formal responsibility? To what extent must we agree to tax ourselves to deal with our shared problems and needs? To what extent can we rely on voluntary giving and voluntary service? How much will our concern for others affect our answer? How much will we be guided by concern for our own self-interest? Should we do more through faith-based nonprofits or private contractors and less through government?

But we should not think of these four responses as starkly distinct and assume that our answers to the questions just raised must always be placed into one of these four categories. In fact, returning to the points from Rockefeller and Maimonides discussed earlier, we can see how the long history of efforts to "help people help themselves" illustrates how the various responses can become intertwined and can be hard to disentangle. These efforts have philanthropic purposes as well as being about "self-help." For instance, in nineteenth-century London, young Octavia Hill wanted to create decent housing for the poor.[21] Lacking capital, she turned to social philosopher and art critic John Ruskin for help. He loaned her five thousand pounds, but with the requirement that she produce a return of 5 percent if she hoped to persuade others to follow his example. Following Ruskin's advice, Hill made payment of rent a first and unwavering demand upon all her tenants. She also insisted on stern self-discipline; her tenants not only paid their rent on time but they also stayed within her range of acceptable social and moral behavior. Influenced by both Christian Socialism and (from the opposite political pole) the Charity Organisation Society approach, Hill was pragmatic. Commenting on Hill's management style, Gertrude Himmelfarb observes: "Her aim was not only to provide the decent housing that was a precondition of independence but to promote the habits, abilities, and sensibilities that would sustain that independence. This meant treating the tenants as equals rather than dependents, and helping them in the same spirit that one might help one's friends."[22] Hill's work is clearly about promoting self-help, but there are also elements of mutual aid involved, and this was all brought about by a voluntary, philanthropic intervention. Hill's response to need—the need for adequate housing for the poor—reveals how it is often in the mix or interaction of responses that we can see fully how society is responding to its problems.

Altruism and Egoism

Many factors influence how we respond to the proverbial request for assistance and how we meet needs and assign responsibility. To start with, we can see that our responses reflect both sides of the recurrent tension in human nature that we identified earlier: the tension between altruism and egoism. Because most of us have some concern about the well-being of others and about the needs of our communities, we answer these questions in terms of our altruistic values. But because we also have needs of our own and a strong sense of fairness—if I work to help myself, others should do the same—we have to recognize that we have egoistic values as well.

Our lives are spent balancing these two human tendencies while trying to address the needs we see. Whether we are asking the self-help question of the panhandler, wondering why we should be singled out for voluntary giving when we already pay taxes to help the homeless, or pondering our felt obligation to be compassionate to all fellow humans in need, our concern for others and our concern for ourselves are in play. Both altruism and egoism influence our judgments of how the four responses should be weighted. The rhetoric of weighting ranges from appeals to pity to appeals to greed, from acting on values to acting on calculations of potential benefit returns, reflecting the influence of both poles. Every answer contains both.

In addition to the decision of whether to give, we must also decide how and how much to give. As we struggle with these decisions, too, we reveal the tension between egoism and altruism. One philanthropic principle that has been in use since antiquity is that one should give to others for whom one has no formal responsibility only out of surplus. To have a surplus means that one has enough for oneself (and presumably for those for whom one does have formal responsibility). But what is "enough"? When does a gift out of surplus begin to cut close to the quick? Often an assessment of one's own resources leads to the conclusion, "I can help, but not enough; others will have to come along on this one." Or "I will give you a hundred dollars toward your scholarship, but you'll have to work for part of the rest, get help from your family, and perhaps get a grant or loan from the college." In other instances we may decide not to follow this principle and instead to be munificent, to "give until it hurts." When should a gift be from income and when from savings? When is a commitment of five hours a week too little, and when is it too much? And how should we give? Should we give directly to individuals, so we can see that the help gets to them? Is it acceptable egoism to want the personal connection with those we help? Is it more altruistic (and therefore better) to pool our help with that of others by giving to an institution, so that more people can ultimately be helped? The point here is that figuring out how to respond—when to act philanthropically and how—requires that we accept the tension between egoism and altruism as a reality and not simply wish that it were not so.

What Is Going On? Where Are We Coming From?

We have to answer the first ethical question, "What is going on?" before deciding whether to act philanthropically, before deciding how to respond to the appeals for help that arise as a consequence of the human problematic. For example, we've seen people on the street holding signs that said, "Homeless and Dying of AIDS" and "Disabled. Want to Work but Can't. Please Help." Each passerby who reads these sorts of signs makes an instantaneous assessment of the credibility of the statement. If what is going on is that the young man holding the first sign is in fact homeless and dying, or that the older man holding the second sign is in a wheelchair, an immediate gift of alms might be called for (even if government assistance is also called for). If one concludes this is simply another familiar deception of the kind newcomers to big cities are warned about, the response may be ironic amusement for some, disgust and anger for others, but probably not sympathy and charity.

So one part of deciding how to respond is looking for information on what is going on. Lacking concrete information, we search for subtle clues or hints from which we can draw conclusions or make assumptions. But in addition to this first question, we also decide how to respond based on factors related to a second, complementary question, "Where are we coming from?" Our response is influenced by our own moral convictions (e.g., whether we believe helping strangers is a moral duty), our own perceptual or ideological biases (e.g., should the government ever be involved in helping the homeless?), the other cultural conventions and concepts we have learned (e.g., is it normal for people in need to ask for help this way?), and the larger social and economic situation we live in (e.g., whether we live in a "social democracy" where the welfare state is responsible for helping the disabled or those with AIDS, or in a neoliberal capitalist state).

Our response is "embedded" in our social and cultural life in these and other ways, and this embeddedness is crucial to our theory of why philanthropy is a preferred response and why it takes the form or role it does in any society. This is similar to what Lester Salamon and Helmut Anheier term the "social origins" theory of the nonprofit sector. They remind us that the philanthropic tradition and nonprofit sector looks different and plays different roles in different societies. What can explain this variation is that—while what we call philanthropy is a response in all those societies—the path taken by the development of nonprofit activities in any society is fundamentally influenced by the "cultural, religious, political, and economic realities" of that society.[23]

A similar set of multiple influences on how we respond can be identified if it is an organization that must decide how to respond or when we think of the choice as a society's choice about how to allocate responsibility. For instance, think about how moral, cultural, and political changes have affected our changing mixture of responses—individual, community, governmental, and philanthropic responses—to poverty in the United States. The idea that the state should care for the poor is almost as old as western civilization and that individuals and religious institutions should help is an ancient idea. But the critical change came when societies and cultures realized that assistance should be regularized and not left to spontaneous expressions of charity, which led to government assistance taking a more prominent role, although it is a role that is still different in different cultural and national contexts.

Of course, despite the way we've been describing this "decision," we should acknowledge that the way we answer these questions, and the responses we offer, are not always the result of a conscious or rational choice. In fact, our answers to the questions are rarely obvious or even simple. Often we decide that more than one response is called for, or we change the mix of responses over time, or we go forward with the response we want and leave the decision about other responses to other people.

Reasons for a Philanthropic Response

The final step in developing a way of thinking about the role of philanthropy as a response to the human problematic—and about the larger question of why philanthropy exists—is to summarize the reasons why, in the context of multiple types of responses, a philanthropic response is warranted, preferred, or perhaps even required and demanded. It helps conceptually to distill these reasons down into three broad categories. Each category relates to a scenario in which some response is needed; in each scenario, the role of philanthropy is considered alongside the others. We identify three categories of reasons:

1. Philanthropy is the only, or the only effective, response.
2. Philanthropy is one response that complements other responses.
3. Philanthropy is the preferred or the most appropriate response.

Philanthropy Is the Only, or the Only Effective, Response

Sometimes we turn to philanthropy when other responses are either nonexistent or not working; we turn to philanthropy *because* the other responses are nonexistent or not working. We give a panhandler a dollar because we figure that self-help and mutual aid and government assistance are somehow not able to help him meet his basic needs. We volunteer as a literacy tutor because we think that if we don't help this person learn to read and they can't help themselves, who will? We donate to public television because we worry about the decline in government funding for it.

Scholars have long offered this sort of "failure" argument as a way to explain, theoretically, the existence of the nonprofit sector. The third sector exists, the theory goes, because of the inadequacy, defects, or failure of the other two. The marketplace provides for the exercise of individual choice but does not provide all the public goods—e.g., clean air—necessary for an operational and healthy society, and it creates costly "externalities"—e.g., air pollution—that must somehow be dealt with. This sort of "market failure" argument has long been a prominent and popular justification for government action and public policy intervention. It helps us to answer the tough question: why does government exist?

But while government provides important public goods, it sometimes does not provide adequate public goods. Recall that this "government failure" is a key reason offered by economists for why the otherwise illogical entity of "not-for-profit" organizations would exist. Further, government is limited in how it can meet needs, both by what James Douglas calls the "categorical constraint"—the requirement that everyone be treated the same can lead government to avoid treating anybody—and by what Burton Weisbrod calls the "heterogeneity" of the population—the more diverse the needs and interests of the people (and, we would add, the more diverse the interpretation of what the "public good" is), the less likely government is to step into the fray.[24]

In the face of this dual failure of the marketplace and of government responses, then, voluntary philanthropic action is needed to fill the void. Philanthropy provides for individual choice like the marketplace and provides public goods like government, but it does so better than these other two responses in conditions of great diversity and in situations when flexibility is key. This theory could be used to explain philanthropic interventions from nonprofit AIDS clinics in poor neighborhoods where the local public hospital cannot handle the demand, to charter schools in suburbs where parents are dissatisfied with their other choices. But we cannot forget the more stark instances in which philanthropy is simply the "only game in town."

While most scholarship has used this sort of "dual failure" theory to explain the existence of the nonprofit (the third) sector, or to explain why nonprofit organizations provide some good that other types of organizations might also provide, we would broaden this theory to fit our broader conception of philanthropy and our conception of the three other responses that we have laid out: self-help, mutual aid, and government assistance. (In a sense, we offer a "triple failure" theory, although the whole idea of "failure" does not really work here, as explained in the next section.)

We would also go beyond much previous work in applying this explanation for why philanthropy exists to the advocacy side of philanthropy as well as to the service side. Philanthropy and the other responses we have been discussing are responding to needs, but we can think of those "needs" as including the need for voice or the need for representation of interests. And philanthropic organizations that advocate for certain populations or for certain ideals and values can be seen as doing so because those populations or values are not, or not effectively, being advocated by other actors—not by the affected or interested parties themselves (self-help), not by their direct networks (mutual aid), and not by the government that is often the target for their advocacy claims.

Philanthropy Is One Response That Complements Other Responses

Our explanation of why philanthropy exists, though, does not require the failure of other responses or other forms of action. In fact, we know that in many (perhaps most) cases, philanthropy exists as a response alongside many other responses in a complex and confusing mix. Life is problematic, and responding effectively (and morally) to the problems of life requires the ability to draw upon all resources of the society—political, economic, personal, familial, philanthropic. This combination of multiple responses is, by most accounts, becoming more common today, particularly as we rethink the roles of the three sectors and develop new cross-sectoral forms of governance.[25] More and more, we respond to things that go wrong, and craft ways of making things better, using "partnerships" between government and philanthropy and the market. More and more we are seeing the four responses described above as complementary, rather than simply fighting the ideological battles over, for example, whether self-help *or* government *or* philanthropy is best.

Take the example of one of the most fundamental needs of any society: taking care of children, particularly those that might be in trouble. Children are an interesting case because in deciding how to respond to their need, we quickly move beyond calling for self-help. Children can certainly help themselves, but their ability to do this is more limited than almost any other group in the society, and no one blames them (as we blame others) for their inability to help themselves. So, moving beyond self-help, we note that in any society the resources that are available to help children are varied and important. The most important, of course, are the family and sometimes close friends. These are the first line of support we expect all children to have, even if many do not or are not well served by their families or other mutual aid networks. Beyond this, there are plenty of others whose careers are devoted to helping children: the pediatricians and other medical specialists; the teachers and coaches and other school professionals; social workers and other therapists; counselors, guides, and mentors. A great many of these are employed by government, and they are charged with implementing a widely acknowledged mandate that the government, if it helps no one else, should help this least vulnerable population.

But beyond these sources of support, there are volunteers and professionals in the vast array of philanthropic organizations that have programs designed for children. Hundreds of thousands and perhaps millions of people in the United States alone are engaged as volunteers in trying to help children by working for these philanthropic organizations: Boys Clubs and Girls Clubs, the YMCA and YWCA, Police Athletic Leagues, 4-H clubs, Catholic Youth Organizations, Boy Scouts, Girl Scouts, and others more recently established. It is important to note that these philanthropic organizations do not simply exist to help children in ways that (or because) government or families have failed to help, although this is sometimes an important reason why such children's organizations exist; they also exist because they believe helping children is for the public good, regardless of what other parts of society do. And these philanthropic responses help children in ways that complement the ways these children are helped by other parts of society—e.g., Girls Clubs can serve at-risk girls better when there is a supportive family involved as well. We should also acknowledge that these philanthropic groups are not always effective and might themselves fail in ways that force a government or family response. Many of the organizations mentioned are now said to be less effective with children than they were fifty or sixty years ago. In particular, they seem to be less effective in reaching ethnic and racial groups and the poor in the often dangerous neighborhoods where the toughest problems always are. This is further evidence for the need to spread the responsibility around and for various actors in society—familial, governmental, and philanthropic—to work together.

Philanthropy Is the Preferred or the Most Appropriate Response

Because we argue in this book that philanthropy is moral action, that it is voluntary action driven by a vision of the public good, we must be sure to remember this last—really the first—reason for philanthropy. Philanthropy is often how we prefer to do our good works. We respond philanthropically many times because philanthropy is deemed, in our culture, as an appropriate way of making things better, an appropriate and normal and expected way of trying to advance the public good. In other cases, we respond philanthropically because the situation seems to call specifically for philanthropy instead of other responses.

Much of what we cover in the next chapter will illustrate this reason for why philanthropy exists, as we will be exploring how philanthropy is distinctively moral action and therefore has a melioristic purpose and philanthropic meaning that make it distinctive. And what we discussed in the previous chapter about the positive roles of philanthropy also demonstrates this notion of philanthropy as the preferred or most appropriate response. Philanthropy is most appropriate when, for example, our action is meant to express or promote religious values and convictions that we want to keep separate from government. Philanthropy is preferred when the goal is to advocate for broad social change or to try out a new idea for achieving change in communities. Remember that philanthropy is in some ways the first sector, that it is the place we prefer to express our vision of the public good or to do our public work regardless of what the other sectors are doing or whether self-help is possible. This fact partly underlies the currently popular recognition of social entrepreneurship as a key role for philanthropy.[26]

We can also imagine many situations in which a philanthropic response is most appropriate. Sometimes we want or need to make a public statement with our generosity (perhaps to leverage the generosity of others). At other times we want to have a personal connection with the people we help, even if they are strangers to us at the start. Both of these somewhat opposing situations are more possible through philanthropy than, say, through mutual aid or government assistance. Sometimes we see a need, like the face of a starving child on television, and we feel the need to do something rather than let others take care of it. Sometimes we give philanthropically specifically to pay back someone who helped us philanthropically in the past.[27] And sometimes we simply do not have time to think or learn about what other responses might be going on; the situation is an emergency and voluntary intervention is clearly the right thing to do, right now.

Philanthropic action is, in most places and times, culturally prescribed and highly valued for its own sake. But, of course, when philanthropy is appropriate versus when government or mutual aid is appropriate is a social choice that is determined in part by cultural traditions, historical developments, and other aspects of our social origins—"where we are coming from."

We also see this reasoning for why philanthropy is appropriate often in the accounts and understandings that people offer to justify their giving. When, for instance, someone says that helping children learn to read or giving money to their local library is "the right thing to do" or "a way to give back," they are not merely expressing their motives but also justifying their particular sort of action, their philanthropic action, in terms that make sense to them given what they have learned from their culture. More generally, social and historical patterns often deem philanthropy the most appropriate way to solve certain problems or address certain needs in any given society. It is "what we do."

The Response to Hurricane Katrina

The fact that things often go wrong is an inevitable part of the human problematic. But sometimes things go very wrong (and for many reasons), and everyone can see clearly just how wrong. These cases, such as the devastating crisis in the coastal areas of Louisiana and Mississippi caused by Hurricane Katrina in 2005, starkly illustrate the points we have been making. The response to the Katrina crisis illustrates the forces affecting our decisions about how to respond and how absolutely vital philanthropy is as one response among many.

Natural events disrupt our lives in dramatic ways, often calling for philanthropic action to relieve the suffering that results. But responding to natural disasters like floods or wildfires or hurricanes far exceeds the capacity of philanthropic assistance and exceeds its proper role as well. Families and relatives play a role in helping people deal with their loss and rebuild their lives. And it is in such situations of utter devastation that we see perhaps most clearly the necessity of government. So natural disasters—and the human disasters or system failure that sometimes accompany natural disasters—demonstrate the need for a full array of responses. Of course, this is also true when the disaster is completely man-made. Think of the crucial role played by all four responses—self-help, mutual aid, government assistance, and philanthropy—in the response to the terrorist attacks of 9/11.

In the case of the Katrina crisis we can see how the massive philanthropic response—an unprecedented response that outpaced the relief giving that following either the attacks of 9/11 or the Indian Ocean tsunami—fit with other responses such as self-help and government assistance. Philanthropy here was clearly seen as filling a void where other responses failed, but if we look closer we can see how philanthropy was also complemented by other responses, and how philanthropy was for many the preferred response regardless of what else was being done.

The failure of the government response to the aftermath of Katrina has been well documented. Seeing this failure portrayed so vividly and horribly on television led many people to reach for their checkbooks and some people to pack their bags to go be a volunteer; that is, the failure of other responses was part of the reason why we turned to philanthropy to deal with the obvious need for help. Government officials acknowledged their failure publicly, in fact, making press statements in the midst of the crisis in which they told those in need to seek out the Salvation Army or the Red Cross for help rather than turning to the overwhelmed Federal Emergency Management Agency (FEMA). But it was not simply government that failed; self-help and mutual aid failed as well. For many residents of New Orleans, self-help was either not an option because of their infirmities or lack of supplies or because they could not return to their homes to get what they would need to survive on their own. And while mutual aid clearly saved many lives in this crisis, as family members stayed together to help each other, many other people lost their lives while their family and friends sat helplessly on the other side of washed-out bridges and roads, and many people (including children) got separated from their families and had to rely on relief workers to care for them until they could be reunited. These are instances in which philanthropy—symbolized by a lone Salvation Army van that for a few days was the only source of aid to reach some of the most rural Mississippi towns—was the only way to help.

Within the philanthropic community itself, we can note similar dynamics that blur the lines between types of responses. While the international relief organizations like Red Cross were clearly responding, local organizations like churches and community groups in Louisiana and Mississippi did what they could amid the rubble in their own backyards. Local foundations such as the Greater New Orleans Foundation and the Foundation for the Mid South helped set up relief funds and coordinate community organizing, even though, in some cases, their own offices had to be temporarily closed. And existing nonprofits in the area were forced to reexamine their missions in light of a changed set of needs in the communities they served. For example, Louisiana Environmental Action Network, an advocacy group that normally focused on toxics issues in communities around the state—many of which were hit by both Hurricanes Katrina and Rita—transformed itself into a relief group providing supplies for homeowners and volunteers who now had to deal with the toxic hazard of returning to their homes.

But while these local groups engaged in this sort of mutual aid/philanthropy hybrid, plenty of grantmakers from outside the region backed them up with a more traditional philanthropic response to the crisis—"traditional" here meaning voluntary interventions, sometimes from far away, in the lives of strangers for whom they have no formal responsibility. For instance, the McCormick Tribune Foundation in Chicago—not usually a foundation that gives to local causes in the Gulf Coast region—set up a special relief fund soon after Katrina hit, and pledged to use foundation funds to match all individual donations and to cover all administrative costs so that the issue of "how much of my check is going to help those in need" would not arise.

However, philanthropy was not simply a response to fill the void left by the failure of others. Despite the struggles we noted, there was clearly a lot of self-help and mutual aid going on, especially in areas (and in early stages) where neither FEMA nor that Salvation Army truck had arrived. Family and friends were in some cases both the "first responders" and the only effective response for days at a time. In the first few days, the people stranded in the Superdome and those waiting for help in flattened towns in Mississippi relied on each other for medical care, supplies, and emotional support. But the point is that while these sorts of responses were ultimately inadequate—the task before them was just too great—we can see the government and philanthropic responses as complementary to this self-help and mutual aid.

And this reliance on multiple responses will continue as the efforts to help move from relief to recovery. After the first anniversary of Katrina, much attention turned to what government can and must do, and this is appropriate. Neither philanthropy nor individuals and families nor even the marketplace have the capacity or organization required to deal with such a problem when it is on such a scale. Government agencies at many levels (including the military) must help provide emergency aid, but they must also provide long-term help of many kinds, from rebuilding infrastructure to providing tax incentives for businesses to return to decimated places. Ultimately, however, recovery from such a calamity depends not on government but on people getting back to their economic work, helping themselves, cooperating in their networks, competing in the marketplace, and only secondarily depending on government subsidies and continued charitable contributions. Mutual aid and self-help—perhaps microcredit loans would work—are essential to long-term recovery.

But we should not overlook the fact that philanthropy was for many the preferred or most appropriate response to the Katrina disaster. Americans saw the crisis and wanted to "do something," and in such cases "doing something" meant donating clothing, or volunteering at a crisis switchboard, or donating money online, or traveling to the region to volunteer, or any number of other philanthropic responses. We would have done this even if the government response had been swift and well-coordinated.

Finally, the response to Katrina also illustrates what we have discussed in this chapter about the multiple influences and considerations that affect our decision about how to respond, such as our assessments of "what is going on" and "where we are coming from." The charitable giving in this crisis was very likely much larger and swifter than others because when we assessed what is going on, we decided such a massive charitable response was needed. Something clearly was going wrong, and the people were clearly in need, so there was no question that philanthropy was called for. But how people responded philanthropically was influenced by factors about who they are and how they could best help. Vietnamese neighborhoods in Orange County, California, held fund-raising drives to assist the Vietnamese fishing communities on the Gulf Coast. Veterinarians and animal lovers rushed to New Orleans in a highly coordinated effort to rescue abandoned and stranded animals. And corporations donated useful in-kind supplies, from satellite phones, to Web services for victim registries, to temporary relief from car payments.

But despite these patterns, it is heartening to note in the end that the massive philanthropic response to Katrina often came from people who live outside the Deep South and who look very different from those they reached out to help. This should come as no surprise to those who know how philanthropy works.

Cultural Patterns in a Universal Response

This chapter has outlined certain fundamental features of the human condition and human nature that call philanthropy into being, in a sense, as a response to the inevitable human problematic. However, it is helpful at the end to remember a point we made at the start: This seemingly universal response is always influenced by cultural and historical context. The response might be impelled by human nature, but the expressions of human nature are culturally prescribed. Some "life chances" circumstances should be considered universally unacceptable, but many times what is considered unacceptable and deserving of philanthropic intervention depends on social definitions or disputed claims of different moral imaginations. And as noted, our choices about how to respond, and what role philanthropy will play, are also influenced by "where we are coming from," which can be seen in the significant variations in the way that different countries conceive of the role of the nonprofit sector. This cultural distinctiveness is what led Tocqueville to focus so much attention on the use of associations in public life by Americans. It was not that they did not have such associations in France, but in France citizens turned first to government to meet human needs or to express the general will, while in America, Tocqueville perceived, citizens turned first to voluntary associations. If Hurricane Katrina had struck New Zealand instead of New Orleans, there would have been a philanthropic response, of course, but it would have looked a bit different.

The distinctive philanthropic tradition in any culture is the history of this response as it took shape in that culture. America's tradition is vibrant and prominent, but the Russian people have a philanthropic tradition, too: even during the time of the Soviet Union there were secret voluntary associations to publish *samizdat* literature. This recognition of distinctive traditions is a point we will explore in the next two chapters as well, as we discuss philanthropy as a difficult moral action that reflects and determines the moral agenda of a society and as the "social history of the moral imagination."

4

The World Can Be Made Better: Philanthropy as Moral Action

*I*n previous chapters, we have made the point that philanthropy is "moral action" and that the moral dimension of philanthropy is the most important. The connection to morality, we argued in chapter 2, is the defining feature of philanthropy and the nonprofit sector, the essential dimension and unifying idea that most distinguishes it from government and the marketplace. But *moral action* and *morality* are terms that could mean very different things to different readers, so it is essential to clarify what we mean by them in our theory of philanthropy.

In essence, we have introduced two general understandings of how philanthropy is moral action, which we now address more deeply in this chapter:

1. Philanthropy is the primary vehicle people use to implement their moral imagination and to shape and advance the moral agenda of our society.
2. Philanthropy is about voluntarily intervening in other people's lives for their benefit, to do them good and to advance the public good, and in this way philanthropic action is inherently moral.

The first meaning of philanthropy as moral action is one that will be illustrated in the following chapter as well. It is one of the positive social roles for philanthropy that lead us to prefer this affirmative conception over other ways of thinking about the sector such as nonprofit. The story of philanthropy in any society is the story of people coming together in voluntary associations around an expression of moral imagination—such as a definition that something is wrong, and a call for a specific response to make things better—and then engaging in voluntary giving and service (including advocacy) to advance that moral mission. Taken together, these philanthropic efforts are a primary and indispensable means by which any society's moral agenda is crafted. The public arena of action that we label philanthropy, as many theorists of the nonprofit sector have noted, is often the place where new causes, new expressions of values, and innovative new solutions to social problems are first introduced, including competing causes and solutions. And so philanthropy deals with the whole gamut of the most important moral issues and debates confronting a society such as the United States, from concerns over growing wealth inequalities to the debate over whether Internet gambling is a vice to be regulated, and on and on.

The second meaning of philanthropy as moral action concerns the practical ethics and principles of philanthropic action. People are acting morally when they presume to come to the aid of others as an act of mercy or they intervene voluntarily to improve the quality of life and advance the public good. To act morally is to act with regard to and for others, beyond one's concern for oneself, particularly when that action is voluntary; voluntary action for the public good is moral action. But such voluntary moral action, as Good Samaritans know, is difficult and fraught with uncertainty or even peril. The middle section of this chapter examines some of the principles, questions, and concepts that can help guide people who engage in this sort of moral action. And we conclude the chapter by outlining a practical philosophy—the pragmatist doctrine of "meliorism"—that we think best expresses the worldview behind philanthropy as moral action and that encapsulates much of what we have been saying about the rationale for philanthropy in human societies. Meliorism is the doctrine that the world can be made better through rightly directed human effort. That is the philosophy of philanthropy at its pithiest. It is also a good answer to the question "Why does philanthropy exist?"

Philanthropy, the Moral Imagination, and the Moral Agenda

Distinctive Expressions of the Moral Imagination

Philanthropy is about the search for the good life and the good society through good works—our own and those of others. Of course, there is no such thing as *the* good life or *the* good society. The "good life" seems to have as many definitions as there are people. The "good society" may have as many definitions as there are communities. Each of us has our own definitions of these ideals or at least our own hunches. We have dispositions and preferences and wishes for something better. And in social life we often find ourselves reaching toward the same goals as other people we know or know about. However we define these ideals, the important point here is that we try to achieve them through philanthropy. Good works are essential to the good life and the good society.

Previous scholarship that has examined the way that people engaging in philanthropy think about this part of their lives supports our view of philanthropy as an expression of the moral imagination. The sociologists Paul Schervish and Robert Wuthnow have both presented extensive evidence from interviews with donors and volunteers. They find that philanthropic action is a meaningful and specifically moral-oriented activity for these people. Through philanthropy, donors and volunteers express their moral (and sometimes spiritual) values and make public their moral opinions on how the world can be made better. Schervish says givers craft what he calls a "moral biography," and they do so by drawing on what Wuthnow identifies as culturally available meanings and vocabularies to make sense of their charitable action as moral action (as well as self-fulfilling activity).[1]

We take this important sociological work on individual philanthropic behavior and expand it into a view of the entire field of philanthropy as moral action. Individuals and groups express their values, advocate for their visions of the public good, work to achieve their missions, and find meaning, purpose, and hope in life through philanthropy. And society's moral agenda, in turn, is imagined, proposed, debated, implemented, and reformed through philanthropy.

Philanthropy is a way that we can work with others toward something better, toward a shared understanding of the public good, or perhaps to preserve something we see as good already. However, we must also recognize that many of the most fervent polarizers of moral issues also band together in voluntary associations, ostensibly to serve the public good. Most of us prefer a climate of openness to controversial ideas and proposals, but in such a climate it is difficult to find common ground on what, if anything, might be ruled off-limits or out-of-bounds, and what is for the public good. Philanthropy is the means we use for polarizing and possibly for finding common ground.

The idea that philanthropy is the primary vehicle people use to implement their moral imagination and to shape and advance the moral agenda of our society is a vital piece of our explanation in this book of why philanthropy exists in any society. But this fundamental rationale for philanthropy also reveals how and why the philanthropic tradition will always contain different content in different societies. Because cultures have distinctive interpretations and mixtures of moral values, public histories, ethnicities, political traditions, and so on, the way that philanthropy plays its role as a vehicle for moral action will necessarily be influenced by those factors in any culture. The moral imaginations of Mexicans are different from those of Moroccans; the moral agenda shaped by philanthropy in Iran will be different from the moral agenda in India. As we noted in the previous chapter, both the definition of what is "wrong" and the decision about how to respond—and, therefore, the nature of philanthropic activity—are influenced by cultural and historical context.

In fact, taking this a step further, we can see here the central role that philanthropy plays in creating and maintaining the enduring and powerful distinctiveness of a culture—recall that we identified this in chapter 2 as the "cultural role" of philanthropy. All one has to do is look at the biggest field of philanthropic action in most societies—the work of religious groups—to appreciate philanthropy's role in making cultures different and keeping them different by passing on traditions, values, rituals, etc. Giving alms to the poor through the collection plate in an American church (which is, after all, philanthropy giving to a voluntary association) reinforces many moral ideals and conventions at the core of American culture; the same could be said for placing food in a monk's begging bowl in rural Thailand.

The moral agenda shaped and debated by philanthropy also varies over time, as social problems rise and fall, as cultures evolve, as science and technology develop, and as philanthropic entrepreneurs pursue their creative passions and bring new moral issues to our attention. Domestic violence is more clearly defined as a "problem" now than in the past largely because of the work of women's advocacy groups and social workers providing aid on the nonprofit frontlines. The same could be said for drunk driving; it would be hard to find a grassroots philanthropic endeavor that has been more successful than Mothers Against Drunk Driving (MADD) in terms of awareness and measurable outcomes. The issue of civil rights has been transformed by various movement organizations to embrace more minority groups, from defending the rights of immigrants to gun owners to prisoners. Scientific developments have revolutionized public health and nutrition to the point where life expectancy is far beyond what was thought possible in the nineteenth century, and so the moral agenda around caring for the elderly is different now than it was in the past—and the role of philanthropy in taking up the slack of government in this area will increase. Euthanasia will only become more prominent as an issue on the moral agenda in the coming decades. The point is that changes in the moral agenda over time reveal and implicate the role of philanthropic actions as we define them.

We turn to philanthropy to alleviate suffering and to improve the quality of life in a community and also to advocate for policy goals, to experiment with new approaches to social reform, to pass on values, etc. But perhaps the greatest benefit of turning to philanthropy as moral action is that it helps us to think more clearly about issues that are more often than not held at a distance, a tidy morality that can be enjoyed without staining one's clothes. Participating in philanthropy provides a way into the messy but enlightening process of figuring out and putting to the test our moral commitments. Those who would reduce philanthropy to narrowly rational processes fail to grasp this fundamental aspect. "The human understanding is no dry light, but receives an infusion from the will and affections," as Francis Bacon put it.[2] Philanthropy serves causes, and causes are compelling, urgent, inspiring, and motivating, but they can also be emotionally draining and, at times, exasperating. Pursuing the moral imagination through philanthropy can be tough, but it can also show us who we are and what we believe.

Mission and Vision

More than a million organizations operating in the United States philanthropic sector exist because something is going on in society that calls forth a response. Some boys in urban neighborhoods have no one to mentor them through the tough choices they face; our most vital institutions need a constant infusion of well-educated leaders; people without health insurance are injured in car accidents; the arts enhance the quality of our lives; affordable housing and community economic development are impossible without adequate financial capital. These social conditions or problems are the reason why those philanthropic organizations exist.

As we noted in the first chapter, this way of thinking about the rationale for philanthropy comes from the idea of "mission" developed by the late Henry Rosso, founder of The Fund Raising School (now a part of the Center on Philanthropy at Indiana University).[3] Rosso taught that the mission of an organization can be found in their particular answer to the question "Why do we exist?" Specifically, the mission is the urgent social issue or problem that calls for a response.[4] Rosso's intention was to force his students to look beyond themselves and beyond their organization to the issues that make philanthropy necessary in society. He wanted them to get away from thinking solely about programs and tactics. He rejected all mission statements that began with *to*, as in "our mission is to provide health care services for poor children." The mission is something about society, not something about the organization. From this starting point of a moral vision for society, a vision of the public good and how society does not match that vision in some way, philanthropic organizations could then derive their programmatic strategies to address their mission.

For example, many children are at risk and disadvantaged; they become ill, experience the consequences of poverty, drop out of school, and suffer from troubles in their family. These problems are the mission of groups like the Children's Defense Fund (CDF). The staff, supporters, and volunteers for the CDF advocate on behalf of increasing tax-supported programs to improve children's health, expanding educational opportunities and school lunch programs, and so on. But merely defining the mission of the CDF in terms of these programmatic activities—"the CDF exists to advocate on behalf of children"—would skip over the crucial point of considering the overarching moral and social conditions that require such activity..

Rosso taught this understanding of mission for many years to many fund-raising professionals and nonprofit leaders, always urging them to focus first and always on the mission if they wanted to be ethical philanthropic professionals. He also believed fervently that this approach was the most effective way to raise money. Getting donors committed to mission, rather than to the organization, was the secret to effective fund-raising.

This perspective on mission expresses in an ingenious way our view that the moral dimension of philanthropy is the most important and distinctive, and it explains the moral rationale for why philanthropy exists. It shows how understanding philanthropic action requires an understanding of the moral and social justification for that action. The importance of this justification is illustrated most dramatically when the justification disappears. This happened most famously in the case of the March of Dimes, which came into being because of the alarming increase in cases of po-liomyelitis. The March of Dimes raised money for research to bring an end to the disease. In time a vaccine was found that vanquished polio, and in doing so the vaccine eliminated the mission of the organization. The March of Dimes faced a choice: it could simply declare itself successful and fold, or it could choose another set of problems or issues in the world and declare that to be its new mission. In a not wholly uncontroversial move, they chose the latter option, and today the organization raises money to prevent birth defects and infant mortality.[5]

Mission is not always cut and dried, and sometimes asking about mis-sion stirs up controversy about philanthropic groups, as we know from re-ports of lavish parties thrown for museum donors or critiques of groups such as Ducks Unlimited, which raises lots of money for wetlands preser-vation and restoration of duck habitat but raises that money from the duck hunters who make up the membership of the organization. But before we are too critical of Ducks Unlimited, we should remember the ambiguity of mission that appears in every church senior citizens socializing group or in every tax-exempt scholarly journal. Philanthropy as moral action is about mission, but mission is not always easy to define, and not everyone agrees that a particular mission is for the public good. Mission can also "drift" away from original intentions.[6]

Mission is not always obvious either. Sometimes it takes the creative use of moral imagination to "see" a problem that requires a philanthropic re-sponse. Sometimes defining mission requires exceptional vision and often a visionary. Sometimes we need a leader who can recognize the urgency of something that others fail to grasp. Such visionaries are key players in the historical story of philanthropy. John Muir saw the natural world differ-ently than most of his contemporaries, as a majestic environment that we shouldn't take for granted; he provided the vision for naturalists and envi-ronmental organizations to follow after him. Elizabeth Cady Stanton saw the situation of women in society as unacceptable and unjust when most people simply took it for granted; she provided women's organizations with a vision of the society they wanted to achieve.

However eloquent the vision or compelling the mission, philanthropy will fail in achieving its moral agenda without organization, resources, and sustained commitment. Another way to put this is that philanthropy re-quires thought, action, and passion. Visionaries are merely "voices crying in the wilderness" if others do not join them in sharing and acting on their moral imaginings. Visionaries must become leaders who work together with others in organizations to convert social visions into social realities and to gather resources, both financial and human, including the all-important volunteer resources. In the civil rights movement, the organizational genius of the religious congregation was the fulcrum on which the movement achieved its first and most important victories. These victories did not arise—as some histories would lead us to believe—from the sheer eloquence of Martin Luther King's statement of the vision or from the sheer righteousness of the cause, even though the passionate commitment those engendered were surely indispensable. But for the civil rights vision to be realized, organization was the key. Rosa Parks was a visionary in her own way, yes, but she was also an active volunteer for the National Association for the Advancement of Colored People before she ever became famous for refusing to give up her seat on the bus.

The example of Rosa Parks reminds us that voluntary action—especially courageous actions like hers—to advance our moral ideals is not only difficult but sometimes dangerous. The challenges of engaging in responsible moral action are addressed below.

Philanthropy and the Good Samaritan

The Christian parable of the Good Samaritan is well known, even to non-Christians.[7] The story is short and deceptively simple; it touches deep emotions and common experience at the same time.

Jesus is being tested by a lawyer, who asks, "Teacher, what shall I do to inherit eternal life?" Jesus draws from him the answer that he must love God and his neighbor as himself. The lawyer persists: "And who is my neighbor?" Jesus then relates this story:

> A man was going down from Jerusalem to Jericho, and he fell among robbers, who stripped him and beat him, and departed, leaving him half-dead. Now by chance a priest was going down that road, and when he saw him he passed by on the other side. So likewise a Levite, when he came to the place and saw him, passed by on the other side. But a Samaritan, as he journeyed, came to where he was; and when he saw him, he had compassion, and went to him and bound up his wounds, pouring on oil and wine; and then he set him on his own beast and brought him to an inn, and took care of him. And the next day he took out two denarii and gave them to the innkeeper, saying, "Take care of him; and whatever more you spend, I will repay you when I come back."

The passage concludes with another question: "Which of these three do you think proved neighbor to the man who fell among the robbers?" The lawyer replied, "The man who showed mercy on him." To which Jesus responded, "Go and do likewise" (Luke 10:25–37).

Jesus is telling the story to people who know personally what things are like on the road from Jerusalem to Jericho. His listeners can readily identify with what happened to the man who fell among robbers. But it is likely that none in the audience would have been prepared for what he said about the Samaritan. Jesus said the Samaritan had compassion toward a stranger and, what is more, toward a Jew.

Samaritans were the mortal enemies of the Jews, and Jesus was a Jew speaking to an audience of Jews. The depth of animosity between Jews and Samaritans is perhaps hard for us to understand, but not for Jesus' audience. Biblical scholar Robert Funk notes that "a Jew who was excessively proud of his blood line and a chauvinist about his tradition would not permit a Samaritan to touch him, much less minister to him."[8] But despite the audience, the hero of the story is the Samaritan. The Samaritan was the one who did the right thing.

The Good Samaritan story is part of our philanthropic tradition and culture in the West, whether we are Christians or not; it has come to symbolize the act of philanthropic helping. This parable captures what might be the purest expression of the philanthropic ideal: the mandate to go to the aid of a stranger in need, even at risk to oneself.

There are many lessons we can draw from this story, including many lessons that help us understand philanthropy specifically as moral action. We can also see in this story an illustration of the ethical questions and challenges and tough decisions we confront in trying to do good works in a responsible way.

Lessons from a Parable about Philanthropy as Moral Action

The most basic lesson we should draw from the Good Samaritan parable is that philanthropy is moral at its core. It is about intervening in other people's lives for their benefit, as the Samaritan did. Another clear lesson is the implicit answer to the lawyer's question, "Who is my neighbor?" Christians are being taught that anyone in need or who might benefit from their help is their neighbor, even those they are taught to avoid or disdain.

A third lesson is that philanthropy is a lived experience that most of us can relate to. The story resonates with many of us not because we would be brave enough to act the way the Good Samaritan did, but because we know that we would want to act that way. Most of us have had experiences, such as coming upon a car accident before the police or ambulance arrive, in which we are confronted with the opportunity to "be a Good Samaritan." The cultural significance of this philanthropic story forces us to think about our response in those terms—are we willing to sacrifice our time and money, to take a risk, to help?

When Robert Wuthnow asked Americans of all sorts to explain their reasons for being compassionate, he found that while most of them thought of these acts in moral terms, many of them struggled to come up with a cogent moral or religious explanation. But when they began to explain their acts in light of the Good Samaritan parable, they became quite animated and articulate.[9] Of course, they also bent the story to fit their circumstances, as many modern theologians have done to maintain the relevance of the parable. In fact, this parable seems to be particularly adaptable. One philanthropic entrepreneur in England, Chad Varah, borrowed the idea in 1953 when he founded the Samaritans, an organization "to befriend the suicidal and despairing."[10]

We all want to believe that we are mature and responsible and virtuous enough to do the right thing, to be Good Samaritans. But we also know that if we spend too much time calculating costs and benefits, we might immobilize ourselves, or we might fail to do the right thing from a simple failure of nerve or fear of risk.

We certainly know of situations in which Good Samaritans were nowhere to be found. We read in the paper about those unlucky souls who experience car trouble—even car accidents—on remote roads and can't get anyone to stop and help. Like the priest and the Levite, most people pass by. But remoteness is not always the reason for the lack of Good Samaritans. Most readers will surely remember the scandalous story of the thirty-eight witnesses to the assault and murder of Kitty Genovese in New York in 1964, when none of the thirty-eight even went so far as to call the police.[11]

In the aftermath of the Kitty Genovese case, psychologists became very interested in examining when "bystander intervention" would occur and when it wouldn't. They found, for example, that we are more likely to help when we think we are the only ones who can help. But when there is a "diffusion of responsibility" among several people, like Ms. Genovese's neighbors who heard her screams, each person is less likely to help. This same sort of problem has been used to explain the lack of community action or humanitarian intervention to stop genocide or human rights abuses.[12] Psychological studies also revealed that we are less likely to help when we are in a hurry. In one famous study, researchers created a scenario in which seminary students were given varying amounts of time to hurry over to a building where they were supposed to give a speech. Some of the students were told they would be talking about jobs for seminary students while others were told to give a speech on the Good Samaritan parable. The genius of this experiment is that, on their way, all the students passed by a man (working for the experimenters) who was slumped in an alleyway coughing and groaning—the proverbial Good Samaritan situation. While 40 percent of the students stopped to offer some kind of help to the man, only 10 percent of those who were in the greatest hurry stopped to help. And even more surprising was that it didn't make any difference whether they were about to give a talk about the Good Samaritan or not, only whether they were in a hurry. In fact, some of the students rushing to give their speech on the parable actually stepped over the groaning man as they hurried by.[13]

Unfortunately, we also know of situations in which those who have intervened have been sued for supposedly causing harm in doing so. Every state in the United States now has some version of a "Good Samaritan" law providing immunity from liability to those who try to help (some state laws only protect doctors). Some of those statutes also include a "duty to assist" clause, making it a misdemeanor to act like the Levite and the priest and just pass by. In fact, these sorts of "Bad Samaritan" laws requiring philanthropic aid have been enacted in places around the globe, from Mongolia in 1781 to Portugal in 1982.[14]

Another lesson from the Good Samaritan parable is about risk: the philanthropic mandate sometimes requires people to go to the aid of others even at some risk to themselves. For those who decide to heed this lesson, there will be no shortage of opportunities—or risks. There are many places in this world that are dangerous, and there are thieves of infinite variety. All of us have heard reports of Good Samaritans who were robbed and murdered after coming to the aid of another. In general, fear based on real or perceived risk constrains the charity of those who might otherwise bring care to AIDS victims or participate in a project in a minority neighborhood—or for a minority person to join a project in a majority neighborhood. And we should remember that anyone caught harboring Jews in Europe during the Holocaust often executed.[15] There are even reports of "Good Samaritan scams," tricks to lure well-meaning Good Samaritans into traps set by decoys feigning injury or peril. When there are risks, courage is called for, a kind of quiet courage that does not masquerade as bravado and machismo—the kind of courage exemplified by Wesley Autrey, the construction worker who dove onto the subway tracks as the train was fast approaching to save someone he had never met. That kind of courage is evident every day among those people—from social workers to shelter volunteers to Teach for America participants—who overcome their fears and live the unprotected life of service in every American city.

Given the risks, why is it that the Samaritan did not turn his eyes away and pass by on the other side of the road? Why did he come to the aid of the stranger in that dangerous place, even when he must have assumed that the injured person was a Jew?

Religious tradition says that God had given the Samaritan the capacity to feel compassion. A nonreligious answer could be that the Samaritan had been socialized by his culture, by his parents, or by some other agent to believe that helping others in need was "the right thing to do." Or perhaps we return to the idea that the capacity to help others is human nature, and it is this innate altruism that helps push the Samaritan past his fear so he can act in the way he has been taught or in the way he wants "in his heart" to act. It is more difficult to use the popular assumptions about humans as calculators of self-interest to explain why he decided to accept the risk and inconvenience of offering assistance; the rational calculators of self-interest here seem to be the priest and the Levite. But perhaps the Samaritan was thinking that someone somewhere would hear of his generosity and he would gain a reputation that might help him in his business or that he might improve the reputation of Samaritans everywhere.[16] As presented, however, the Good Samaritan represents the true philanthropic spirit: he has compassion, and he voluntarily intervenes.

The parable also provides a lesson about vulnerability. It reminds us that everyone is vulnerable; we all face the possibility of needing the help of others, perhaps even the help of a hated enemy. We can be minding our own business one minute and be pinned inside our cars in desperate need of help the next. When we realize that we are all vulnerable to such unpredictable and sometimes dreadful experiences, we realize why we believe in philanthropic principles like the Golden Rule or what we will label here—following the economist Kenneth Boulding—the principle of "serial reciprocity," which says that we repay good deeds done for us by doing good deeds for others, for third parties rather than for those who helped us.[17] Our own need for help is likely to be remote in distance and time, but we all hope that the strangers going by us in our time of need will believe in the Golden Rule or that they will want to help someone like us because they anticipate that they might be in our dire situation someday. Moreover, when our accident occurs, somewhere else at some unpredictable time, the persons we have helped are not likely to be there. What we might count on instead is that someone will be there, willing and able to help, because they were previously helped and want to give back in some way, which is the principle of serial reciprocity.

But another way of thinking about the need of the other is not reciprocal at all, even indirectly. It is the simple and powerful feeling of shared suffering and a shared sense of vulnerability; it is the feeling that causes us to say—or at least to think—"I can imagine how you feel" or even "I know how you feel; I've been there." That experience of shared suffering may be the most effective motivator for philanthropic activity. Some experience of suffering, even suffering of a different kind, is a reason why many people are able to sustain compassion even in extreme circumstances. Being a victim, knowing pain and suffering and despair, is often the experience that causes us to think philanthropically. Just knowing that we could be a victim can do this as well.

The Challenges of Responsible Moral Action

A final lesson from the Good Samaritan parable deserves our extended attention: the story forces us to confront the reality that philanthropy is problematic. It offers a short course in responsible service to others. The Samaritan doesn't foolishly give the victim money and then ride on; the victim can't use money at that point. The Samaritan applies first aid and then helps to get the injured man to a place where he can recover. This is the appropriate form of charitable intervention, even if it is not the most convenient.

But while the parable of the Good Samaritan sounds like a simple tale, acts of charity are seldom simple. They are almost always fraught with questions and uncertainties. In order to help others, we should clarify what we know. We should answer the first ethical question of "What is going on?" We must know facts about the situation, about the victim, about our own capability and character, about other people's responsibilities, and about the likely consequences of our own action or inaction. Yet in some situations calling for our intervention we will have neither information nor time to acquire it. We will have only the preparation of our past experience. In those circumstances, our values and our rules of thumb rather than our calculations guide us.

In the parable, the Samaritan knows little about the victim, but he knows he has the capability to assist. The man has been robbed and can't pay for what he needs, so the Samaritan pays the innkeeper to care for him long enough to get him on the way to recovery. Then the Samaritan says that he'll come back—not to collect what is owed him by the victim but to make sure that all the bills are paid. And that prompts us to ask: When does an act of charity end? For instance, who should pay the extra bills that pile up if the victim's recovery takes longer than expected?

And then there are questions surrounding the Samaritan's arrangement with the innkeeper. The cooperation of the innkeeper is essential for the Samaritan's philanthropy to be effective. What if he had chosen not to cooperate? Should we expect persons who are involuntarily involved in a philanthropic act to behave philanthropically? Does the innkeeper have a right to a reasonable profit for his efforts, or would we expect him to be content with breaking even? Should he accept a loss? Should we view the innkeeper as simply an "interested party," caught in this act of mercy whether he wants to be or not? He might simply view the victim as a customer. Someone will have to pay—and pay the going rate. On the road from Jerusalem to Jericho (or from midtown Manhattan to the South Bronx), victims may be numerous. We might ask at what point voluntary hospitality can no longer be sustained.

Philanthropy relies heavily on trust. In the parable, the Samaritan trusts the innkeeper to care for the victim until he recovers. What if the innkeeper thrusts the man out before he is completely well? Or what if the innkeeper pads his bills? People who are street-smart often fleece those who show compassion. Perhaps the innkeeper reasoned that if the Good Samaritan was willing to put up two denarii to help this man, he would be willing to pay another denarius or two when he returned. The philanthropic values shared within the American tradition suggest that we would expect the innkeeper to be trustworthy in this case and that we would expect him to share some of the burdens of the Good Samaritan's act. The Good Samaritan, in one sense, can be thought to be acting on behalf of all of us; he is behaving in a way that we all applaud. Because the Samaritan is acting for all of us, we expect others who happen into the situation, like the innkeeper, to act for us, too.

Another concern of philanthropists is to ask whether there are some people who aren't worth helping. What if the victim were found to be drunk? What if we discovered that the victim was still wearing his robe, apparently on the way home from a meeting of the Ku Klux Klan?

The Good Samaritan parable suggests that we are not to deny help to either a stranger or an enemy. Every human being may qualify as a neighbor—even thieves. If the Good Samaritan scenario occurred today, how would the thieves be treated? The moral imagination is always at work, challenging us. Perhaps this was a first offense. Perhaps the thieves were young hoodlums on drugs. Could they be held responsible for their behavior when they were themselves victims of a drug pusher or an abusive father? There are philanthropists and philanthropic organizations on all sides of this issue. There are those whose goal is to rescue thieves from a life of crime; there are others whose call is not for compassion or rehabilitation but for retribution.

Some philanthropic organizations work with the victims of crime, helping them to recover from the trauma of the experience, to regain the use of muscles and limbs that were injured in the attack, and to get back to work. Working with the victims of crime may be a strong motivator for continued philanthropic activity, because it develops the ability of law-abiding people to put themselves imaginatively in the place of others. The human response to the suffering of others is the most basic and powerful of the forces at work in philanthropy throughout history. The extraordinary outpouring of concern for starving children in Niger or Ethiopia, for the victims of catastrophic events like earthquakes in Pakistan or tsunamis in Indonesia, for the struggling parents on the evening news who cannot afford toys for their kids for the holidays—all reflect an immediate and personal response to suffering. People want to do something, and one thing they can do is give money to organizations at work on the scene.

The problem of philanthropy is that the emotion of compassion has little staying power; the human attention span is limited. And we now know more than we want to know about "compassion fatigue," when the media confront us with more catastrophes than we can grasp and more suffering than we can absorb.

Questions about the moral imagination have interested and frustrated scholars for centuries. We don't know whether visual observation of others' suffering on our television sets enhances our sensibilities or deadens them through repetition and familiarity. Does the repetition of appeals lead to a change in our behavior? If natural and human disasters seem to have been more common in the ancient world, did they become commonplace and fail to elicit humane response as they seem to do today?

Another question that troubles givers is whether anything should be done beyond attending to the immediate needs of the victim. In some situations, the giver may feel called upon to offer advice to the recipient of his assistance. For example, a Good Samaritan of the scientific philanthropy school might use the occasion to give a gentle lecture. "Next time," he might say, "take a different road." Or—more severely—"I'll help you this time, but no more." We expect people to learn from their misfortune, just as children do. It tests our patience and our generosity to respond again and again to people who never seem able to make it on their own. A century ago, both liberals and conservatives believed that most people in need were in that condition through their own weakness and failure. That thread persists throughout the modern history of philanthropy. Good Samaritanism is all right in some circumstances, we may say, but prevention is the best answer. People may have to be encouraged, perhaps even compelled, to take care of themselves.

In the interests of compelling people to take care of themselves, the modern Samaritan might draw from the school of philanthropy which holds that people should be required to behave in ways that make them independent and thus advise the victim that he must pay for the service. As Octavia Hill sought to do in her philanthropic work in nineteenth-century London, perhaps requiring payment while offering aid is a way to help victims cultivate the "habits, abilities, and sensibilities" that can sustain independence. To discourage the victim from being a victim a second time, the Samaritan might consider the payment to the innkeeper a loan and ask the victim to repay it. Or, desirous of simultaneously fostering independence and traditional philanthropic values, the Samaritan might also say, "Go and do likewise."

These possible requirements created by the Samaritan remind us that there is a thin and sometimes barely discernible line between help and intrusiveness. Philanthropy as voluntary interventions in the lives of others is moral action that can sometimes offend or disturb. This is the dilemma facing all potential Good Samaritans, especially in a culture that values both help and independence. As Morton Hunt points out, "We are taught: 'Help those who are in trouble,' but also: 'Don't stick your nose into other people's business.'"[18] Knowing when and to what extent to intervene is the philanthropist's challenge. Again, we must address the question, "What business is it of ours?"

These ruminations on the lessons and dimensions of the Good Samaritan parable illustrate for us why this parable can help us think about more than mere acts of individual charity. It reveals much about all sorts of philanthropic acts and about those acts as complex and difficult moral actions. We have also discovered in this exploration of the parable that religious teachings are important for the philanthropic tradition beyond their strictly religious message. Religion, of course, is a major part of philanthropy, both as recipient and initiator. This is particularly true in the United States, but philanthropic teaching and practice are found in all the great religions. As a shaper and transmitter of ethical systems and a guide for moral action, religion often provides the cultural underpinnings for philanthropy as moral action. So religious teachings about philanthropy such as this parable take on broader significance, beyond the walls where believers gather.

Ethical Questions and Guiding Principles for Philanthropy as Moral Action

We argue that philanthropy is moral action because it involves voluntary interventions in the lives of others, presumably with the intention of doing them good. Our reflections on the Good Samaritan parable raised many questions, implications, and challenges of engaging in moral action of this type, and we now consider these at a more general level.[19] We discuss some of the general ethical questions and guiding principles for philanthropy as moral action, and consider some of the common criticisms of philanthropy that also focus our attention on the tough ethical choices that philanthropists face. These questions and principles are often at work in actual philanthropic practice, but they are also useful normative guidelines for improving that practice.

Ethical Questions in the Practice of Philanthropy

What Is Going On?

The question "What is going on?" is the ethical starting point for moral action. If we propose to change things for the better—to relieve suffering or to improve the quality of life in the community—it seems reasonable to expect that we should know what is going on as well as what people are doing about it. We need to know about problems, about organizations and actions, and about ourselves.

One way of thinking about this ethical question refers back to the way of thinking about "mission" that we introduced earlier. What is it that is going on in the world that should be defined as a compelling mission and that calls forth a philanthropic response? How are children "at risk," and why? How many? Closely related to this is asking, "What else is being done?" to address this mission? Which problems are being addressed, and which are being overlooked? Which children are being helped, and which are falling through the cracks? To intervene philanthropically, we must know what other philanthropic actors are doing. How much is being given, and who is volunteering? What are the government and corporations doing? This, then, leads us to ask, "Why philanthropy?" What is going on that requires this particular sort of voluntary intervention?

In addition to looking at what is going on in the world, outside of our philanthropic organizations, we need to look inside our organizations. Is our work directed to the mission or to something else? That was the question everyone asked of Jim and Tammy Faye Bakker, the disgraced televangelists in the 1980s. What was the true end of their organization, which was soliciting charitable donations from so many? Was the end directed to others or to themselves? More intimately, this look inward involves examining ourselves. As we noted in the last chapter, how we respond to the world through philanthropic action is influenced by our answer to the question, Where are we coming from? What are our strengths and weaknesses? What is it about our culture or political situation or socialization that leads us to respond, in a philanthropic way, to help endangered children?

What Business Is It of Ours?

Deciding to intervene in the lives of others pushes up against the boundary between what is helpful and what is intrusive. Ethical philanthropic practice requires reflection. What right do we have to intervene in strangers' lives or to advance our view of the public good? Why should we be the ones to intervene? Why should we take the risk? A shelter worker who intervenes to help a woman escape from her abusive husband takes a significant risk. Should the woman's other family members be responsible for taking that risk instead? Should the police? For that matter, why was it the Samaritan's business to help the man on the side of the road? Should he have just called some public agency that deals with bleeding people on the side of the road? What is the extent of his moral obligation to this man? These are the sorts of ethical questions that often require careful consideration when acting philanthropically, even if in daily practice we do not have the time to reflect on them fully.

In some instances, of course, philanthropic intervention is welcomed, but in others it can be roundly rejected. What business is it of ours to intervene to do what we think is good, even if we aren't sure that others see things this way, or perhaps even if they say they don't need or want our help? The prisoner awaiting execution on death row might gladly accept help from any quarter, whether invited or not. But many parents would likely be less interested in the philanthropic efforts of reformers trying to change the way their kids are educated, especially about subjects like sex. This sort of intervention is more likely to be resented or turned away, perhaps with the comment "Mind your own business."

We know from research that philanthropists often answer this question of "What business is it of ours?" by saying that we are all human beings with attachments to other human beings. Kristen Renwick Monroe studied altruists of many sorts—from those who rescued Jews in Nazi Europe, to a grandmother who saved a young girl from being raped, to people who devote their lives to traditional charities. She found that while there were significant economic, religious, ideological, and other differences among these people who intervened, what they had in common was a shared worldview, specifically their "perceptions of a common humanity." What can best explain altruism, Monroe concluded, is that "altruists share a view of the world in which all people are one."[20]

That humans are in some way deeply connected is a bold idea. Yet it is so familiar to us that we can't see the boldness of it. It might even be the essence of philanthropy, this article of faith that humans everywhere share a transcending and unifying bond. Of course, focusing on this common bond does not mean philanthropy should ignore differences among us, which is what gets some modern, well-intentioned "communitarians" in trouble with the "multiculturalists."[21] Philanthropic action must find the narrow, ethical middle way between celebrating our differences and yet seeing everyone as similar in their humanity. This is particularly important when those who are different from us are in dire need of help.

There is a similar ethical hierarchy that ranges from meanness of spirit and selfishness to generosity of spirit and a sense of oneness even with "genetic strangers." That feeling of unity carries with it a large responsibility because it carries a large claim: Yes, peace in the Sudan is to some extent my business; yes, the same is true of Bosnia and Venezuela and inner-city Atlanta. We are, in a sense, authorized by what we might call a "voluntary association of spirit" to engage in voluntary action. But we must proceed cautiously. Feeling a voluntary association of spirit does not guarantee wise voluntary action or ethical philanthropic leadership.

So we return to the question posed in the Good Samaritan parable: Who is my neighbor? Is a Sudanese refugee woman who lives in daily fear of being raped by the Janjaweed militia the "neighbor" of, say, a university professor in Los Angeles? If we share the perception that we are all part of a common humanity, is everyone our neighbor?

Guiding Principles

The challenges and uncertainties suggested by those ethical questions about philanthropy as moral action make it seem all the more important to have some principles to guide our attempts to intervene voluntarily in other people's lives for their benefit. We discuss three such guiding principles here, though we admit from the start that this is a very incomplete list—for instance, a principle that is becoming more popular in the philanthropic world these days (but not listed here) is something like "give strategically to make a measurable impact." We should also note that principles for philanthropy, like principles in most fields, are more like rules of thumb than like laws grounded in science.

Seek to Do Good, but Do No Harm

Perhaps the most fundamental principle of philanthropy is to be found in the Hippocratic Oath as applied to the philanthropic act: "Seek to do good, but do no harm." The seeking is a declaration of intention; doing good rather than harm is the intended result. But this principle also implies a warning about consequences: good results do not always follow from good intentions. Another way of connecting this principle to philanthropy is to return to the distinction between benevolence or "good will" and beneficence or "good action." "Seek to do good" is about benevolence. "Do no harm" is about beneficence. Both are important for ethical philanthropy.

Philanthropy is about morality because of its voluntary nature (even if motivated by felt obligation) and good intentions, but this moral act does not always lead to moral outcomes. Intentions are harder to discern and measure than concrete results, yes, but results should not then be the only way we define "good." The problematic of philanthropy is in knowing what "good" versus "harm" is. If philanthropy is about the virtue of charity, reflection on the virtues would suggest that we act charitably under the constraint of the virtue of prudence. And prudence calls for thinking about the consequences of action before acting. Thought about action means thought not only about expected consequences but also about possible unintended consequences. The most familiar form of unintended consequences in philanthropy is reflected in the charge that almsgiving cultivates dependency, reinforcing poverty by rewarding the poor without requiring them to work.

The Hippocratic Oath is very often truncated just to the second part, "do no harm," which is of course absolutely essential from an ethical standpoint. But it is the first part, "seek to do good," that best reveals the relevance of this maxim for philanthropy. This first part is an admonition to be philanthropic; it is the social and moral obligation that impels us to help the bleeding man by the side of the road, to give the alms, or to advocate in

Washington, D.C., for disadvantaged children. As we explained in chapter 2, philanthropic actions are voluntary, but this does not mean they are not also often driven by feelings of obligations or even the fear of social sanctions for not "seeking to do good." Being moral in helping others voluntarily very often means doing what we feel required to do, in a sense.

Related to this admonition to "seek to do good" is the idea that philanthropic action should seek primarily to benefit other people and should not be done in order to get something in return. This does not mean that all philanthropy must be altruistic in a pure sense or even solely benevolent in intent. It also does not mean that philanthropists should shun all intangible rewards of their actions, such as the heartfelt thanks they might receive or their good feelings about themselves. This principle simply says that the primary focus should be on the needs of others or on the larger good rather than one's own needs or interest. Philanthropy should be "allocentric" (other-directed) in contrast to "egocentric." Perhaps the purest expression of this principle is anonymous giving. In the ethical hierarchy of types of charity (*tzedakah*) offered by the Jewish philosopher Maimonides, anonymous giving to anonymous recipients is the next to highest type, just below helping people to help themselves by giving them employment or a loan.

A final variation of this principle that is worth mentioning applies the principle to the recipient rather than the donor. It is a principle of philanthropy that the rights and intentions of donors should be recognized and honored; failing to do so can be considered "doing harm" to the donor. Recipients should use gifts for their intended purpose and in a responsible way. Donors also have a right to expect that financial integrity and parsimony will be observed in the way their gift will be used. The importance of this version of the principle is revealed by the frequent questions raised by watchdogs who judge the ethical standing of philanthropic organizations. They ask, "How much of donations are being spent on administration or fund-raising?" and "Are gifts that are earmarked for one purpose being used for another?" We see this clearly in the criticisms leveled against the Red Cross in the wake of the September 11 attacks and Hurricane Katrina. The Red Cross practice of using excess donations to fund other parts of their operations violated this implicit ethical rule, which many donors apparently felt strongly about.

Give All You Can

There is certainly a philanthropic mandate to give, but in many traditions there is also some version of a mandate to give as much as you can, and perhaps even to "give 'til it hurts." This is the mandate to be not only beneficent but also munificent.

In the western philanthropic tradition, this directive is definitely found in religious teachings. We see this in the biblical parable of the rich young man who was advised to give all that he had to the poor. And a famous sermon on "The Use of Money" by John Wesley summarizes the following rules for believers: "Having, First, gained all you can, and, Secondly saved all you can, Then 'give all you can.'"[22] But this principle has a secular version as well. In an equally famous statement in his decidedly nonreligious essay "The Gospel of Wealth," Andrew Carnegie declared, "The man who dies thus rich dies disgraced."[23] This generalized obligation to give away all your money (or at least all you can), philanthropically, before you die was revealed in the criticisms made for years against Bill Gates, before he (in partnership with his wife) turned his attention to giving. He now gives more than Carnegie ever did.

This principle again raises the issue of how to weigh the claims of others against the claims of self. There is such a thing as selfishness, being too concerned with oneself, and there is such a thing as sacrificial giving, giving that might go too far. Cicero advised his son Marcus not to be so generous that he brought harm to himself.[24] In the parable of the rich young man just mentioned, the assumption is that he would survive somehow. Of course, voluntary poverty can be a calling of its own; it is sometimes thought to be the highest form of the charitable life, partly because so few people choose it.

Give Back and Pass It On

More and more these days, you hear people who are acting philanthropically say that they are "just giving something back." In some cases, what this means is that the philanthropic activity is directed toward the general community that somehow benefited those doing the philanthropy. There is a recognition that one's resources are earned in the community and that, in some meaningful sense, we are obligated to return something to the communities that make our lives possible. A common illustration of this is in corporate giving, when businesses make philanthropic contributions—of money or of time—to the communities where they do business; many corporate giving programs have "giving back" as their slogan.

A similar sentiment was expressed by Warren Buffett when he described his motivations for deciding to commit much of his vast fortune to philanthropy:

I won the lottery the day I was born. . . . I had terrific parents. I had a good education. I was wired in a way that paid off disproportionately in this particular economy. . . . If I had been born long ago or born in some other country, the wiring I had would not have paid off the way it has. I'm lucky that I accumulated it, and all along I felt like it should go back to society.[25]

In acknowledging the obligation he felt to give back to society some of the results of his own good fortune, Buffett was echoing another famous philanthropist, Albert Schweitzer. Schweitzer wrote often about how being the recipient of "good fortune" carries with it the responsibility to do good works, and he cited this as part of his own motivation, at age thirty, to give up his privileged life as a scholar and noted organist and become a doctor providing medical care in Africa for the rest of his life.[26]

In many cases, what people mean by "giving back" is more like "giving forward." They are doing something good for someone other than the person or entity who did something good for them. The well-known phrase "pass it on" captures this principle. Or as a popular novel and film recently labeled it, we should "pay it forward."[27] As we have said earlier, we borrow the term *serial reciprocity* from Kenneth Boulding to denote this principle, and we see it as a significant notion underlying philanthropy, particularly in American culture where reciprocity is highly valued.[28] Serial reciprocity as a principle of philanthropy says that we should reciprocate for what we have received—e.g., from parents, friends, a mentor, strangers, previous generations—by providing something to a third party, regardless of whether a return is given or makes its way back to our original benefactor. And serial reciprocity is not simply a common justification for giving or an ethical principle. It is also a highly effective mechanism for perpetuating philanthropic acts; it is the genius of the system that good works multiply.

Serial reciprocity is particularly important because most of us, when we think about it, are both donors *and* recipients. We give to help others, and we receive the gifts of others in the enrichment of our own lives. Everyone, in a sense, is deeply in debt philanthropically—debts that cannot be settled by repayment but only by imitation or replication through serial reciprocity. In some situations, serial reciprocity is the only way to "repay" this philanthropic debt; this is the case for debts we owe to previous generations that we can only repay by doing things for future generations. In other situations, serial reciprocity is the most appropriate way of repaying our philanthropic debt; this is the case when a donor says, "Don't give me anything; just do the same for someone else when you get the chance," or when our mentor says, "Be a mentor yourself someday."

This reminds us that, as the saying goes, "It is better to give than to receive." Being an ethical recipient of philanthropy can be difficult, particularly when the gift is overwhelmingly generous or when it comes with high expectations. Just ask any recipient of an organ transplant. Or ask the people at *Poetry* magazine, a prestigious but financially struggling journal (and small nonprofit) which in 2002 received without warning a bequest from Ruth Lilly that will eventually total well over $100 million. We must also be sensitive to the dignity of recipients in the course of giving, to defray the unpleasant feelings that sometimes arise when someone feels like a "charity case" or feels resentful that their benefactor placed such a burden of gratitude upon them. Gratitude and reciprocity are key philanthropic virtues, but they can make life difficult for those on the receiving end.

A very important philanthropic principle that is closely related to serial reciprocity, but is slightly different, is stewardship.[29] Stewardship is also about "passing it on" but more in the sense of caring for, perhaps improving, but then passing on valuable things that you have been entrusted with. Stewardship has both religious and secular variations in the western philanthropic tradition. John Calvin derived the practical philanthropic responsibility of stewardship from a spiritual source: "Let this, therefore, be our rule for generosity and beneficence: We are the stewards of everything God has conferred on us by which we are able to help our neighbor and are required to render account of our stewardship."[30] In Christian churches in the United States today, the term *stewardship* has become synonymous with the responsibility to give money to the church. But some notion of stewardship, and its variant "trusteeship," is also invoked by many secular philanthropists—including environmental groups and historic preservation societies, for instance, and on many nonprofit boards of trustees—to describe the principle behind their work. They have inherited good things of various sorts, and they have a duty to preserve those, perhaps improve them, and pass them on. Being a steward, as we will see in the final chapter, is not an easy task. There is no job description. But this could be said for all of these principles of philanthropy.

Some Criticisms and Potential Pitfalls of Philanthropy

Teleopathy

A quality of aspiration about philanthropy, of high-mindedness if you will, stirs all the moralistic juices of editorial writers, politicians, and others who turn a critical eye on the field. But these critics are certainly not wrong to hold philanthropy to a higher standard. And in their criticisms, they reveal a great deal about the potential pitfalls of philanthropy and the ethical principles and considerations that can be followed to avoid those pitfalls. We have touched on some of these common criticisms throughout this book, and we discuss a few more here. But again, this list is incomplete.

One way of summarizing a number of potential pitfalls of philanthropy is to classify them under the notion of teleopathy. *Teleopathy* is a term coined by business ethicist Kenneth Goodpaster that joins the Greek words *telos*, meaning end or purpose, and *pathy*, meaning illness or disease.[31] Teleopathy is a disease of purpose, a sickness of mission. Teleopathy, as Goodpaster uses it, occurs when there is a lopsided fixation on achieving certain goals without regard for ethical considerations such as what means are being used to achieve those goals.

In philanthropic organizations, this concept could apply to the "disease" of focusing on the needs of the organization to maintain itself—e.g., a focus on fund-raising as the primary task—and a resulting neglect of the core purpose. The organization comes to think of itself as its own justification rather than being justified by its moral mission. The staff might say that they are working to advance multicultural education or to provide care for the elderly, when in fact they are more concerned about their jobs, their retirement plans, or the size of their office or salary. This is a danger in lots of organizations. As John Gall argued, in many organizations, "intrasystem goals come first."[32] But in philanthropic organizations that are defined by their moral mission, this danger is particularly troublesome, especially when their mission is fairly ambiguous or ambitious. This makes effective and ethical leadership to avoid teleopathy even more important in philanthropic institutions.

Teleopathy may take the even more insidious form of outright corruption in the form of using philanthropy to line one's own pockets. Televangelists are suffering from the disease of teleopathy when they exploit the religious faith of their viewers to indulge their own personal needs. There are, sadly, too many other examples of this to list here.

Other possible, more general forms of teleopathy can also be identified. Well-intentioned people laboring in the trenches of philanthropy can sometimes lose sight of the original mission and find themselves off in a programmatic cul-de-sac. The "sickness" in this case is simply losing sight of mission in the hubbub of activity. This should also remind us of what we mentioned earlier about Hank Rosso's lesson for fund-raisers and non-profit leaders: mission comes first. When constructing the case or justification for why someone would give money to your organization, Rosso taught, do not focus on the benefits you will provide to them or the programs that might help their friends and neighbors or their reputations; rather, get them committed to the mission. This will avoid teleopathy down the line. A final meaning of teleopathy might be the most difficult illness to cure: there are simply some nonprofit organizations whose very purpose is something most of us would define as morally diseased. The Ku Klux Klan is one of those.

Tough Questions about Philanthropy

Perhaps the best way to analyze some of the criticisms of philanthropy is to list some of the questions that critics raise. Again, this is a partial list, but it should evoke reflection on the problems that ethical philanthropists must try to avoid and the choices they make. Some of these have to do with the tax treatment of philanthropy, which raises questions about the rationale for philanthropy in the first place.

- Should the fund-raising practices of philanthropic organizations be regulated by government as "speech"? Should nonprofits be required to publish details of their finances? Should there be a cap on how much of the money they raise can go for "overhead" expenses?
- Should there be a ceiling on what CEOs of nonprofit organizations can be paid? Should trustees be paid?
- Should tax policy encourage us to direct more of our giving to agencies that help the poor? Should some donations, such as gifts to the schools where our children attend, be treated differently by tax policy?
- Should organizations that most Americans find repulsive, like the KKK, receive the benefits of tax-exempt status? What about groups that slightly more than half of Americans find repulsive?
- Should the vast amount of individual philanthropic giving that goes to religion be considered philanthropic in the same way as money given to secular organizations? Is any giving to "member benefit" organizations like the Lions Club truly philanthropic?
- Should private foundations be required to pay out more of their endowments each year in grants? Should private foundations invest their endowment assets only in companies that meet "social responsibility" guidelines in line with the foundation's areas of giving?

- Should business corporations be allowed to deduct charitable contri
  butions when they simply seem to be using philanthropy to promote
  their public image?
- Should nonprofit entities be allowed to make a profit—i.e., to run
  profit-seeking enterprises like YMCA health clubs—as long as they
  do not distribute the profits to their employees and boards?
- Should recipients of our philanthropic dollars be required to dem
  onstrate measurable results? Should their supporters—individuals,
  foundations, government, whomever—demand results?
- Should advocacy nonprofits, such as pro-life or pro-choice groups,
  be allowed to use money they receive from the government to lobby
  the government? If so, should there be a cap on this?
- Should students be required to perform community service, or
  should community service be voluntary in the purest sense of the
  term? Should young people from poor families, or those on need-
  based financial aid, be paid for community service?
- Should international NGOs—unofficial, private organizations,
  perhaps based in the United States—be allowed to intervene in the
  internal affairs of other countries in whatever way they can, such as
  promoting Christianity in China or building bridges in Bangladesh?

And on, and on, and on.

Meliorism: The Pragmatic Philosophy of Philanthropy

We conclude this chapter on philanthropy as moral action by proposing a
way of conceptualizing the practical philosophy that is embodied in most
philanthropic action. We propose that the worldview underlying philanthropy—whether made explicit by philanthropic actors or not, usually
not—can be thought of as *meliorism*. The doctrine of meliorism fits what
we have been saying about the rationale for philanthropy in human societies.

"Meliorism," as one definition in the *Oxford English Dictionary* has it,
is "the doctrine, intermediate between optimism and pessimism, that the
world can be made better through rightly directed human effort." That
sentence largely captures what philanthropy is about. It captures a way of
thinking that makes voluntary action for the public good a reasonable response to the world we live in, that explains philanthropy as an attempt to
make things better even though things often go wrong. It captures the un-

derstanding of philanthropy as a moral effort to voluntarily intervene in other people's lives to improve the quality of life or relieve suffering.

It is significant that the concept of meliorism is found in the most famous single work on the philosophy of pragmatism, William James's book *Pragmatism*, because pragmatism is probably the most congenial philosophical home for philanthropy. James writes:

> [T]here are unhappy men who think the salvation of the world impossible. Theirs is the doctrine known as pessimism. Optimism in turn would be the doctrine that thinks the world's salvation inevitable. Midway between the two stands what may be called the doctrine of meliorism, tho it has hitherto figured less as a doctrine than as an attitude in human affairs. . . . Meliorism treats salvation [of the world] as neither inevitable nor impossible. It treats it as a possibility, which becomes more and more of a probability the more numerous the actual conditions of salvation become. It is clear that pragmatism must incline towards meliorism.[33]

Individuals who believe that undesirable social conditions can be modified to improve life chances and advance the public good are meliorists. These meliorists can often be found engaging in philanthropy as the human effort directed toward such improvements. This does not mean that philanthropy is the only thing meliorists do. There is certainly an element of meliorism behind the work of, say, policy analysts who study how government should intervene to make the world better. And there are certainly philanthropists who are more idealistic optimists than meliorists, and even some philanthropists who are pessimists at heart. But we would argue that the attitude of meliorism—that "salvation of the world" is "neither inevitable nor impossible" but will come from "rightly directed human effort"—is the one that best fits the mindset of most philanthropists. Meliorism appears in politics and economics, but it is the guiding philosophy of what we might call "philanthropics."

Reflections on Meliorism and Meliorists

We discuss below some of the affinities between meliorism and philanthropy by looking at the definition of meliorism—"meliorism is the doctrine that the world can be made better through rightly directed human effort"—piece by piece.

"Meliorism is the doctrine"

The novelist George Eliot reportedly coined the word *meliorism* more than a century ago, again as midway between optimism and pessimism. The word is from the Latin: *melior* means better and is compared with *bonus*, good, and *optimus*, best, in contrast with *malus*, bad, *peior*, worse, and *pessimus*, worst. Perhaps *meliorist* should be contrasted with *peiorist*, a person with an inclination to look on the dark side, but not convinced that doom is inevitable. Eliot, like James, saw meliorism as a hopeful but more realistic perspective than optimism or pessimism.

"Meliorism is *the doctrine*"

We take the word *doctrine* to mean a teaching, but in this case not a settled and authoritative teaching. Doctrine seems to mean a point of view with a center of gravity, not a dogma spelled out in language that is fixed and inflexible and immutable. Philanthropy needs an emerging doctrine, an attitude thought of as a sense of direction, rather than a dogma. Philanthropy has no foundational text or definitive set of proclamations by original sages. Meliorism is not an algorithm of philanthropy but a heuristic tool for philanthropy, not a fixed rule but a rule of thumb. Perhaps meliorism simply emerges as a pragmatic social philosophy made manifest in the activities called philanthropic.

"*The world* can be made better"

Philanthropy requires, as we have argued, an honest attempt to answer the question of what is going on in the world. But philanthropy proceeds on the assumption that "the world" is one in which things often go wrong and things could always be better, a world in which life is problematic. The world of meliorism and philanthropy is a real world of success and failure, vice and virtue, good and evil, right and wrong, that is never finally complete. The world is also a place where trade-offs must be faced and choices made, where scarcity is an essential quality of material reality, where there are limits. For example, the world is a place at the moment where we must weigh population growth and economic development and the alleviation of poverty in a balance with environmental depletion and pollution.

"The world *can be made better*"

Meliorism finds its bearing in pragmatism. Pragmatism suggests that the truth of philanthropy will be found in its actions and their results. But actions are not always easily chosen or enacted. It seems easier for us to see how things are going wrong than how they might be made better and to visualize how they might be better without doing much to make them so. It is easier to lament families falling apart than it is to reassemble them. It is also sometimes easier to try to make the world better than to succeed.

To declare oneself a meliorist is to put oneself usually on the side of moderation and compromise, but not always. Meliorism sees the world being made better gradually and incrementally, in most cases, but more quickly and dramatically if possible. Techniques like conflict resolution and mediation are melioristic. Meliorists would try to find some useful truth in both sides of polarized debates such as the classic one between Paul Ehrlich and Julian Simon over our environmental future. Ehrlich is an environmental pessimist who says doom lies ahead if we continue on this road, while Simon is an environmental optimist who says human ingenuity is the "ultimate resource" that will make up for any potential problems caused by extensive use of natural resources.[34] A meliorist would adopt neither view definitively and would emphasize the need for a plan to try to make things better regardless of predictions.

The belief that things can be made "better" suggests a bias toward hope, a disinclination to despair. The meliorist reasons that some things are probably acceptable as they are but could be improved, that many things that go wrong and appear to be out of our control—e.g., famine, floods, wars—could be prevented, and certainly that most things that go wrong can be "ameliorated" through philanthropy. But, while hopeful, the meliorist is a realist. The meliorist knows that things often go wrong in the world. As the residents of Los Angeles know, earthquakes happen and riots happen; the melioristic response to such misfortune is to lessen the destructiveness by building better, stronger, and more flexible structures, both architectural and political. Optimists would presumably assume that the future will be better and might even ignore the probability of earthquakes or riots; pessimists have already moved somewhere else.

"Making the world better" means attention to the possibilities across the spectrum from absolute misery to self-actualization and beyond. Education and the arts make the world better; so does providing blankets to refugees. Life can be made better for some families if the adults in them are helped to overcome alcohol and drug abuse. Life can be made better for many people with physical disabilities if they are provided with prosthetic devices—and prosthetic devices can be made better and cheaper and more accessible. Sometimes the marketplace is the creative engine that produces such things as prosthetic devices or drug treatment. Sometimes government is the mechanism that makes these things accessible to those who could not afford to pay for them. But very often it is philanthropy that makes life better by providing these things; and it is also philanthropy that often makes the market and the government know there is a problem to begin with.

"The world can be made *better*"

Philanthropy is one forum in our world in which we debate good-better-best and bad-worse-worst scenarios and propose answers to such conundrums. "Better" means that we can discriminate between good and bad, right and wrong, at least in the sense that we can know, on average, whether people's life chances are improving or getting worse. The assumption is that we know something about what "better" means in life. "Mental health," for instance, is thought generally to be a better condition than "mental disorder." Perhaps the most authoritative catalogue of human mental misery is the *Diagnostic and Statistical Manual of Mental Disorders* (*DSM*) published by the American Psychiatric Association.[35] But this example is a reminder that we often disagree, sometimes passionately, about what is better, and that we change our minds over time about what is better. Homosexuality was listed as a disorder in the *DSM* until it was removed in 1973; heterosexuality was, before then, defined as better and healthier.

The moral imagination is the means by which we visualize "the better." And as we have seen, philanthropy is often how we express our moral imagination by pursuing our ideas about the public good. Philanthropy advances conflicting points of view that affirm (sometimes competing) visions of the public good as well as the rights and responsibilities of individuals in pursuit of the public good. Philanthropy is a good way for meliorists to pursue "the better," even while some of them may disagree over it. Philanthropy is also a good way for meliorists to pursue different types of "better," from tangible and measurable material progress to the much more tenuous ethical, aesthetic, and spiritual progress. Progress is a measure of a movement toward a desired end, but as Columbus and others have found, the better end may not be the one in mind in the first place.

While lying between the poles of optimism and pessimism, meliorism, like philanthropy, is certainly not at the midpoint; it is inclined toward optimism. There is much in the culture of philanthropy that is nearly utopian or at least so enthusiastic about grand-scale, ambitious reforms that it pushes the boundaries of pragmatism. Again, philanthropy and meliorism rely on hope. The meliorist is hopeful even in the face of adversity. The meliorist may be baffled by the scope and depth of human inhumanity and cruelty, but for her, the worst savagery and barbarism call not for despair but for renewed commitment to civility and community. Still, in the meliorists' enthusiasm to find ways to make things better, they may become too convinced that they know the way and the truth. Meliorists need a touch of humility when engaged in philanthropy. This is especially true given the nature, severity, and complexity of the problems that appear on the philanthropic agenda.

"Through *rightly directed* human effort"

The meliorist as philanthropist believes in action and seeks a constantly improving sense of direction and purpose. The meliorist uses baselines and guidelines and projections that sketch out patterns and estimates of what "improvement" or "human betterment" might mean. This presumably encourages the meliorist to study history for signs of progress. In this way, the recent push by many new, business-minded leaders in the philanthropic world to encourage more strategic giving that achieves measurable results fits with the pragmatic meliorism that has long been the orientation of philanthropic work.

The meliorist seeks balance between the claims of inclusion and the needs of exclusion, between rights and responsibilities, among the claims of past, present, and future, between the claims of justice and the claims of compassion, among rescue, relief, return or relocation, development, toward freedom and autonomy. But the balance the meliorist seeks may at times require correction of mission, purpose, or objective. The meliorist as leader uses the insights of cybernetics to make good use of feedback and the arts of the sailor tacking in capricious or turbulent weather. The meliorist accepts the complexity of things within a search for simplicity. The goal may be clear, but the path may be obscured by the underbrush. It is possible to lose one's way and then find it again. Progress is not an irreversible commitment, as an optimist might see it. One can take the wrong fork in the road and then come back and take the other fork if the first choice is mistaken. If the meliorist is hopeful, the meliorist is also humble, alert to mistaken assumptions, to human error as well as to human capacity and potential, to things going wrong as well as to things getting better.

However, "rightly directed" still means purposeful rather than meandering without a compass through a Slough of Despond. The direction comes from within (from thought and reflection) and from without (from lessons taught and learned about human history) and through past experience. The meliorist is aware that human effort can be and often is *wrongly* directed. The comparative measure of good implies bad; the measure of *phil*anthropy implies *mis*anthropy. The meliorist's conception of the human implies the ability to know the difference between such things and the capacity to seek the better through voluntary action. "Rightly directed" also implies that sometimes the direction can be imposed on us—by the community, by others seeking to limit us "for our own good" or "for the public good," etc. What is the right direction can, of course, be open to dispute.

"Through rightly directed *human effort*"

This does not imply a denial of divine intervention or guidance, but focuses our attention on what we can do regardless of such intervention. Humans have many ways of understanding and responding to the world, and we have more capacity and efficacy than we sometimes think.

The meliorist accepts the diversity of the human—biologically, physiologically, genetically, ethnologically, geographically, psychologically, morally, philosophically, aesthetically, spiritually. But the meliorist believes that collective action to make things better is possible amid this diversity. The meliorist has enemies and accepts this fact. The question is not whether we have enemies but what we do about them. The meliorist is reluctant to dehumanize enemies because of their faults or their attacks. The meliorist struggles to be tolerant and fair and openminded, but to be a meliorist carries the responsibility to come to conclusions, to come to closure, to judge, to make choices, and then to act. Sometimes this action is in concert with former enemies; sometimes it is in opposition. But the meliorist always values civility and the open society over brutality and the closed society.

The meliorist accepts the counterintuitive sense that humans are defined not only by their self-interest but also by their capacity to see and act beyond it. Human nature is such that we manifest both traits in greater or lesser degree at different times and in different circumstances. And while ethical values can be shared and developed across our diversity, the meliorist expects and accepts a wide range of ethical understandings, not all of which will be compatible. Meliorism, then, will be expressed through many different efforts to improve the world.

Finally, meliorism accepts the reality that "effort" is required if the world is to be made better. Defining, describing, and diagnosing the world and its problems are important but preliminary, necessary but not sufficient to the action and hard work to relieve suffering and to improve the quality of life.

A Modest Doctrine for Moral Action

Meliorism is, then, the philosophical foundation for philanthropy and good works. It is a normative ideal: if the world can be made better through human effort, the world should be made better. However, this does not mean meliorism is an empirical reality in full, despite all of the good works it engenders. If all these statements about what meliorism is and what meliorists do were in fact complete descriptions of reality, the world would already be a much better place than it is and would not need much more meliorism. Meliorism is an aspiration rather than a fact. It is a guiding attitude or doctrine that applies only to some human efforts, some of the time, even if we wish it applied all the time. Philanthropy exists because things go wrong, but also because people do wrong. People can be misanthropic instead of philanthropic; people can be apathetic instead of melioristic.

What we gain by explicating the values a meliorist might advance is a banner to rally around, even if meliorism is not a brash or flashy banner that inspires us to take to the streets. Meliorists are not radicals or reactionaries or extremists; they might, under extreme circumstances, go to the barricades, but never with joy and usually with great reluctance. Meliorists in Selma, Alabama, in 1965, were required to direct the human efforts to the streets. But in most cases, meliorists risk being condemned not as radicals but as compromisers and relativists—as do-gooder reformists who will be "run over like the other skunks in the middle of the road." But again, how meliorism is expressed in philanthropy depends on time, place, and context.

Meliorism is a point of view; it is a doctrine, not a dogma. It must be thought of as one worldview among many. Cynicism and utopianism are two views, but we ultimately find fatal flaws in those ways of looking at the world. Cynicism, utopianism, and meliorism are all perspectives inevitably colored by emotions of hope and fear. Meliorists are no more immune to such emotions than anyone else, even though they are ostensibly committed to rational, pragmatic behavior.

Meliorism is a modest doctrine rather than a triumphant one, but it is the best guide for philanthropy. It is the doctrine of the Good Samaritan and of others who use voluntary moral action to enact their visions of the public good and to intervene in the lives of others. Despite the existence of evil and human weakness of will, philanthropy assumes an underlying human capacity for compassion and virtuous moral action. Philanthropy is a modest act of faith in human effort, a modest will to believe that the world can be made better, that suffering can be reduced and the quality of life improved by the exercise of the moral imagination and human reason through collective as well as individual acts.

Philanthropy holds this melioristic view even though life is problematic and there are no certain or final solutions. Philanthropy proceeds as moral action—guided by principles such as "seek to do good, but do no harm" and "give back"—despite the fact that we cannot know with certainty that our intended good works will have good results. In the face of such uncertainty and of things continuing to go wrong in the world, philanthropy is our best hope to make the world better.

5

The Social History of the Moral Imagination

*W*e have noted how the practice of philanthropy is common to all of the great religions and civilizations of the world. But each culture develops a distinctive philanthropic tradition that reflects other aspects of that society and the unique ways in which the people exercise their culturally shaped moral imaginations.

As a relative newcomer, the United States has absorbed the teachings of philanthropic traditions that preceded ours, and it continues to absorb new elements as we practice, pass on, and reinvent the tradition in our increasingly pluralistic society. American philanthropy is a mosaic of cultural influences, emanating primarily from the ancient Middle East and from classical civilization, but also from Native American tribes and from the Far East. Basic teachings of the Buddha and Confucius blend here with the folk wisdom of slave culture. Different variations of the "Golden Rule," and of the adage about teaching a poor person how to fish rather than simply giving them a fish, commingle in the American philanthropic tradition.[1]

To understand philanthropy in any culture, we have to understand the sources of the philanthropic tradition, both ancient and modern, and how these influenced philanthropic actions and meanings over time. We trace some of these sources for the American tradition here; it is the one we know best. However, doing so requires that we look at the philanthropic tradition in western civilization in general, as this is the primary influence on American philanthropy, so we venture far outside the borders of America here, too.[2] This exploration will help us understand the historical development of the American philanthropic tradition, as well as how a philanthropic tradition develops out of the exercise of the moral imagination in any culture. We will also understand better where the idea and practice of philanthropy as moral action comes from.

Understanding the Use of the Moral Imagination

The course of philanthropic history in any civilization can be thought of as "the social history of the moral imagination." This phrase is loosely borrowed from anthropologist Clifford Geertz, who used it to refer to the imperfect process of "translating" other cultures, other people, and other times.[3] The way we use the phrase here relates to this definition, but also expands the notion in order to describe the development of a philanthropic tradition.

Social history, for Geertz, is the result of translations, both by anthropologists and by others who observe and engage with other cultures. These translations try to understand how those "others" are interpreting and engaging in their own lives and contexts, how they are using their own moral imagination. But translating itself is an act of moral imagination, trying to see through the native's moral eyes. In the case of colonialists in the previous centuries, this act of translating sometimes had dire consequences, for example, when colonialists failed to understand the cultural meaning of rituals such as the *suttee* in Bali, in which young concubines sacrifice themselves upon the death of their rajah. According to Geertz, interpreting these ceremonies—through a non-native moral lens—as merely "barbaric" led to increased pressure and justification for colonization. Anthropologists, Geertz believed, need to work harder to stretch their moral imaginations when constructing accounts and histories of other cultures.

How does this apply to the task we undertake in this chapter of reviewing our own philanthropic tradition? Any tradition is a history of culturally bound social actors (natives) using their moral imaginations in order to act philanthropically for what they (as natives) deem to be morally just causes. Understanding this history of the moral imagination requires stretching our own moral imaginations, either because those philanthropic actors engaging in moral action were living in a very different time from us, or because their lives are very different from ours, despite our shared status as "natives" of American culture. Our translation also involves, in a sense, a reflection upon our own deeply held understandings and taken-for-granted cultural themes. We have inherited these from our traditions but we might not know their complex and multiple origins.

The other meaning of this phrase as we borrow it from Geertz is more straightforward and relates to how we used the term *moral imagination* in the last chapter. Philanthropy is the social history of the moral imagination because philanthropic action in any time and place requires the use of the moral imagination by philanthropists. They must use moral imagination to understand other people who may need help or to imagine some way in which the world might be made better. In philanthropy, as in anthropology, the moral imagination helps us understand other people's lives, but in philanthropy it helps us also to respond creatively to human needs and to see the possible public good. When humans want to put into action the vision of their public good, they engage in the social practice of philanthropy. So the history of philanthropy in any society is the social history of the moral imagination.

As the examples in this chapter will indicate, the moral imagination has applied itself throughout history to a vast array of social issues, from universal and ever-present concerns, such as alleviating poverty, to local concerns, such as setting aside land for parks. It has not always been a success story. In too many instances the philanthropists' moral imagination has been feeble, and the resulting actions have been inappropriate or intrusive. But the moral imagination remains a necessary philanthropic tool, even as its limits remain unavoidable.

Many people in the history of American philanthropy can be seen as effective entrepreneurs with vivid moral imaginations, from Benjamin Franklin founding the Junto club for political discussion to Ralph Nader founding consumer watchdog groups. Many institutional innovations throughout that history can themselves be seen as the products of creative imaginations thinking about how to better serve the public good. This list would include the barn-raising as mutual aid with a touch of charity; the invention of the general purpose endowed philanthropic foundation and, later, the community foundation; the creation of the tax deduction to encourage charitable giving; the development of the "community chest" idea that became the United Way; the design of the tools used in the business of fund-raising—capital campaigns, charity balls, cause-related marketing, planned giving, etc., and the ingenious grassroots programs being developed by "social entrepreneurs" around the globe.

We do not intend to cover all of these pieces (and more) of our philanthropic social history in this chapter. The range of history we cover here is long, but our treatment of it is more interested in concepts than in events and dates. This is not a comprehensive narrative history of philanthropy, but an episodic and thematic history of those philanthropic innovations, ideas, people, and movements that illustrate key elements of the philanthropic tradition and representative applications of the moral imagination.[4] Like all *social* history, the history here tries to consider how life was lived, and thought about, by the people of those times as well as their leaders; it considers the history of everyday action as well as extraordinary events, and the history of organized social action as well as stellar individual achievements.[5]

Two Strands in the Social History: Compassion and Community

The philanthropic tradition we have inherited in America—which has determined the course of the social history of our moral imagination—has essentially two strands, one based on a core value of compassion and the other on a core value of community. This is a useful heuristic to think about the earliest origins of the philanthropic tradition in the larger history of western civilization.

It is *compassion* that moves us to perform acts of mercy to relieve suffering, acts which we sometimes refer to as "charity" or—especially with reference to foreign aid—as "relief" or "humanitarian assistance." We find this value of compassion exemplified in the classic tale of the Good Samaritan and in such efforts as finding shelter for the homeless or setting up centers for the distribution of food to the hungry. Many in the West trace this core value to the religious teachings of the ancient Jews and Christians.[6]

The core value of community moves us to perform acts intended to enhance the quality of life in our social worlds, both large and small. Such acts are what the word *philanthropy* refers to in one of its narrower meanings (that is, development as contrasted with relief). We are guided by the value of community when we join an organization to plant trees on public boulevards or when we advocate setting aside space for public parks. Community values underlie our voluntary efforts to support scientific research or scholarship in the humanities. The core value of community, in the western philanthropic tradition, is derived primarily from classical Greece and Rome. At the heart of the idea of community is the Greek notion of *polis*, from which the word *political* is derived. Philanthropy is often the moral goad of the political. Other times philanthropy is political itself, or steps into the life of the *polis* when political action fails.

Compassion and the Religious Origins of Philanthropy

The branch of the American and western philanthropic tradition that is rooted in compassion emerged from the early culture of the ancient Middle East. It was a hard world, where suffering was a routine and unremarkable fact of life. Yet it was a world, its inhabitants believed, created by a God who declared that he wanted his creatures to make it a better place —to act philanthropically. He even began to tell them how: "When you reap the harvest of your land, you shall not reap right into the edges of the field, neither shall you glean the loose ears of your crop; you shall not completely strip your vineyard nor glean the fallen grapes. You shall leave them for the poor and the alien. I am the Lord your God" (Leviticus 19: 9–10). Thus began the idea and practice of "gleanings," an enduring part of our philanthropic social history.

Two principles of philanthropy—discussed in chapter 4—are affirmed in this Old Testament passage: giving to others out of one's surplus and helping persons beyond those for whom one is immediately and formally responsible. Both are grounded in the core value of compassion for others.

The first principle, that philanthropic gifts are to be drawn from surplus wealth, was consistent with a tradition that, while it encouraged almsgiving, cautioned that it should not be done to excess, to avoid the risk of putting oneself into poverty. "Give all you can" means, in this view, do not give too much. The question of how much to give was addressed in various ways, including the Christian principles reviewed in the previous chapter.

The Islamic tradition resolved this question by imposing exacting guidelines. The medieval Islamic philosopher and mystic al-Ghazali offered this very precise guide: "No *zakah* is due on less than five camels, on which is levied a sheep in its second year or a goat in its third year. On ten camels two goats are levied, on fifteen camels three goats," and so on, with increasing levies up to 131 camels, at which point the levy becomes fixed.[7]

The word *zakah* is the almsgiving required of all free Muslims by their faith. *Sadaqah*, by contrast, refers to voluntary, meritorious giving that goes beyond what was required. *Zakah* is legal and obligatory. "*Zakah* is one of the Five Pillars and is in effect a tax on one's possessions. It may be paid directly to the poor as alms, or to travelers, or to the state."[8] Derived from a word that means to purify, *zakah* is a tax that served to purify the possessor, purification here being an avoidance of excessive wealth by almsgiving. One finds a similar point of view in Jewish law as given in the Mishnah, "The Sayings of the Fathers," which offers the advice that "tithes are a fence for wealth."[9]

The *nisbah*, or schedule for determining the *zakah*, provides an indication of the gradual but inexorable movement from spontaneous and irregular giving to the adoption of established norms for giving. One might infer a tendency of people to watch one another to be sure of fairness and equity of effort, quite apart from the needs of the poor. Similarly, among the Hebrews, the charitable allocation became a "tithe," an obligatory tenth of the harvest, divided between ritual sacrifice and aid to the poor and homeless.

> Every third year you shall bring out the full tithe of your produce for that year, and store it within your towns; the Levites [priests], because they have no allotment or inheritance with you, as well as the resident aliens, the orphans, and the widows in your towns, may come and eat their fill so that the Lord your God may bless you in all the work that you undertake. (Deuteronomy 14: 28–29)

The second, and more radical, principle related to compassion—to help persons for whom one bears no formal responsibility—appears in numerous Old Testament references and in Egyptian and Babylonian texts that are even older. It reveals itself in the ancient appeal of philanthropy—the appeal to come to the aid of the widow, the orphan, the stranger, the poor. In the ancient world, widows, orphans, refugees who had been driven from their homes, the poor, old people unable to fend for themselves—in short, people without land in an agricultural society—were those by definition most dependent on the compassion of others.

However, accepting responsibility for persons beyond one's family and circle of close friends is a difficult mandate to fulfill and one that has often not been followed. In fact, in the endless number of maxims and guides and rules that shape the culture of giving, there appears to be a consensus that "charity begins at home." One's first responsibility is to self and family, to friends and neighbors, and to those of similar ethnicity or class—what we talked about in chapter 3 as self-help and mutual aid. Al-Ghazali, for instance, affirmed that "both friends and the brethren of good [friends] should be given precedence over acquaintances, just as relatives are given precedence over non-relatives."[10]

Another aspect of philanthropy that appears in ancient Middle East culture, introduced by the Old Testament prophets, was the role of advocacy and the concern for justice. When human action and oppression is identified as the source of human suffering, Christians were told to seek justice and pursue "righteousness." The prophets spoke on behalf of the poor and downtrodden, calling for justice as well as charity and blaming the powerful for the condition of the oppressed. "The Lord enters into judgment with the elders and princes of his people: 'It is you who have devoured the vineyard; the spoils of the poor are in your houses. What do you mean by crushing my people, by grinding the face of the poor?'" (Isaiah 3:14–15). Believers were told to "do justice" rather than simply offer kindness in a passage from the Old Testament that is popular among "faith-based" social justice activists: "What does the Lord require of you but to do justice and to love kindness" (Micah 6:8).

The New Testament adopts and extends the Old Testament edicts on charity, providing the charitable agenda for Christendom for the subsequent two thousand years, an agenda best embodied in the famous passage: "For I was hungry and you gave me food, I was thirsty and you gave me something to drink, I was a stranger and you welcomed me, I was naked and you gave me clothing, I was sick and you took care of me, I was in prison and you visited me" (Matthew 25:35–36). More than simply reinforcing the Old Testament pronouncements on charity, the New Testament calls for a more rigorous philanthropy with respect both to how much to give and to whom to give.

Jesus' radical instruction to "give all you have to the poor" goes far beyond the decree that one should provide for the needy out of one's surplus wealth or goods. The parable of the widow's mite (Mark 12:41–44; Luke 21:1–4) makes this clear—the widow who gave her only two coins to the Temple gave "more" than the wealthy men who gave their larger sums in an ostentatious way. Jesus' advice is also grounded in the view that riches are harmful to the soul, a view similar to some Asian traditions in which property and possessions are seen as barriers to a higher life that is gained through escape from this world. From that perspective, the poor are seen not just as objects of need but also as opportunities to move toward liberation from the world or toward eternal salvation. The parable of the Good Samaritan, we have seen, also offers a more radical understanding of who should be recipients of our philanthropy. The message there is "Everyone is your neighbor."

Christianity placed two additional requirements on the way philanthropy was to be practiced. The first was that givers were to be attentive to the spiritual as well as to the material condition of the recipients of their assistance. The second, described by historian of philanthropy Merle Curti, was that "giving, in order to be pleasing to God, must be an outward manifestation of a genuine feeling of justice and a true act of love."[11] We see this in the frequent use in the New Testament of the Greek word, *agape*, that was once translated as "charity" but is now usually translated "love." Recall that in chapter 2 we explained how this meaning of "charity" as "love" has strayed a bit from the original meaning of the term as found in Paul's first letter to the Corinthians, ending "and the greatest of these is love" (I Corinthians 13). The original meaning of *agape* in that now-famous passage is not so much about romantic love (as it is used in weddings) as about charitable regard toward others and selfless affection as the proper spirit for compassion. Consider the meaning of the passage if we reinsert *charity:* "If I give away all my possessions . . . but do not have charity [*agape*], I gain nothing. Charity is patient; charity is kind; charity is not envious or boastful or arrogant. . . . It does not rejoice in wrongdoing, but rejoices in the truth" (I Corinthians 13:3–4, 6).

By the end of the ancient world, the framework of philanthropy that is still with us had been established. Prominent pillars in the general framework were the principle of giving at least out of surplus, the inclusion of the stranger among those whom one helps, and the recognition of a link between the need for charity and the fact of economic oppression. Specific to the Christian framework were the mandate of sacrificial giving, the obligation to provide spiritual as well as material assistance, and the principle that alms should be given out of selfless love, *agape.*

The medieval church perpetuated and extended these ideas. In 1250, acknowledging the obligation to provide both material and spiritual help, St. Thomas Aquinas summarized the thinking of the church in lists of the two kinds of almsgiving: "corporal works of mercy"—*visito, poto, cibo, redimo, teco, colligo, condo*—(visit, give drink, feed, rescue, clothe, gather, bury) and "spiritual works of mercy"—*consule, solare, castiga, remitte, fer, ora* (instruct the ignorant and give advice to those in doubt, console the sorrowful, reprove sinners, forgive offenses, put up with people who are burdensome and hard to get on with, and pray for all).[12] Earlier in the same century, in his codification of the Talmudic rules, Maimonides had provided the standards for charity that have been addressed previously in this book.

In the belief that all gifts come from God and are to be used to his glory, the church assumed jurisdiction over philanthropic practices, claiming the right to be a mediator between God and humankind in matters of claims on the use of God's property. In the twelfth century, the *Decretum* declared that "the needy had a right to assistance, and those better off had a duty to provide it."[13] Under the *Decretum*'s formula for giving, the bishop had "a specific responsibility for dividing up the total revenue of the diocese in such a fashion that a due portion was distributed to those in need. . . . The classical division of ecclesiastical revenue was into four parts," of which one part was to be allocated to the poor.[14] This belief that all gifts come from God and are to be used to his glory, as directed by the church, are the religious origin for two core ideas that continue to guide philanthropic practice: stewardship and trusteeship.

There were other sources of assistance in the Middle Ages—the feudal system in which masters supported serfs, guilds in which members supported each other, and hospitals that served the sick, the elderly, the poor, orphans, and travelers—but the church remained the most important and reliable source, its charity funds being acquired through a compulsory tithe on parishioners. The imposed charity "tax" of the church served as a forerunner to the Poor Law; when the church was absorbed by the state in the mid-sixteenth century, civil authorities became responsible for administering charity.[15] Nevertheless, the pattern of ecclesiastical responsibility, established in the Middle Ages, persisted, and the church has continued to be the source of a substantial portion of charitable funds.

Community and the Classical Origins of Philanthropy

The second strand of western philanthropy we owe largely to classical Greece and Rome. In contrast to the philanthropy of the ancient Middle East, which emphasized acts of mercy to individuals, the primary classical contribution to philanthropic thought was to see philanthropy as a way of improving community and enhancing the general quality of life. In contemporary philanthropy, these two strands are often differentiated as relief and development. More broadly, they clarify further the distinction we have already discussed between charity and philanthropy.

The culture of classical Greece and Rome was a civic culture and its religion was a civil religion. Its highest aspirations were expressed in terms of honor and dignity in the community. In the classical world, wealth was the means by which honor, power, and privilege were obtained, and the calculus of self-interest was measured in mundane rather than celestial benefits. Historian Paul Veyne uses the Greek neologism *euergetism* to refer to the practice of honoring "persons who, through their money or their public activity, 'did good to the city.' . . . *Euergetism* means the fact that communities (cities, *collegia*) expected the rich to contribute from their wealth to the public expenses, and that this expectation was not disappointed: the rich contributed indeed, spontaneously or willingly."[16]

Gifts were made for a variety of civic events and facilities—for games and festivals, for theaters, baths, and stadiums. Private philanthropy contributed funding for the Lyceum and Academy.[17] Classical philanthropists were patrons of the arts, benefactors of their communities; they are the prototypes of the modern American philanthropist.

Veyne cites a variety of motivations for acts of public service in ancient Greece and Rome: "careerism, paternalism, kingly style, corruption, conspicuous consumption, local patriotism, desire to emulate, concern to uphold one's rank, obedience to public opinion, fear of hostile demonstrations, generosity, belief in ideals."[18] When Cicero advises his son Marcus about being generous, he observes that philanthropic contributions are sometimes used to win public favor and that too much ambition can impoverish a family. Some people, he says, will go so far as to steal from one to give to another, using their gifts in order to buy advantage for themselves. The point begins to be made here that it is difficult to give intelligently.

The guidelines for philanthropy that Cicero sets forth are still useful today. He advises that "we should see that acts of kindness are not prejudicial to those we would wish to benefit or to others; second, we should not allow our generosity to exceed our means; and third, it should be proportionate to the merits of the recipient."[19] The first and third principles in this list figured prominently in the scientific philanthropy movement of the nineteenth century, and are part of the current welfare debate as well. The second principle hearkens back to the perennial question, raised earlier, of how much to give and whether self-sacrificial giving is wise.

Cicero is an apt representative of the classical tradition of philanthropy, which is founded on what Aristotle called prudence and what we might now call *enlightened self-interest*. The donors expected that their gifts would redound in some way to their benefit. By contrast, the Hebrew and Christian traditions of charity seem to have been more clearly founded on altruism; rewards for philanthropic deeds are not to be anticipated, at least in this world. Classical civilization gave us *philanthropy*, defined as acts to advance the welfare of the community; the culture of the ancient Middle East gave us *charity*, defined as acts of mercy to individuals. As we have explained, we prefer now to use the former term as our umbrella term, but we should remain cognizant of the dual strands in the tradition behind that umbrella term.

Transition to the Modern Era

In the late Middle Ages, the economic transformation of Europe expanded the cities and improved the standard of living, but it also caused large population migrations and a temporary increase in the unemployed poor. By the late sixteenth century, economic conditions for increasing numbers of people had deteriorated to a crisis point.[20]

In the latter part of the sixteenth century, responding to the rising levels of poverty and growing ranks of unemployed, the English Parliament passed several pieces of legislation relating to charity, which culminated in the Statute of Charitable Uses of 1601, the so-called Poor Laws. The Poor Laws mark the watershed between medieval and modern philanthropy; they represent the first time that the problem of poverty was addressed in an organized and official way. The relief provided by traditional almsgiving was too limited in scale to ameliorate the worsening conditions creating poverty, and the traditional institutions of the nobility and the church lacked the organization and leadership to address such fundamental social problems. As W. K. Jordan observed, with the passage of the Poor Laws there was a "striking change in the pattern of men's attitude towards the problems of poverty, misery, and ignorance. . . . The mediaeval system of alms, administered principally by the monastic foundations, was at once casual and ineffective in its incidence, never seeking to do more than relieve conspicuous and abject suffering."[21] By contrast, the Statute of 1601 offered a wide-ranging and organized method for dealing with poor relief, including measures calling for a local tax for support of the poor and encouraging the creation of private charitable trusts.

But this statute was not the only significant change in philanthropic practice in Elizabethan England. In addition to the public legislation supporting philanthropy, there was a new spirit of private philanthropy. In fact, Jordan assigns more symbolic than actual importance to the enactment of the Poor Laws; he argues that the private sector response to the need for increased philanthropy is what makes the period most distinctive. "Two classes of men," Jordan asserts, "the gentry and the newer urban aristocracy of merchants, assumed an enormous measure of responsibility for the public welfare."[22]

The private philanthropy of the sixteenth and seventeenth centuries was ambitious in its aims as well as practical in its methods. Its objects included an attack on poverty, not only through traditional charitable avenues like expanding and improving the system of almshouses and assistance for the aged and infirm, but also through municipal betterments ranging from fire protection to public parks and the maintenance of roads and bridges. Workhouses were built, loan funds were established, and education at all levels won new attention and emphasis, most significantly in efforts to improve schools for the poor—education being recognized, then as now, as the best means to escape from poverty.

The combined wealth and vision of private citizens, especially as it issued in the charitable trusts, effected a revolution in the approach to philanthropy.[23] The modern charitable trust seems to have been definitively created in sixteenth-century England. A persistent failing of prior philanthropy had been the absence of such a mechanism to permit the establishment of permanent endowments. Individuals had only friends and family to rely on to preserve the intention of their bequests. The medieval church had provided some assistance in that respect, but the creation of the charitable trust, with its carefully rationalized claims against the future, provided a more stable institutional mechanism.

As early as the sixteenth century, then, several "modern" features had been added to the philanthropic tradition: the assumption of responsibility for the poor by both government and wealthy private citizens, the institution of charitable trusts, and the creation of devices such as workhouses and schools to enable the poor to assume responsibility for their own welfare.

Philanthropy in Early America

In the American colonies, the church and the governing agencies followed the English model, taking responsibility for providing for those in need. There was also the informal assistance of neighbor to neighbor, a result of what sociologist Robert Bellah calls "a strongly social, communal, or collective emphasis in early New England political thought." Bellah traces the origins of that communal consciousness to both strands of the philanthropic tradition:

> That collective emphasis was derived from the classical conception of the *polis* as responsible for the education and the virtue of its citizens, from the Old Testament notion of the Covenant between God and a people held collectively responsible for its actions, and from the New Testament notion of a community based on charity or love and expressed in brotherly affection and fellow membership in one common body.[24]

Perhaps the best known example of a religiously grounded concern for community is John Winthrop's sermon "A Modell of Christian Charity," written in 1630, in which Winthrop declares, "We must be willing to abridge our selves of our superfluities, for the supply of others necessities, we must . . . make others Condicions our owne."[25] Writing in the next century, Baptist minister Isaac Backus echoed that communal focus, arguing that "each rational soul, as he is part of the whole system of rational beings, so it was and is, both his duty and his liberty, to regard the good of the whole in all his actions."[26] In the same century, Benjamin Franklin expressed his "regard [for] the good of the whole" by contributing to the establishment of a library, a hospital, a volunteer fire department, the Junto, and the educational institution that is now the University of Pennsylvania. These are important cultural sources for the current ways that American philanthropic actors conceptualize the "public good."

Another aspect of philanthropy in America, the voluntary association, was already important in the early decades of the American republic. Tocqueville, of course, famously marveled at "the use which the Americans make of associations in civil life" during his visit in the early 1830s.[27] Historian Robert Bremner echoes this assessment: "The principle of voluntary association accorded so well with American political and economic theories that as early as 1820 the larger cities had an embarrassment of benevolent organizations." William Ellery Channing proclaimed that "there was scarcely an object, good or bad, for whose advancement an association had not been formed."[28] Channing could make the same assertion today.

"Scientific Philanthropy"

The "scientific philanthropy" movement, which was introduced in America in the nineteenth century, was a response to current criticisms of philanthropic practices, but the issues with which it was dealing were not new nor have they faded with time. One particular criticism it addressed has been familiar to every age, and that is the charge that philanthropy has a deleterious effect on its recipients. We referred earlier to Cicero's caution that "we should see that acts of kindness are not prejudicial to those we would wish to benefit or to others." Likewise a commentary on the *Decretum* advised against giving alms to able-bodied beggars: "If the one who asks . . . is able to seek his food by his own labor and neglects to do so, so that he chooses rather to beg or steal, without doubt nothing is to be given to him, but he is to be corrected."[29] And in 1531 in England a statute was instituted that differentiated between the worthy poor who could benefit from assistance and the idle poor whose bad habits would only be encouraged by charity.[30]

From the sixteenth century through the nineteenth, the growing role of the state, the diminishing role of the church, and the expanding influence of a new commercial class wrought changes in the philanthropic agenda; specifically, more attention was focused on the question of whether charity actually *worked*. So while "scientific philanthropy" emerged in full force in the late nineteenth century, it dealt in a thoroughgoing and innovative way with age-old issues. It will be discussed in detail here because its principles and strategies continue to be at the heart of the debate about and principles of philanthropy.[31]

Scientific philanthropy was organized, tough-minded, moralistic, and intrusive. Like their predecessors in the social history of philanthropy, supporters of scientific philanthropy were motivated by the fear that philanthropy might reinforce the very conditions it sought to eliminate, that it might "pauperize" the recipients. They wanted to distinguish the "deserving" poor from the "undeserving." They thought giving alms to those who could work to support themselves would encourage them to take the easy way of not working, and some argued that the able-bodied—the undeserving poor—should be punished for not working. Rather than give alms to the able-bodied poor, Andrew Carnegie argued in "The Gospel of Wealth" in 1889, it would be better to throw one's money into the ocean.[32]

Influenced by the new social sciences of psychology and sociology, promoters of scientific philanthropy were confident that philanthropy could be improved through the application of scientific principles. They urged those engaged in charitable activities to stop acting on emotion and impulse and to start acting on hard evidence, careful analysis, and planning. They took the view that it was better to reform someone's behavior than to permit that person to become dependent on others, and that it was better to prevent social problems than to try to alleviate them. As a political and economic philosophy, scientific philanthropy assumed that requiring the poor to help themselves would reduce the need for public charity. The parallels to our contemporary public welfare debate are significant, as are the connections to contemporary philanthropic efforts to build "capacity" rather than merely give charity.

Wealthy men like Andrew Carnegie and John D. Rockefeller were highly influential in the development of this new scientific philanthropy. Overwhelmed by individual requests for assistance, and unwilling to give assistance without knowing if the recipient deserved help or really needed it, they hired staff to systematize the review of appeals for philanthropy. Eventually they created philanthropic foundations and staffed them with the first specialists in giving money away.[33] They also encouraged research into the causes of social problems and the development of well-defined strategies to solve those problems. Instead of tying their foundations' funds to specific problems, they designed an instrument that could be adapted to changing circumstances and that could continue "in perpetuity."

This professionalization of grantmaking and focus on solving root problems was, not surprisingly, encouraged by the concerns of other wealthy businessmen and entrepreneurs who figure prominently in the history of philanthropy. Education, both formal and informal, has been a particularly important focus for business-generated philanthropy; education is the quintessential avenue for fulfilling the scientific philanthropy dictum "Help people to help themselves." One of the first businessmen to be involved with philanthropy was Stephen Girard, who paved streets in Philadelphia, risked his life helping the sick in the plague, and founded a school for poor boys (regrettably with a racial bias). Perhaps the most famous example of philanthropic largesse by a businessman is Andrew Carnegie's gift of 1,689 public libraries in the United States.[34] This was his way of repaying a debt to a wealthy man who had permitted Carnegie and other boys to use his personal library and thereby to "help themselves."

Gifts to institutions of higher education have historically been especially popular among wealthy business leaders. In 1821, local business and professional people joined with other citizens of western Massachusetts to contribute $35,000 to found Amherst College, and in 1861, gifts from the wealthy brewer Matthew Vassar supported the establishment of the women's college named for him. Another early American philanthropist, George Peabody, made his fortune in England and then returned to the United States where he was among the first to concern himself with the education of African Americans. The Peabody Education Fund, established in 1867 and sometimes distinguished as the first American foundation, was devoted to southern education. John D. Rockefeller used some of his wealth to transform a bankrupt Baptist college into the University of Chicago at the turn of the century. Other institutions of higher education established by wealthy entrepreneurs include Cornell, Stanford, and Johns Hopkins.

The Charity Organization Movement

Out of the view that charity should be organized along scientific principles arose what was called the "charity organization" movement. This was first institutionalized in Great Britain in 1869 with the founding of the Charity Organisation Society. Charity organization owed much of its conceptual framework to the extraordinary genius of Scottish pastor and theologian Thomas Chalmers, who, a generation earlier, had developed a system of charitable service and neighborhood social reform in Glasgow. The first charity organization societies were founded in the United States in the late 1870s, and soon there were such organizations in dozens of cities. For example, Indianapolis records the establishment of a Charity Organization Society in 1879, which makes it one of the earliest. It was founded in the offices of Benjamin Harrison (later President Harrison), at the instigation of Oscar C. McCulloch, a Congregational minister.

Building on the principles of scientific philanthropy, the charity organization movement sought to be both more efficient in the use of resources and more effective in helping the poor to achieve self-sufficiency. To improve efficiency, it proposed that requests for service should be handled at a central location and that charitable organizations should share information and expertise. To improve effectiveness, it proposed that clients should be interviewed about their circumstances and then visited in their homes to verify the accuracy of their information, thereby weeding out the undeserving. These reforms raised charity to a new level, developing a method that was organized, disciplined, and purposeful. It was also, at times, intrusive, condescending, and narrow.

According to this new perspective, what was needed more than alms was advice, instruction, training, and motivation to learn the coping skills necessary for survival in the new society. Volunteers called "friendly visitors" were sent into the homes of families in distress to counsel mothers about becoming better housekeepers, and to offer advice about keeping children in school, to bring pressure to bear on fathers and husbands to seek work and not waste the family's income on alcohol. Friendly visitors were sometimes cruel and snobbish, but they were also often courageous and determined.

The poor were encouraged to live frugally and to save whatever they could. They were never thought to be wholly without resources; they always had something to give (the parable of the widow's mite was a powerful lesson) and something to save for a rainy day. What the poor lacked was access to the established financial institutions, which had scant interest in those whose wealth was measured in coins rather than bills, in IOUs rather than stock certificates. To encourage saving by the poor, some communities established "dime banks" or "penny banks" specifically for the deposit of small sums of money, to enable the poor to share the responsibility for accumulating funds to help themselves.

In *How to Help Cases of Distress*, published in 1895, Charles S. Loch, a key figure in the British charity organization movement for more than forty years, summarized five principles of charity:

(1) As a rule, no work of charity is complete which does not place the person benefited in self-dependence. . . .

(2) All means of pressure, such as the fear of destitution, a sense of shame, the influence of relatives, must be brought to bear, or left to act on the individual. . . .

(3) . . . Family obligations—care for the aged, responsibility for the young, help in sickness and in trouble—should be cast, as far as possible, on the family.

(4) Further, as material charity is only a part, and a small part, of efficacious charity, a thorough knowledge is necessary both of the circumstances of the persons to be benefited and the means of aiding them; and the element of personal influence and control must very largely predominate over the monetary and eleemosynary element.

(5) The relief, to effect a cure, must be suitable in kind and adequate in quantity. Charity must [consider its beneficiaries] not as the recipients of gifts, but men and women whose standard of life has to be raised.[35]

Loch measured charity by its results, and its results must show the individual standing on his or her own two feet. These principles have continued to be at the heart of discussions about charity and would resonate well with many current proponents of "strategic giving."

Not everyone was convinced of the value of this new approach to philanthropy, even with its newfound adherence to scientific principles and to weeding out abusers of the generosity of others. To get a glimpse of the debate at the time, it is helpful to balance the passage from Loch with one from Herbert Spencer, the nineteenth century's preeminent spokesman for social Darwinism and a libertarian critic of charity. Spencer pointed out that those who believe in philanthropy

suppose that nothing more is required than to subscribe money for relieving it. On the one hand, they never trace the reactive effects which charitable donations work on bank accounts, on the surplus-capital bankers have to lend, on the productive activity which the capital abstracted would have set up, on the number of labourers who would have received wages and who now go without wages—they do not perceive that certain necessaries of life have been withheld from one man who would have exchanged useful work for them, and given to another who perhaps persistently evades working. Nor, on the other hand, do they look beyond the immediate mitigation of misery. They deliberately shut their eyes to the fact that as fast as they increase the provision for those who live without labour, so fast do they increase the number of those who live without labour; and that with an ever-increasing distribution of alms, there comes an ever-increasing outcry for more alms.[36]

So Spencer shared Loch's goal of a community of self-reliant citizens, but he thought charity failed to reach it and was harmful to the larger economy. Like Loch's, Spencer's argument has continuing relevance; these two views of the philanthropic coin are still offered in contemporary discourse.

Still, many reformers were convinced that the adoption of scientific principles would correct philanthropy's failings, particularly if those who were serving the needy were trained as professionals in the new field originally called "philanthropy" but soon referred to widely as "social work." If charity organizations were to be based on scientific principles, they would require professional workers with formal knowledge of social behavior as well as specific skills. These professionals would then be both more effective and more accountable than volunteers, in the same way that lawyers and engineers were because of their formal and regulated training.

So charity organization leaders began to establish "schools of philanthropy." The profession was seen at the time as the domain of strictly nongovernmental professionals, so "philanthropy" fit as a label until the profession began to call itself "social work." In 1893, under the sponsorship of the National Charity Organization Society, the Summer School of Applied Philanthropy was begun in New York City.[37] This evolved into the New York School of Philanthropy, founded in 1898, which later became the Columbia University School of Social Work. A similar evolution occurred at the University of Chicago and elsewhere. Soon this spirit of professionalism, which dovetailed with a similar celebration of expertise in the Progressive Movement in these years, reached into every aspect of philanthropic practice, producing managers of nonprofit organizations, specialists in grantmaking, paid advisers to wealthy philanthropists, professional fundraisers, etc.

Scientific philanthropy and the charity organization movement altered the practice of philanthropy in significant and long-lasting ways. Momentous as those changes were, they did not sever philanthropy from its roots of compassion and community. We can see how these remained influential in the form that philanthropy took in another key development in the "social history of the moral imagination": social reform campaigns and modern social movements.

Philanthropy, Social Reform, and Social Movements

Expressions of compassion for the vulnerable members of society and concern for the welfare of communities both appear in many forms in the rhetoric supporting social reform and issue-based social movements in America. Starting in the mid-nineteenth century, people attempting to act on their moral imaginations to address both human suffering and social problems—for example, the abolition of slavery, the elimination of child labor, the amelioration of conditions in asylums and hospitals, etc.—have turned to the social movement as their philanthropic vehicle of choice. Social reform campaigns and social movements are clearly philanthropic and charitable actions, for they begin through private, voluntary initiative and seek to advance a vision of the public good, whether that is relieving suffering or improving the quality of life. What is more, many social movements possess another trait common in many philanthropic activities: they are often inspired by religious values.

The Settlement House Movement

The settlement house movement was motivated both by religious principles and by the principles of scientific philanthropy that were altering the charitable landscape at the time. In the late nineteenth century, within London, New York, and the other great new cities of the modern world, there had developed vast areas of abject poverty and alienation. Responding to those conditions, using a keen moral imagination, the Reverend Samuel Barnett established Toynbee Hall in London in 1885.[38] His intent was to create a place in a poor section of the city where university students could help to improve the lives of the residents. He believed that settlement houses would create an opportunity for educated young Christians, who were privileged by their education, to come to the assistance of those less fortunate.

A young, well-educated, idealistic, upper-middle-class American woman named Jane Addams visited Toynbee Hall during a European trip and decided upon her return to Chicago to borrow, but amend, Reverend Barnett's idea. Along with her friend Ellen Starr, Addams established Hull House on Halsted Street in Chicago in 1889. Like the Reverend Barnett, Addams was religiously motivated; it was her aspiration to be part of "a certain renaissance of Christianity." But she also saw Hull House as a way to "extend democracy beyond its political expression."[39] Also like Reverend Barnett, Addams chose a location for Hull House in a deteriorating urban neighborhood, believing strongly in the principle of being close to the people one presumes to help. She wanted to share in the life of the people while simultaneously dispensing the cultural and social knowledge that she and her friends had acquired. So in addition to enriching the lives of the working poor, Addams saw Hull House as a place where educated young women could add meaning and purpose to their own lives by serving others.

The settlement house philosophy was described by Addams and Robert A. Woods—the director of a new university settlement in New York City known as Andover House—in 1893 in a book Woods edited entitled *Philanthropy and Social Progress*. The book reflected the new mode of philanthropic thought in which social science was the acknowledged authority. Modern philanthropy must be scientific, Woods wrote: "The close, scientific study of the social conditions in the neighborhood about a Settlement is indispensable to its success." Woods discussed the need for settlements to be established in those parts of the city that were largely untouched by both public and private charity. "It must come close to the lives of the people themselves," he wrote. The new philanthropy was a rejection of traditional almsgiving: giving aid to people whose circumstances one neither understood nor cared about was more likely to do them harm than good. To be serious about doing good meant getting closer to those in need and understanding their circumstances. To achieve that understanding one had to gather solid information about the community as well as about the individuals asking for assistance. "[The settlement worker] must be a neighbor. He must join freely in the neighborhood life."[40]

The settlement house movement was an impressive success. Hundreds of neighborhood settlements were established between 1890 and World War I. Hull House grew into a massive and permanent institution, as did the Henry Street Settlement in New York. The settlement house idea has been carried on in numerous programs throughout the rest of the century that sought to place college students in neighborhoods that need their help—from the Economic Outreach and Action Project of the otherwise politically focused radical group Students for a Democratic Society (SDS) in the late 1960s, to the student volunteer programs operating on most college campuses today.

The settlement movement is often dismissed today, though, because of its aim of bringing "high culture" and mainline religion to the masses. Those involved in the movement indeed assumed there was such a thing as high culture, but that it could be passed on to, and be beneficial for, the "uncultivated." But Addams and her colleagues also had a democratic spirit, as well as an ethic of service that became increasingly professionalized as she and others sought to develop social work's methods and training. One can also see a shift in the movement over time away from the original friendly visiting approach to more comprehensive and social democratic solutions; this is evident in the changes in Hull House itself over the years, as sewing classes were replaced with seminars to train new immigrants in useful trades.

The Temperance Movement

Another social reform movement that was rooted in the private, voluntary efforts of individual citizens acting philanthropically to exercise their moral imagination was the temperance movement. This is both one of the greatest success stories in the history of American philanthropy and, ultimately, a failure in the eyes of history.

The first voluntary temperance organization in the United States was founded in 1807. Starting as a fragmented and scattered protest, it became a powerful social force. It plateaued before the Civil War and regained momentum after the war. Along the way, abstinence rather than temperance became the goal. We know that goals evolve like this over the lifespan of most movements, as the vision of the public good proclaimed by the movement changes to fit the political opportunities, the cultural climate, or the mentalities of those people who assume the mantle of movement leadership.[41] Later still, emphasis shifted from arguments supporting abstinence to a campaign to prohibit the consumption of alcohol entirely and legally. The campaign peaked in 1920 with the adoption of the Eighteenth Amendment, mandating Prohibition across the land. The ambition of the Prohibitionists in their heyday was almost boundless; after conquering America, they intended to conquer the world. They even formed a political party and ran a candidate for president in the election of 1896.

The temperance movement was significant not simply for this amazing, but temporary, success, but also for several other features that we see in other movements later in the century: it was international; it sought women's involvement and leadership; it focused on education and the socialization of children; it promoted scientific research on alcohol; and it gradually took on the character of an evangelical Christian movement. Perhaps most extraordinary, however, is the fact that the temperance movement shifted the focus of social reform from simply trying to persuade people to change their behavior to trying to change government policy and to lobby for major legislative change, a focus that is key for almost every major social reform movement today. In fact, directly across the street from the Capitol in Washington, D.C.—in a location envied by every lobbyist on "The Hill"—is a prominent building known as "the house that Prohibition built." It was once the headquarters for temperance advocates who wanted to be as physically close to Congress as possible. The building now houses the Washington offices of the United Methodist Church, as well as several other religious nonprofits that routinely engage in policy advocacy to push their philanthropic agendas. To do so, they simply have to walk next door.[42]

The temperance movement mobilized large numbers of people and overcame both the fierce resistance of the marketplace and the inertia of government. It achieved its goal of changing the law of the land and imposing its moral will on the nation as a whole. But this victory was short-lived, and it was all over by 1933. Its importance to the social history and future of the moral imagination remains, however.

The Social Present and Future of the Moral Imagination

This review of the social history of the moral imagination could continue up to the present, tracing the continued developments in the philanthropic tradition throughout the twentieth century. We might even lead up to predictions for the future—for example, where will our moral imaginations take us, philanthropically, after the tragedies of September 11, 2001?

The rise of the welfare state and social democracy after World War II revived and altered the debates over how to provide "relief" for the poor, who was responsible for organizing the compassionate response to need, and whether social welfare was as much about "justice" as compassion. The relationship between government and philanthropy became much closer but also much more complicated, as we will see in the next chapter. Philanthropic actors, like civil rights organizations, continued to advocate programs of social change to government, as temperance lobbyists had. But philanthropic actors also received money from government to provide social services beyond their previous capacities. This complex relationship continues today, as witnessed in the debates over "devolution" of government services to nonprofit providers, perhaps especially to faith-based ones.

Business leaders—the modern-day Carnegies and Rockefellers—have also continued to play a prominent role in the social history of philanthropy, and the well-established practice of corporate philanthropy has made the old adage that "charity has no seat in the corporate boardroom" seem quaint. Like in ancient Athens and Rome, prominent citizens of every community continue to be called upon to support local programs and boost development through charitable activities. More than ever before, their role in such efforts is also routinely challenged by those worried about elite domination or corporate control. These critics, often hailing from social movements, also question corporate and foundation philanthropy at a national and even global level. The questions now, though, are less about whether philanthropy "pauperizes" those it is trying to help—the target of those questions is now usually government—and more about whether philanthropy reinforces class inequality or corporate power.

The impulse to make philanthropy more scientific and strategic, and to borrow practices from business to improve giving and focus nonprofit work more on results, continues today. When Warren Buffett gave most of his money to the Gates Foundation, he said he did so because this made good business sense. The Gates Foundation was already a proven success and was the institution best equipped for achieving results. It is fascinating to note the similarities of this strategic philanthropic approach to that espoused by Carnegie and Rockefeller and other wealthy philanthropists in the previous "golden age" of wealth and giving.

We also see similarities in various well publicized developments in the world of grantmaking that have arisen under banners like "strategic philanthropy," "venture philanthropy," or even "new philanthropy." While these "new" innovations in the philanthropic universe position themselves as departures from "traditional philanthropy," they have a great deal in common with certain strands of the American philanthropic tradition. Like scientific philanthropists, charity organization society operatives, and others in the past, these new philanthropists seek to give effectively and in ways that achieve results and address causes rather than just providing "Band-Aids." What Barry Karl and Stanley Katz write about philanthropic foundations in the early twentieth century—that they "sought out the root causes of social problems and developed strategies for their solution"—could have been taken verbatim out of the annual report of a contemporary foundation that practices strategic philanthropy.[43] Perhaps what is new about the contemporary strategic philanthropy is their unprecedented advancement and extension of this historic emphasis.

The scope of modern philanthropy is more extensive than ever before, and more professionalized than ever before. But even with this professionalization, volunteering and individual giving remains the core; individual giving still accounts for the majority of money given philanthropically in America. This is why the place of almsgiving in our social history, to take one example reviewed in this chapter, remains relevant to understanding the practice of giving today.

The philanthropic tradition is the social history of the moral imagination, the history of efforts to improve human society and the lives of others through imagining a vision of the public good and inventing forms of voluntary action to advance that good. The history of philanthropy is the story of humans exercising their moral imagination in particular historical contexts to bring forth "good works." In the same way, the future of philanthropy will be the social future of the moral imagination.

As we have seen in this chapter, the moral imagination also permits us to make connections across time as well as across space. It helps us not only to bridge the gap between ourselves and, say, a six-year-old girl in slum in Jakarta, but also to connect the moral claims of three thousand years ago in the Middle East, or in ancient Athens and Rome, with the moral claims of the current time and place. In our own social future of philanthropy, we will continue to use our moral imaginations to translate these moral claims of others from the past into moral action agendas that make sense in our own lives.

6

Philanthropy, Democracy, and the Future

$\mathcal{T}$his chapter provides the final piece of our explanation of why philanthropy exists and, moreover, why it *should* exist. It describes a vital role of philanthropy in society and considers how to ensure the persistence of that role in the future. The first half discusses how philanthropy is essential to a free, open, and democratic society. The second half looks to the future and considers the need to be good stewards of the tradition of philanthropy and to pass it on through expanded education about philanthropy. Like all traditions, philanthropy in any society must be actively preserved and transmitted, or else it is in jeopardy of decline, a decline that would have far-reaching consequences. Understanding how philanthropy is essential to the sorts of democratic societies that we want is a crucial step in the process of preserving it for the future.

Philanthropy Is Essential to a Democratic Society

The future of free, open, and democratic societies is directly linked to the vitality of the philanthropic tradition in those societies. It is not possible for a democracy to thrive without a healthy philanthropic sector. This is an important part of the rationale for philanthropy that we present in this book. While we have emphasized elements of this role for philanthropy in previous chapters, we elaborate on these contributions here and consider their constitutional basis and democratic consequences. We illustrate our assertions mostly with reference to the example of how philanthropy helps ensure a healthy democracy in the United States, but similar arguments can be made about other democracies.[1]

The "advocacy role" and the "civic role" of philanthropy are clearly essential in democracies. But other activities—helping to meet public needs and responding to human problems, shaping the moral agenda, and expressing cultural values—also play a vital role in maintaining (and reforming) effective and stable modern democracies. While philanthropic institutions like the League of Women Voters or the American Civil Liberties Union help to make American democracy work, other groups assist in their own way. The private university trains future civic leaders. The American Medical Association maintains a trusted profession that every citizen depends on (while, of course, also lobbying extensively to shape health care policy). The faith-based community group is able to counsel and reform gang members in a way the police or other parts of government cannot. The historical preservation society works with planners in city government and private developers to protect a shared heritage so it can be passed on to future generations.

We have argued in this book that philanthropy plays an essential role in defining, advocating, and achieving the *public good*. Philanthropic actions are a key part of the ongoing public deliberation about what the public good is and how best to pursue it, and we also know that philanthropy advances the public good through other activities like providing services the public needs or wants, from daycare to opera. Of course, philanthropy makes this sort of public good contribution to democracy alongside government. *Both* government and philanthropy provide public goods. Sometimes they do so in partnership—government money is a primary source of funding for nonprofit organizations—and other times philanthropy steps in to provide public goods—goods that are vital to a democratic society—when both the market and government fail to do so.

Philanthropy is also essential to democracy because voluntary associations are essential to democracy. The freedom to form voluntary associations is a First Amendment freedom that, as Tocqueville noted, has multiple benefits for making democracy work, including the somewhat perverse benefit of providing a vehicle for citizens and civic leaders to voice their concerns and criticisms and to advocate for their factional interests. This is why we say philanthropy is essential to the *free, open,* and democratic society. Such a society allows its citizens—even encourages and empowers them—to form associations, trumpet their causes or their values, give their money to support what they believe in or to help whomever they want to help, and so on.

Philanthropy helps to build the *trust* among citizens that is necessary for legitimate democratic states to survive. It serves this vital civic role in times of both national triumph and national crisis.

Another way of summarizing what we argue here is to say that philanthropy is essential to the democratic task of public problem-solving. For instance, it plays a key role in all parts of the policymaking process. Advocacy organizations arising in the philanthropic sector set the agenda and define the problems that policymakers and democratic institutions must address, propose solutions to those problems, and collaborate and negotiate over the adoption of solutions. And nonprofit service organizations play a crucial role in implementing those solutions; they are often the ones on the street level, the frontlines of addressing public problems. Finally, philanthropic organizations are watchdogs that assess whether policy solutions are working.

Democracy needs philanthropy because democracy is not simply a political phenomenon; it is a cultural one as well. Many of the values that uphold the culture of democracy are fostered not in government or in the marketplace but in philanthropy. It is particularly unfortunate, therefore, that our democratic society is largely ignorant of the vital philanthropic tradition which has been a part of America's history since its beginning. And it is all the more unfortunate in this period of government downsizing in the United States—as the government debates about what it should and should not provide for its citizens, and political figures are talking about the philanthropic sector taking up the slack when government programs are reduced or eliminated—that the voice of the philanthropic sector and the values it represents have played too small a role in the conversation. We hope our discussion can help correct this lack of understanding of philanthropy's essential and appropriate role in a democracy.

Philanthropy and the Goals of Constitutional Democracy

The Preamble to the United States Constitution provides a famous summary of the goals of establishing this sort of democratic governance system, and the goals it lists provide a wonderful summary of the meaning of the "public good" or "good society."

We the People of the United States, in Order to form a more perfect Union, establish Justice, insure domestic Tranquility, provide for the common defense, promote the general Welfare, and secure the Blessings of Liberty to ourselves and our Posterity, do ordain and establish this Constitution for the United States of America.

As a powerful normative statement, the Preamble challenges us to translate its aspirations into the substance of a good society. Of course, the public good— Justice, Tranquility, the general Welfare, our Posterity—is the end that we think government should promote and pursue. But the Preamble implies a plan of work that goes well beyond what government and the economy can accomplish. It invites us to take a comprehensive view of American society, a view that includes a role for all sectors of society. Certainly achieving the goals of the Preamble includes a significant role for philanthropy, though more in some areas than others. The Preamble is a vision that motivates voluntary action for the public good.

Translating the ideals of the Preamble into an existing "good society" is an ambiguous enterprise, however. It is not uncommon for philanthropic initiatives to cause dissension rather than harmony. In working toward objectives like establishing justice, promoting the general welfare, and securing the blessings of liberty, philanthropic associations frequently assume ideological positions, which can generate factionalism. In an imperfect world, philanthropy may be compelled to disturb the peace in order to keep the peace; advocacy and reconciliation are both legitimate functions of philanthropy. But still, in spite of their adversarial stance, most philanthropic organizations would declare their ultimate goal to be "a more perfect union." The voluntary action of philanthropy is oriented toward some vision of the public good, even if people disagree on the definition of this general goal of the Preamble.

Shared Responsibilities of Philanthropy and Government

We have discussed how a key rationale for the philanthropic sector arises out of the failure of the other two. Voluntary associations are often formed simply because the government and the market do not provide all the things that people want, or do not provide enough of those things in an affordable way, or do not give voice to all the concerns and interests that yearn to be represented, or do not protect all the people who have a claim to be protected, and so on. Voluntary associations are often relied upon extensively by government as their partners in serving the public, especially as governance and public problem solving have become even more "cross-sectoral" in recent years.[2] These rationales for philanthropy raise again the general question of how we allocate responsibility in our society between philanthropy and government. Philanthropy is essential to democracy because it shares responsibility with government for meeting the goals of democratic society, for providing public goods and advancing the general welfare, for responding when things go wrong in democratic societies.

Government, as the entity with the power to use certain forms of coercion to ensure the public good, has distinct responsibilities for dealing with certain problems, especially large-scale problems and problems that require strict control. When entire nations are in desperate conditions, as the cases of Rwanda during its recent outbreak of devastating genocidal violence, government is required to provide the necessary assistance. Less well accepted is the idea that we have our own inner-city Rwandas that require extensive governmental intervention: communities in the United States without justice, without tranquility, and without order. But these too need help on a scale that is so extensive and so severe that it exceeds the capacity of voluntary action. Voluntary action must, of course, play a role, but philanthropy cannot be the lone battalion deployed in America's troubled cities.

Similarly, the route by which drugs travel from Colombia to the South Bronx or South Central Los Angeles crosses dozens of police and military jurisdictions. We don't expect Save the Children or Catholic Relief Services to enlist soldiers of fortune to enable these charitable groups to do their work. From the local police precinct to the international agencies trying to control the drug traffic, the role of government appears at every step. The same can be said of the traffic in guns and more ambitious weapons, of traffic in girls for prostitution, and of the problems of refugees and others caught up in "involuntary migration" in too many places around the globe.

In such grim matters, philanthropy plays a modest but critical role; most commonly it involves helping victims, but it can involve making the case on behalf of victims as well. The principal voice of conscience for victims, the defenseless, and the oppressed is the voice of philanthropy. Much of its shouting and haranguing and persistence is because those in need of help lack language or literacy or education—or all three—and those in government won't pay attention. This is the advocacy role of philanthropy that we return to later.

In less dramatic but no less pressing matters, we know that philanthropy and government—and philanthropists and taxpayers—share responsibility for such things as providing health care and housing, training people for jobs, and helping them care for their pets. This sharing seems to work, particularly because philanthropy cannot do it all. Some public goods require more money or more reliable money than private philanthropic giving can provide. In the debate about welfare shifting from governmentally funded to charitably funded, for instance, those who argue for tax-funded programs contend that giving for charitable purposes will not be sufficient to meet the growing need. One reason is that people have other philanthropic interests and don't want to direct all their giving to helping the poor. A second reason is more of a claim than a reason—that the poor have a legal and moral right to share in the resources of the society. A third reason is that the heavy costs of relief should be borne by the state, freeing up more of philanthropy to concentrate on development. Philanthropic investment might then lead to new solutions to social problems, but the funds for that investment won't be available unless the state provides maintenance and relief assistance to the poor.

Just as government expects philanthropy to supplement governmental efforts on behalf of the general welfare, philanthropy turns to government to advance its objectives. Private philanthropy created parks and then leveraged public funds to make them public, but other examples are everywhere. Philanthropic organizations expect public subsidies through tax exemptions to ease their financial burdens, and individual givers expect the government to encourage their private philanthropy by granting a tax deduction, even though that reduces tax revenues to the state. One argument for these tax advantages is that philanthropy does some of the work of the state, but there is no definitive test to be sure that happens. Many tax-exempt and tax-deductible activities would never win tax subsidy if more overt justification by public opinion were required, for instance; their view of the public good is not shared by most of the public.

The Democratic Importance of Voluntary Associations

Although most of us, when we think of the First Amendment to the U.S. Constitution, think of the protection of free individual speech or the freedom of the press—or perhaps, for some, the free exercise of religion comes first to mind—the hidden power of the First Amendment is in the notion of freedom of assembly. This particular right is essential for the whole democratic system to work, for it guarantees the right of voluntary associations to do many of the things that we know are necessary for democracy to flourish. Yet the words *voluntary association* do not appear in the Constitution.

For the authors of this new Constitution, "assembly" may have been envisioned as a group of people gathering on the village green to listen to orators denounce taxes on, say, tea. In that sense, an assembly seems little more than a crowd. A voluntary association, however, is an assembly that takes on continuity of form and purpose. Some members of the crowd decide to associate themselves with the views of one of the orators and to form an organization to advance that position. And certainly when we consider our own contemporary experiences with voluntary associations, we see that the most democratically important assemblies are those that continue over time, those assemblies that become associations.

These associations enjoy the same right as other assemblies, the right to intrude themselves into the public's business with no official public mandate. And the role of such voluntary associations in the public's business is crucial. Both parts of the term *voluntary association* are key: one person acting alone cannot have much impact on public policy, and so an association of persons is necessary; one person cannot command allies to join in, and so allies must be persuaded and recruited to join as volunteers.

Once brought together, the members of a voluntary association cannot be effective without resources, and here we see the importance of another aspect of the First Amendment, the right to free speech. Implicit in this right of speech is the right to raise money—remember that this is the crux of the whole debate over campaign finance, the protection of political contributions as "speech." The protected right to raise money in the form of voluntary gifts for philanthropic purposes is essential to voluntary associations.

The democratic importance of voluntary associations might not have been recognized explicitly by the authors of the First Amendment, but it certainly was forty years later by Alexis de Tocqueville. Tocqueville is often cited as saying that Americans are joiners who constantly form associations, but his intention in pointing out this penchant was to make a larger point about the essential role played by these associations in America's emerging democracy. Tocqueville argued that associations were an antidote to several potential problems of democracy, particularly in societies like the United States that had a widespread equality of conditions. In such societies, associations mitigated against the threat of despotism, the tyranny of the majority, and the antidemocratic impulses of individualism.

Tocqueville also made a more sociological and cultural argument about the democratic contributions of voluntary associations. In *Democracy in*

America, he said that associations are the "great free schools" where civic and political socialization occurs, where civic leaders and citizens are trained. Through involvement in voluntary associations, Americans learn civic skills and knowledge such as "the general theory of association" and the "knowledge of how to combine." And these skills and types of knowledge, along with others learned in voluntary associations, can be used in all sorts of other democratic activities outside of the "civic associations" in which they were learned. In this way, Tocqueville explains, "civil associations pave the way for political ones" and participating in civil associations helps "spread a general habit and taste for association," which is a crucial element of democratic culture—a "more."[3] Being involved in forming voluntary associations, even for various nonpolitical purposes, makes citizens more capable and often more likely to engage in all sorts of democratically beneficial activities and engagements, including participating in the public conversations about public issues that are seen as so vital to a health democracy.[4] So, in the end, there are many reasons, both cultural and political, why the guaranteed, if implicit, right to form voluntary associations in the First Amendment is perhaps its greatest contribution to making democratic governance work.

Advocacy and Social Movements

The First Amendment right to free speech, when we think in terms of group speech rather than merely individual speech, also relates to another crucial democratic role played by voluntary action for the public good: advocacy. Voluntary associations appear on all sides of critical social issues; often it is these associations who define those issues, who advocate solutions, and who decisively influence the outcome of public policy debate.[5] First Amendment rights to speech allow voluntary associations to do many things that we label advocacy. They can badger legislatures and government agencies. They can intrude technologically into our homes and our patience with their endless, insistent clamor for our signatures, our money, our time, and our blessing. They can picket and boycott corporations. They can sermonize against the churches and protest against the protesters.

Data suggests that this advocacy type of voluntary association has become a much bigger part of the nonprofit landscape since the 1970s. Jeffrey Berry calls this the "advocacy explosion."[6] Robert Putnam points to this trend as an indicator of "decline" in our "civic life," as it is becoming more common for Americans to "belong" (at least by way of sending a check or filling out a form on a Web site) to a single-issue, Washington-centered, professionalized advocacy group that engages in direct lobbying, than to belong to a local service club, neighborhood watch group, or bowling league.[7]

But we should perhaps not discount the democratic contributions of the growing cadre of advocacy groups, if we consider their role in placing crucial moral issues and social problems on the public agenda, and in fueling the democratic conversation about just what is the public good we wish to advance. Their form of voluntary action is to advocate a particular vision of the public good, and even if the visions of different associations conflict—as they always do—their participation in the democratic practice of advocacy helps reinforce the fundamentals of a free, open, and democratic society.

Activities undertaken by advocates of social causes—from feminism to civil rights to farm worker safety—often go beyond traditional public rhetoric, courtroom eloquence, or lobbying campaigns. Advocacy also calls to mind marches, banners, demonstrations, interrupted traffic, occupied buildings, and people hanging limp while being dragged somewhere by the police. This particular form of advocacy activity, which has come to be called the "social movement," has a democratic importance that is hard to deny, even by those who disdain the more radical tactics of movement actors in the third sector. Social movements arising in the public space we call philanthropy have fundamentally shaped the duties and reordered the priorities of government. The abolition of slavery, the amelioration of conditions in asylums and hospitals, the reform of prison administration, and the reduction and eventual elimination of child labor are cases in point. Like their lobbyist counterparts, social movement advocacy groups often have the deliberate intention of influencing public policy. As we saw in the last chapter, in fact, perhaps the greatest triumph of voluntary action in translating its influence into legislation was the Eighteenth Amendment, which had been so effectively advocated by the temperance movement. This social movement sought to control moral behavior like so many others, but they did so by making it a matter of law and policy rather than conscience or custom.

Social movement advocacy symbolizes both the exhilarating struggle for freedom and the repellant excesses of people who never seem to have anything good to say about what the majority holds most dear. Advocacy spawns its own opposition, of course; the more extreme the advocacy, the more extreme the opposition.

The social movement supporting the homeless provides a good illustration of how philanthropic organizations turn to government to advance their objectives. Advocates for the homeless have organized themselves, without being asked and without any formal mandate from anyone, to intervene as patrons in the lives of other citizens. They argue that it is demeaning for the homeless to have to beg for our questionable mercy, that they should not have to depend on the unreliable reception they will receive if they show up on our doorstep, hungry, thirsty, ragged, dirty, and desperate. They argue that it is the whole nation's responsibility to see to it that the homeless find permanent housing, that adequate housing can only be provided by the government, paid for by taxes that you and I will not be able to refuse to pay. In short, advocates for the homeless are applying their influence to bring to bear the coercive power of government.

Philanthropy and Trust in Democracies

Trust is an essential element of the constitution of society, and it is required for healthy democracies. It is also an essential element of morality, for morality requires the persistence and predictability that accompany trust. Morality also reaches beyond self-interest to conscious and deliberate concern about the rights and well-being of others, a concern that is manifested in the voluntary association. The voluntary association is one of the most effective instruments for enabling people to develop trust in one another and in the larger society, and its effectiveness derives from its essentially moral character: organized interventions in the lives of others for their benefit, justified in moral rather than political or economic terms.[8] This is a particularly important role for voluntary associations to play in democracies because of the dramatic decline in public trust in government since the 1970s.[9]

We do not want to minimize the direct contribution of democratic government to the development of trust, nor ignore the important contribution of a responsible marketplace in building trust. Yet each of those sectors is strengthened by the presence of a vigorous third sector. Association for purposes that go beyond self-interest provides a different dimension of trust than that gained by experience in the marketplace or by the government's imposition of trust. Government efforts to require behavior that is trustworthy develops different values from those that grow out of voluntary initiative. The continuing struggle of affirmative action and ritualized claims of equal opportunity in employment have not resulted in increased trust in the laws and regulations, nor in those who implement them. Trust is voluntary. Trust cannot be required.

One of the paradoxes of voluntary associations, however, is that, although they are mechanisms for the development of trust, many of them function as voices of *distrust*. That is, many voluntary associations come into being as *critics*. Some take as their mission the protection of consumers from abuses of trust in the marketplace; Ralph Nader symbolizes the extraordinary power of well-timed and carefully targeted initiatives of this sort. Some voluntary associations have as their central mission the close monitoring and public criticism of government policies and marketplace practices around a single issue—that of the environment or social security, for example. There are even voluntary associations whose criticisms are aimed at other voluntary associations—at grantmaking foundations and corporations, for instance, for not contributing enough to address the problems of the homeless or of AIDS victims.

Yet at work in all these voluntary associations is a rhetorical claim of credibility based on a moral concern for the public good. That is, such associations are accorded trust by the public because their mission and purposes are moral rather than more narrowly political or economic. In the case of the *Exxon Valdez* oil spill in Alaska, for example, neither the government agencies nor the business corporation immediately involved were seen as reliable sources of information. The corporation's lack of prudent supervision seemed intertwined with imprecise agency regulations and monitoring laxity. So the public turned to respected environmental organizations for information. The public trust in those organizations rested on the organizations' moral claims to represent the public interest as well as on their claims of expertise. Of course, we must not forget that many people actively distrust many philanthropic groups; some people consider many environmental organizations to be run by "wackos." Trust, again, is voluntary.

The Threat of Faction

When they are associated with divisive issues, voluntary groups can contribute to the development of a problem famously identified by James Madison in his defense of the new Constitution in the *Federalist Papers*, Number 10: the threat of faction. Madison defined a faction as a group of people—a voluntary association, if you will—united around a common "passion" or "interest" that is "adverse to the rights of other citizens, or to the permanent and aggregate interests of the community." To deal with this threat, Madison said that while it was unacceptable to curb liberty simply because it leads to factions, the Constitution had to somehow provide a framework within which people could pursue their passions and interests without destroying social unity and justice. He argued this framework was provided in the form of a representative democratic structure in which the power to decide what sorts of policies were in the public good was delegated to a group of elected elites, men who had education, virtue, "patriotism," "love of justice," and the "wisdom [to] best discern the true interest of their country."[10]

We take issue with the notion that all voluntary associations pursue passions or interests that are "adverse to . . . permanent and aggregate interests of the community." Some factions pursue interests that are both passionately held and seeking the good of the whole. We also reject Madison's implication that (in most cases at least) elites have more wisdom about the public good than the general public. But Madison was surely right to worry about the possibility of some factions causing problems for democracy. Some factions—some voluntary associations—are more factionalizing than others, and these divisive groups do tend to make things difficult in a free and open democracy. Both sides of the abortion debate, for instance, arose in the philanthropic sector and use voluntary associations to advocate strongly for divisive goals. Also, as we have noted throughout this book (and as we are loath to admit), there are plenty of voluntary associations whose mission is meant to exclude others. While voluntary associations can be the vehicle for mobilizing disadvantaged communities and expressing nonmajority points of view in a pluralist society, they can also be the vehicle used by advantaged communities to express views meant to suppress diversity and to stigmatize minority identities.[11]

However, it is important to keep in mind that "factions" in the form of voluntary associations were the forces that brought an end to slavery and that initiated the civil rights movement when those were fairly unpopular and disruptive causes. In a sense, philanthropy must always be at work rebuilding the society it throws into such confusion. Although philanthropic organizations can promote factionalism, they can also serve the interests of the entire community. The common weapon available to every battler for justice or every angel of mercy is the right to persuade others to come together around a cause, to form an organization, to raise the funds to advance the cause, and perhaps to influence and cajole and even harass the political establishment to change its ways. This can be divisive, but it can also be the only way to foment social change. Philanthropy is about activism and reform, certainly, but it is also about building community, transmitting values and tradition, respecting the past, and believing in the future.

Passing on the Tradition of Philanthropy through Stewardship and Education

If philanthropy is essential to the future of a free, open, and democratic society, and if it plays such a crucial moral role in all societies as a response to the human problematic, then we must make sure that philanthropy is passed on to the future. This will happen chiefly through education. To return to the point of the first chapter, if philanthropy is interesting and important, it must be studied more and taught more. Its meaning and mission must be better understood.

If we think about philanthropy as a tradition, we can think also about the responsibility of preserving this tradition for the future, and in doing so we invoke a philanthropic principle we have discussed earlier: the idea of *stewardship*. Unlike the general population, stewards have concrete moral responsibility for the welfare of traditions. Whether philanthropy remains alive and vigorous as a tradition in any society rests largely with those who are its stewards.

Traditions can lose energy and meaning, especially through neglect but at times also through active abuse. There is a real risk that the philanthropic tradition will be sufficiently misunderstood by our generation that we will pass it on to coming generations in a hardly recognizable state from when we first assumed our stewardship of it.[12] This risk calls for both active stewardship and increased study and teaching about philanthropy.

Traditions can also become stale. For them to survive and thrive in the future, there needs to be a conscious effort to keep them fresh and perhaps even to challenge the tradition and reform it. As T. S. Eliot puts it:

> Yet if the only form of tradition, of handing down, consisted in following the ways of the immediate generation before us in a blind or timid adherence to its successes, "tradition" should positively be discouraged. We have seen many such simple currents lost in the sand, and novelty is better than repetition. Tradition is a matter of much wider significance. It cannot be inherited, and if you want it you must obtain it by great labour.[13]

Stewards of the philanthropic tradition, Eliot would suggest, must labor to preserve the core ideas, values, and practices of that tradition even as they develop innovative programs and challenge outdated elements. Fortunately, then, philanthropy is a public space that welcomes both those who want to preserve what is good from the past—e.g., the docents of our museums—and those who want to instill a wholly new way of seeing the world—e.g., the activists in our social movement groups.

The Responsibilities of Stewardship

Who are the stewards of philanthropy, and what is the nature of their responsibility? One group of obvious stewards of philanthropy are those who live not only *for* philanthropy but who also live *off* philanthropy. That is, the stewards of philanthropy are found first among those whose livelihood is earned inside the philanthropic sector: the managers of nonprofit organizations, their fund-raisers, the administrators of voluntary hospitals and private colleges and museums, the accountants and business managers, the editors and writers of brochures and promotional literature, the planners and organizers of special events. We saw at the beginning of the book just how many of these people there are—although many do not think of themselves as working in this sector per se—so their potential for effective stewardship is great. One could make the argument that they bear the most immediate responsibility for the philanthropic tradition because it makes their own careers possible.

The second group most immediately involved in the obligation to preserve and continue the philanthropic tradition are the unpaid volunteers who accept the responsibilities of trusteeship. Members of boards of trustees are at the top of the philanthropic pyramid; it is their right and obligation to hire and fire the paid staff, especially the executives who run the organizations. The argument might be made that in moral terms no group has a higher duty to philanthropy itself. Trustees, after all, accept the leadership responsibility for representing the rest of us. Trustees are not only stewards of their own organization, they are also representatives of the people. They testify to the integrity of the organization, its mission, and its performance. Trustees take upon themselves the mantle of trustworthiness and the honor that goes with it.[14]

A third group of likely stewards of the philanthropic tradition are the educators. We talk about their responsibilities later.

To ask, "Who is responsible for philanthropy?" is like asking, "Who is responsible for religion?" And the former question is even harder to answer than the latter. There is no institutional framework for philanthropy comparable to that of religion. Nor is there any agreement about its doctrine and rituals or a body of canonical texts that might serve as scriptural sources of authority. There seems to have been a great deal more thought given to the stewardship of the religious tradition than to the stewardship of the philanthropic tradition. It is as if being a steward of the philanthropic tradition lacks an adequate job description; it has no definition or guidelines. A steward of the philanthropic tradition must make rash assumptions about who asked or authorized him or her to serve, about what tasks are to be performed, and about how the work is to be done. Below are two attempts to list the responsibilities that stewards of the philanthropic tradition might volunteer to accept and perform.

A steward of the philanthropic tradition manages the ideas, values, and practices that

(1) constitute the underlying assumptions of philanthropy
(2) provide the structure and functions of philanthropy itself
(3) link philanthropy to the other major sectors of society
(4) define and develop the idea of philanthropy
(5) illuminate philanthropy from other perspectives and sectors
(6) challenge, question, contradict, modify, or even attack philanthropy

To protect, strengthen, and pass on the philanthropic tradition with these qualities, its stewards need to do three things:

(1) encourage education about, and understanding of the tradition of philanthropy
(2) become public teachers of the ideas, values, and practices of philanthropy
(3) contribute to shaping appropriate public policy about philanthropy

Philanthropy in Education

Perhaps the most important method of stewardship (for many reasons) is stewardship through education. We want to argue strongly here for increased and sustained attention to the academic study of philanthropy. The conceptual framework for understanding philanthropy provided in this book is meant to help inform and orient further study. We also want to argue for a commitment to both teaching *about* philanthropy—courses on the philanthropic tradition, public teaching about the role of philanthropy in public problem-solving—and teaching philanthropy— teaching students how to do philanthropy as well as guiding them in their reflections about the reasons for doing philanthropy.

More and more of the best and brightest of the young people of college age are thinking seriously about how good works might be essential to the good society and the good life. These socially committed and civically curious young people are a major audience for this book. Some of these future leaders who study philanthropy—both about it, and how to do it—will accept quite willingly the lesser material rewards of life in the third sector in order to try to find lives of meaning, purpose, and hope. Others will follow careers in government and the marketplace rather than in the philanthropic sector, but they will take their philanthropic knowledge and values with them.

The key question, then, is where and how "philanthropic studies" fits in the educational system and especially in higher education. Teaching about philanthropy as a component of what we call "general education" makes sense, at least as much sense as teaching students about politics and markets is currently done in general education. Philanthropy can also be taught as a vocational field, as many universities are now doing under the rubric of "nonprofit management" studies. The former is much less advanced at the moment than the latter, but we feel that a general liberal education about philanthropy is essential—even if simply incorporated as a component of professional training—for sustaining the tradition and the field long term.

Philanthropic studies might survive as a field in higher education at the graduate and professional levels. Under some other name it might next work its way into the undergraduate curriculum as an elective or as a minor. Parallel to that development might be the process of integrating philanthropy into teacher education and from thence into elementary and secondary education. When that happens, it will be because we have finally realized that informal socialization into philanthropy as a social virtue is not enough, that philanthropy needs to be studied just as society and the workplace are studied. We say philanthropy belongs in the mix of general education at all levels. We hope that the rudimentary understandings of a book like this will become more deeply and sensitively understood and taught as a matter of course.

The study of philanthropy takes us back to the core ideas of liberal education. Conceptually, liberal education is grounded in the classical notion of education for responsible citizenship and the good life—that is, for participation as a citizen in the good society. The end of liberal education is preparation for action in society. The study of philanthropy, then, is pertinent to liberal education precisely because it examines the role of good works in shaping the good society and the good life. And, conversely, liberal education is a felicitous context for the study of philanthropy because liberal education seeks an understanding of open-ended social issues. Liberal education, as Karl Weintraub used to put it to new freshman at the

University of Chicago, focuses on "the complexity of things," especially the complexity of ethical and social values with their dilemmas, paradoxes, and ambiguities. This is the stuff of philanthropic studies.

Philanthropy can also be thought of as one of Clifford Geertz's "blurred genres."[15] The study of philanthropy must therefore also be interdisciplinary, drawing on the insights and methods of all the humanities and social sciences and on many of the professions to explore open-ended social issues—those persistent and recurrent questions that dominate public consciousness and discourse. Such issues are often confused rather than clarified by the narrow focus of specialization. They do not lend themselves to treatment in the tidy categories of departments and schools, disciplines and professions. We should use history to teach about philanthropy and use philosophy to teach about philanthropy. We should feel free to borrow (if not shamelessly, at least unapologetically) from economics, political science, and law. We should wander into comparative religion, comparative politics, and comparative institutions. We should also encourage those fields to think about the philanthropic aspects of their subjects; this will enrich their research agendas, as it has for many other scholars.

Some people will contend that teaching about philanthropy amounts to indoctrination into an ideology, the very antithesis to what a university education should be about. This charge has been made from both the political Right and Left. Jacques Barzun, for example, in *The House of Intellect*, labeled philanthropy as one of the three enemies of intellect.[16] Philanthropy, in his view, brings an uncritical compassion into the university, compromising the integrity of thought and discourse. But although philanthropic discourse in the world is sometimes conducted as a form of persuasion or advocacy, if one proposes the *study* of philanthropy, one is calling upon the rigors of logic rather than those of rhetoric.

The proper study of philanthropy in an academic setting strives to capture the inherent tensions of voluntary associations as they seek to advocate for or against social change. "Advocacy" is thus a subject rather than a goal of study. Learning how philanthropy works is analogous to learning how politics works or how economics works. Some political scientists study the work of the Democratic Party without committing to its platform; some economists study business corporations without committing to those companies' market strategy. Some students of philanthropy may study the United Way or the Ford Foundation without committing themselves to the missions of those organizations.

The study of philanthropy should include the principal critiques of voluntary action. What must be avoided is the easy politicization of the subject. The philanthropic establishment should be treated no more deferentially than its peers in business and government. We must avoid the dangerous tendency to assume that persons engaged in philanthropy are compassionate and decent so that we will not be blinded to any evidence to the contrary. Fortunately, almost every field of philanthropic activity generates diverse points of view, and it is easy—even unavoidable in some cases—to find alternative perspectives and values that must be considered. Properly open as a field of inquiry, philanthropic studies will have to explore contrasting philanthropic values—Mother Teresa's notion of service as well as Christopher Hitchens's attack on Mother Teresa.[17]

Far from sullying the integrity of a university education, as Barzun would have it, philanthropy can be seen as advancing the mission of the university in society. In fact, to bring the study of philanthropy into the university is to call more attention to the mission of the university. Voluntary action for the public good leads to consideration of basic human needs and eventually to human well-being more generally. Bringing the concerns of philanthropy into the university introduces the burning social, economic, and political issues of the day; the study of philanthropy engages the university in a reexamination of its relationship to the urgent issues of society.

The relationship between philanthropic studies and the university as a whole is symbiotic. Philanthropic studies provides a larger purpose to education itself, and it may offer insights into ways to bring theory and practice into some meaningful and balanced relation. If educators become more informed about good works and how they happen, more astute and self-conscious in their critique, more open to the synthesis of knowledge and values in reflective practice, education will be doing more of what it ought to be doing. In turn, the university can help the philanthropic sector to better understand its tradition and to improve its practices. The university provides guidance in the exploration of the complex issues, issues that the third sector insists society should confront.

Finally, the introduction of philanthropy into the curriculum can also alter society in several ways. The idea of community service—that everyone owes some sort of service to the community and that much of that service will be in the form of uncompensated voluntary service—will become part of the larger concept of the educated person. Beyond rudimentary political education, technical economic competence, and the coping skills of life, everyone will be presumed to know something about the place of philanthropy in the way society works, to understand at some level why philanthropy exists. And in conjunction with that knowledge, there will be a growing knowledge base of hard statistical and empirical data about philanthropy of the same kind that we now collect about housing and medical care and defense expenditures.

The Future We Want

When we think about the future we want for our children, grandchildren, and others coming in the successor generations, we cannot help but place a vibrant philanthropic tradition at the center of that vision. What we want most is for them to live in a free, open, and democratic society. Philanthropy is essential to ensuring the future and vitality of this sort of society, and so what we want for future generations is a healthy philanthropy. This is a problematic future to wish for, though, because philanthropy commands neither the power nor the wealth to ensure its own future, much less to ensure a good life in a good society. But that is why we need stewardship and education. The better we understand philanthropy, the better we can pass it on.

Notes

1. Introduction

1. Rick Bragg, "She Opened the Door to Others; Her World Has Opened, Too," *New York Times*, November 12, 1996, A1.

2. Lauren Gard, "Ordinary People, Extraordinary Gifts," *Business Week*, November 29, 2004, 94.

3. Zlata Filipovic, *Zlata's Diary: A Child's Life in Sarajevo*, trans. Christina Pibichevich-Zoric (New York: Viking, 1994).

4. Donald Schön, *Reflective Practitioners: How Professionals Think in Action* (New York: Basic Books, 1983).

5. For example, Peter Frumkin's *Strategic Giving: The Art and Science of Philanthropy* (Chicago: University of Chicago Press, 2006) offers a useful and sophisticated model—informed by empirical findings—for understanding and improving the effectiveness of giving. Our theory of philanthropy is meant to address a different though complementary set of questions about why giving exists and what is essentially distinctive about it as an activity.

6. There is widespread agreement that this field is in need of much more theoretical development in general. Helmut Anheier and Lester Salamon, reviewing research findings on voluntary sector activities in many countries outside the United States, make the interesting point that theories developed in the West do not hold up so well in the face of international evidence. They suggest we need theories that better account for varying cultural, religious, social, and political conditions. See Helmut K. Anheier and Lester M. Salamon, "The Nonprofit Sector in Comparative Perspective," in *The Nonprofit Sector: A Research Handbook*, 2nd ed., ed. Walter W. Powell and Richard Steinberg (New Haven: Yale University Press, 2006), 89–114.

7. Gilles Deleuze and Félix Guattari, *What Is Philosophy?* trans. Hugh Tomlinson and Graham Burchell (New York: Columbia University Press, 1994 [original French publication, 1991]), 2.

8. Robert L. Payton, *Philanthropy: Voluntary Action for the Public Good* (New York: American Council on Education/Macmillan, 1988).

9. Deleuze and Guattari, *What Is Philosophy?* 15.

10. On the challenges confronting and shaping this field, see Charles T. Clotfelter and Thomas Ehrlich, ed., *Philanthropy and the Nonprofit Sector in a Changing America* (Bloomington: Indiana University Press, 2001).

11. We should be clear that joining together to create the biggest foundation was not their original strategy. The Bill and Melinda Gates Foundation was already well established and already the largest before Buffett, in 2006, decided to break with the norm and give the bulk of his philanthropic money to the Gates Foundation instead of forming his own separate foundation.

12. This dollar estimate and the prediction of a "golden age" has come notably from researchers at the Center on Wealth and Philanthropy at Boston College. See John J. Havens and Paul G. Schervish, "Millionaires and the Millennium: New Estimates of the Forthcoming Wealth Transfer and the Prospects for a Golden Age of Philanthropy," research report, Social Welfare Research Institute, Boston College, October 19, 1999.

13. See Burton Weisbrod, ed., *To Profit or Not to Profit: The Commercial Transformation of the Nonprofit Sector* (Cambridge: Cambridge University Press, 1998).

14. See Alex Nicholls, ed., *Social Entrepreneurship: New Models of Sustainable Social Change* (New York: Oxford University Press, 2006); and David Bornstein, *How to Change the World: Social Entrepreneurs and the Power of New Ideas* (New York: Oxford University Press, 2004).

15. See Peter Frumkin, "Inside Venture Philanthropy," *Society* 40, no. 4 (2003): 7–15; and Michael Moody, "'Building a Culture': The Construction and Evolution of Venture Philanthropy as a New Organizational Field," *Nonprofit and Voluntary Sector Quarterly*, in press. Venture philanthropy is sometimes connected to or relabeled "high-engagement philanthropy"; some practitioners prefer the latter term. See Mario Morino and Bill Shore, *High-Engagement Philanthropy: A Bridge to a More Effective Social Sector* (Washington, D.C.: Venture Philanthropy Partners and Community Wealth Ventures, 2004).

16. For a sum of recent research on the global associational revolution, see Anheier and Salamon, "The Nonprofit Sector in Comparative Perspective," 89, 95–103.

17. See Lester Salamon, *The Resilient Sector: The State of Nonprofit America* (Washington, D.C.: Brookings Institution Press and the Aspen Institute, 2003). Salamon borrows the term *distinctiveness imperative* from Bradford Gray and Mark Schlesinger.

18. In 2005, 76.5 percent of charitable contributions were classified as coming from living individuals, and 6.7 percent came from bequests. These figures are from *Giving USA* (Glenview, Ill.: Giving USA Foundation and Center on Philanthropy at Indiana University, 2006).

19. The exact amount or percent of revenue coming from various sources for the entire set of nonprofit organizations in the United States cannot be reported here because of limitations in the data available and because of the incredible diversity in this sector. The best data is available for "reporting public charities," one subset of the total number of organizations, albeit the subset that probably fits closest to what most people have in mind when they hear the term *nonprofit organization*. These are the tax-exempt entities registered under IRS category 501(c)(3) (see chapter 2 for a description of these categories) that also have over $25,000 in gross receipts in a given year and so must report using a Form 990. (Most religious congregations are excluded from this group, however.) The latest figures on this group of organizations reveal that they receive 12.5 percent of their revenues from "private contributions" (which is where the measurement of $1 out of $8 comes from), compared with 9 percent from "government grants" and 70.9 percent from fees. These figures are compiled by the National Center for Charitable Statistics (NCCS) at the Urban Institute. See Thomas H. Pollack and Amy Blackwood, "The Nonprofit Sector in Brief: Facts and Figures from the *Nonprofit Almanac 2007*" (Washington, D.C.: Urban Institute, 2006). (Note that the *Nonprofit Almanac 2007* is still forthcoming at the time

of this writing.) But there are many other types of nonprofit organizations that do not fit in the category of "reporting public charities." These include most religious congregations, nonprofits classified under other 501(c) categories such as many groups focused primarily on advocacy, and all private foundations. If we include those groups, the percentage of revenues from private giving would probably go up to around 20 percent or so. Also, "government grants" is just one way of measuring government money flowing to nonprofit groups, and when all sources are included (and including other categories of organizations), the percent coming from government is higher than from private donations—e.g., see Murray S. Weitzman et al., *The New Nonprofit Almanac and Desk Reference* (San Francisco: Jossey-Bass, with Independent Sector and the Urban Institute, 2002). In general, we try to use the latest data and best available measurements in this book, whether we are talking about nonprofit organizations or giving and volunteering. But the reader should be aware that any measurement is necessarily complicated by the diversity of activities and organizations that fall under what we call "philanthropy," not to mention other limits in the data gathered itself. For a good explanation of the data limits in this field (and a good summary of the best data), see Elizabeth Boris and C. Eugene Steuerle, "Scope and Dimensions of the Nonprofit Sector," 66–88, and John J. Havens, Mary A. O'Herlihy, and Paul G. Schervish, "Charitable Giving: How Much, by Whom, to What, and How?" 542–67, both in *The Nonprofit Sector*, ed. Powell and Steinberg.

20. See Anheier and Salamon, "The Nonprofit Sector in Comparative Perspective." For instance, outside the United States, government generally plays a larger role as funder (relative to other revenue sources) of what we call "philanthropic" institutions.

21. "Persons of the Year: The Good Samaritans," *Time*, December 26, 2005, 38–88.

22. See Payton, *Philanthropy*, 132–39. Mike W. Martin, *Virtuous Giving: Philanthropy, Voluntary Service, and Caring* (Bloomington: Indiana University Press, 1994), argues against the idea of philanthropy as itself a virtue, although he offers an extensive and useful analysis of philanthropy from the perspective of the philosophy of virtue ethics. For Martin, because philanthropy as an activity can potentially be harmful or bad, it is not a virtue in itself, but "all the major virtues are important to philanthropy" (30). The long list of "philanthropic virtues," then, includes virtues connected to making philanthropy work for good, including benevolence, reciprocity, respect for others, and so on.

23. Much of the scholarship on philanthropy is similarly focused more on givers than receivers. One attempt to remedy this by two noted scholars argues for conceptualizing philanthropy as a "social relation" between a donor and a recipient, which both deserve empirical attention to understand this interactive relationship. See Susan A. Ostrander and Paul G. Schervish, "Giving and Getting: Philanthropy as a Social Relation," in *Critical Issues in American Philanthropy*, ed. Jon Van Til (San Francisco: Jossey-Bass, 1990), 67–98.

24. H. Richard Niebuhr, *The Responsible Self: An Essay in Christian Moral Philosophy* (New York: Harper and Row, 1963), 60.

25. It may be that, for some, informal philanthropy is considered morally but not politically or economically important enough to measure and evaluate. We dis-

agree with this position, but for reasons of space—and sometimes of clarity—we focus principally on organized philanthropy in this book. We do not intend this to mean formal is more important than informal.

26. We offer here only some of the more basic or impressive facts and figures about the scale of organized philanthropy, as our primary purpose in this book is not to document the current state of philanthropy but to discuss a rationale for philanthropy that transcends the present. But looking at the current numbers does provide a good sense of philanthropy's considerable scale, especially relative to other sectors.

27. Virginia A. Hodgkinson and Murray S. Weitzman, *Giving and Volunteering in the United States 2001* (Washington, D.C.: Independent Sector, 2001). We should point out that these percentages—while always impressively high—vary depending on the methodology used in the survey. For example, the Current Population Survey conducted by the U.S. Bureau of Labor Statistics consistently yields a lower estimate of the percentage of Americans who volunteer—they estimated 28.8 percent in 2005 (http://www.bls.gov/cps/). Also, it is important to remember that more informal giving and volunteering is not fully captured by these surveys.

28. These measures also vary a bit across different sources. For instance, the Independent Sector survey cited above gives the average as 3.1 percent of household income, while *Giving USA* reports that in 2005 average household giving was 2.2 percent of average household after-tax income, and this 2.2 percent is exactly the same as the 40-year average. Michael O'Neill, *Nonprofit Nation: A New Look at the Third America* (San Francisco: Jossey-Bass, 2002), 25, gives slightly lower but similar estimates for both figures and points out that itemizers give more like 3 percent.

29. The first figure comes from Virginia Hodgkinson et al., "Individual Giving and Volunteering," in *The State of Nonprofit America*, ed. Lester Salamon (Washington, D.C.: Brookings Institution Press, 2003), 389. The second comes from Havens et al., "Charitable Giving," 548.

30. However, while Havens et al., "Charitable Giving," 46, generally support this assessment, they also argue that the wealthiest households, especially at the highest levels, give a higher percentage of their income than families at lower levels.

31. The figures on immediate 9/11 giving are based on an Independent Sector survey conducted in October 2001. See also Hodgkinson et al., "Individual Giving and Volunteering," 390.

32. Hodgkinson and Weitzman, *Giving and Volunteering*. The total estimated value of volunteer time here is from 2000, while the total amount of charitable giving is from 2005; in fact, the total value of volunteer time for 2005 most likely exceeds the $260.3 billion given in money or property. However, not all of this volunteering is for nonprofit organizations, as Hodgkinson and Weitzman make clear. They estimate 67 percent of volunteering is directly for nonprofits, while the other 33 percent is either informal or for corporations or government (e.g., at the local public school). For a review of the research on volunteering, see Laura Leete, "Work in the Nonprofit Sector," in *The Nonprofit Sector*, ed. Powell and Steinberg, 159–79.

33. *Giving USA.* We should also remember that there is a lot of individual philanthropic giving that goes not to organizations but to friends, relatives, and other individuals. See Havens et al., "Charitable Giving," 556–60.

34. The latest NCCS compilation of IRS figures come from Pollack and Blackwood, "The Nonprofit Sector in Brief." The 2 million estimate is ours, although we make it in light of similar estimations made by other scholars using detailed information and sophisticated methods. Lester M. Salamon, *America's Nonprofit Sector: A Primer*, 2nd ed. (New York: Foundation Center, 1999), figured there were about 1.6 million nonprofit organizations in 1995 (when only 1.1 million were registered with the IRS). O'Neill, *Nonprofit Nation*, 11, estimated that there were around 1.8 million organizations in the late 1990s. See Boris and Steuerle, "Scope and Dimensions," 67–72, for an explanation of the issues involved in making size estimates of such a diverse sector; and see note 19 above on the limitations of any such measurements.

35. Boris and Steuerle, "Scope and Dimensions," 69, report that the number of IRS registered nonprofit organizations of all types increased 37 percent from 1989 to 2000, while the number of 501(c)(3) organizations increased 77 percent and private foundations (listed as a subcategory under IRS category 501(c)(3)) increased 87 percent.

36. Pollack and Blackwood, "The Nonprofit Sector in Brief." These amounts are for all reporting nonprofits in any IRS 501(c) category. O'Neill, *Nonprofit Nation*, 12, reports that nonprofit revenues exceed the GDP of "all but six foreign countries."

37. NCCS data on the reporting 501(c)(3) public charities organizations (299,033 of the total 1.4 million registered organizations), given in Pollack and Blackwood, "The Nonprofit Sector in Brief," reveals the dominance of these two subsectors. In 2004, health care charities received 58.7 percent of the revenues and held 41.1 percent of assets, while education reported 16.3 percent and 29.4 percent, respectively.

38. See note 19 for important caveats to remember on financial measurements of this sector.

39. Hodgkinson et al., "Individual Giving and Volunteering," 394.

40. In "Scope and Dimensions," 76, Boris and Steuerle give 2000 data on reporting public charities (again, this is one piece of the whole universe of nonprofit groups) showing that religious groups receive 57 percent from private contributions while health care organizations receive 85 percent from fees (and only 4 percent from contributions). However, in the *New Nonprofit Almanac*, Weitzman et al. try to estimate revenue sources for a larger subset of nonprofits, and they find that religious organizations receive 95 percent of their revenues from donations, while health organizations receive only 4 percent. Salamon, *America's Nonprofit Sector*, 37, finds that the overall percent of revenue for the sector coming from private giving goes down to only 10 percent if you exclude religious organizations.

41. The figures comes from *Employment in the Nonprofit Sector* (Washington, D.C.: Independent Sector, 2004), a report based on U.S. Bureau of Labor Statistics data.

42. This comparison is based on figures from the Census Bureau's *Statistical Abstract of the United States*.

43. See Leete, "Work in the Nonprofit Sector," 160; and *Employment in the Nonprofit Sector*.

44. Gertrude Stein, *Everybody's Autobiography* (Cambridge, Mass.: Exact Change, [1937] 1993).

45. L. P. Hartley, *The Go-Between* (New York: Knopf, 1953).

46. See George Trumbull Ladd, *Philosophy of Conduct: A Treatise on the Facts, Principles, and Ideals of Ethics* (New York: Charles Scribner's Sons, 1902), xii, for the earliest mention of this idea of "public teacher" that we know of.

47. Alfred North Whitehead, *The Concept of Nature* (Cambridge: Cambridge University Press, 1920), 163.

2. Voluntary Action for the Public Good

1. See Martin, *Virtuous Giving*, 12–14, for a summary of the range of definitions of philanthropy in the literature and in common usage. Martin prefers the term *philanthropy* for many of the same reasons as we do, and although his definition—"voluntary private giving for public purposes" (ix)—is similar, it only includes giving time and money and not the third element of voluntary association. He also argues for using the terms *voluntary giving* and *voluntary service* in general ways that encompass the other and make them nearly interchangeable.

2. Another way of looking at this is to combine two words we inherited from the Latin that clarify an important distinction: *benevolence* means "good will," *beneficence* means "good action." In our definition, philanthropy is about *benevolent beneficence*—good actions that are based on good will, good actions that seek to do good. Of course, as we will argue later, we should always remember that good does not always result from philanthropic action and that good people often disagree on whether good has resulted.

3. W. B. Gallie, "Essentially Contested Concepts," *Proceedings of the Aristotelian Society*, n.s., 56 (1956): 168, 169.

4. Adil Najam, "Understanding the Third Sector: Revisiting the Prince, the Merchant, and the Citizen," *Nonprofit Management and Leadership* 7, no. 2 (1996): 205.

5. See Najam, "Understanding the Third Sector," 208.

6. Henry Hansmann's seminal writings are famous for putting the emphasis on the nondistribution constraint. See Henry Hansmann, "The Role of Nonprofit Enterprise," *Yale Law Journal* 89 (April 1980): 835–98; also Richard Steinberg, "Economic Theories of Nonprofit Organizations," in *The Nonprofit Sector*, ed. Powell and Steinberg, 117–39. Peter Frumkin has attempted to expand on this perspective by defining what he prefers to call the "nonprofit and voluntary sector" in terms of not just the nondistribution constraint but also other constraints, other things that nonprofit entities do not or cannot do. He specifically lists "they do not coerce participation" and "they exist without simple and clear lines of ownership and accountability." See Peter Frumkin, *On Being Nonprofit* (Cambridge: Harvard University Press, 2002), 3. Similarly, Paul DiMaggio and Helmet Anheier are careful to add two other "distinctive features" of nonprofit organizations beyond the economists' nondistribution constraint: "collective purpose" (which we see as most important) and "tax advantages." See Paul DiMaggio and Helmut Anheier, "The Sociology of Nonprofit Organizations and Sectors," *Annual Review of Sociology* 16 (1990): 137–59.

7. Roger Lohmann, "And Lettuce is Non-Animal: Toward a Positive Economics of Voluntary Action," *Nonprofit and Voluntary Sector Quarterly* 18, no. 4 (1989): 367–83. Najam, "Understanding the Third Sector," echoes our argument by saying that a "non" definition obscures the incredible diversity within this sector.

8. The IRS classification of nonprofits defines them as "corporations," which confuses things even further.

9. To deal with this confusion, the organization from its inception has been officially named INDEPENDENT SECTOR, all capitalized, but many find this cumbersome. Also, this organization makes a distinction between the "nonprofit sector" and the "independent sector"—the latter is a subset of the former and only includes IRS category 501(c)(3) and 501(c)(4) organizations as well as other religious organizations.

10. Frumkin, *On Being Nonprofit*, 8.

11. Roger Lohmann, *The Commons: New Perspectives on Nonprofit Organizations and Voluntary Action* (San Francisco: Jossey-Bass, 1992). See also Michael O'Neill, *The Third America: The Emergence of the Nonprofit Sector in the United States* (San Francisco: Jossey-Bass, 1989), on the importance of including mutual-benefit organizations.

12. See Jon Van Til, *Growing Civil Society: From Nonprofit Sector to Third Space* (Bloomington: Indiana University Press, 2000), for an extensive discussion of these sorts of boundary-setting and terminiological issues. Van Til advocates the idea of a "third space" of activity infused with a "voluntary spirit."

13. According to the Internal Revenue Code, 501(c)(3) and 501(c)(4) organizations differ in terms of deductibility of contributions—yes for (c)(3)s, no for (c)(4)s—and restrictions on lobbying/advocacy activities—(c)(3)s are limited to only using part of their budgets for this, though (c)(4)s are unlimited, except that they too cannot participate in candidate electoral advocacy.

14. There are twenty-seven subcategories beneath 501(c) as well as 501(d), (e), (f), (k), and (n).

15. Lester M. Salamon, *America's Nonprofit Sector: A Primer*, 2nd ed. (New York: Foundation Center, 1999), 10–11 [emphasis added]. Salamon's research on non-U.S. countries led to a slightly different but largely similar set of basic definitional elements that could encompass voluntary activity around the globe. See Lester M. Salamon and Helmut K. Anheier, eds., *Defining the Nonprofit Sector: A Cross-National Analysis* (Manchester: Manchester University Press, 1997).

16. Salamon, *America's Nonprofit Sector*, 9–10.

17. Lester Salamon, "The Resilient Sector: The State of Nonprofit America," in *The State of Nonprofit America*, ed. Salamon (Washington, D.C.: Brookings Institution Press, 2003), 4.

18. See Ralph Kramer, *Voluntary Agencies in the Welfare State* (Berkeley: University of California Press, 1981).

19. Alexis de Tocqueville, *Democracy in America* (New York: HarperPerennial, [1840] 1988), 522. For a good summary of the various civic roles of nonprofits in a democracy, including their essential role in citizen socialization, see Elisabeth S. Clemens, "The Constitution of Citizens: Political Theories of Nonprofit Organizations," in *The Nonprofit Sector*, ed. Powell and Steinberg, 207–20.

20. Frumkin, *On Being Nonprofit*, 25.

21. The function of local, participation-based voluntary action in creating the so-called social capital that is necessary for democracy—a very neo-Tocquevillian perspective on the role of voluntary associations—has recently become a dominant way of thinking about the positive purpose of these associations, particularly among scholars adopting a "civil society" framework. This perspective is chiefly based in Robert Putnam's argument that such civic participation–generated social capital is in decline (at least in the United States). See Robert Putnam, *Bowling Alone* (New York: Simon and Schuster, 2002).

22. The recurrent attempts in Congress to tighten regulations on the allowable advocacy activity of nonprofit groups that receive federal funds is an example of the criticism of this role. But we should remember that many others also argue that advocacy and participation in the public debate over vital issues is a central and beneficial role for nonprofit groups. Some research has also confirmed this crucial democratic role of voluntary groups participating in public sphere discourse. For a comparative analysis of this in several countries, see Robert Wuthnow, ed., *Between States and Markets: The Voluntary Sector in Comparative Perspective* (Princeton: Princeton University Press, 1991).

23. See the work of Marvin Olasky, an advisor to George W. Bush on his faith-based initiatives, for a good example of the argument that "charity" is better than government. Marvin Olasky, *The Tragedy of American Compassion* (Washington, D.C.: Regnery, 1992). For the classic statement of the "mediating structures" view, see Peter Berger and Richard John Neuhaus, *To Empower People: From State to Civil Society*, 2nd ed. (Washington, D.C.: American Enterprise Institute Press, 1995).

24. The *Oxford English Dictionary* defines *philanthropia* as love "to" mankind rather than love "of" mankind, which strikes us as a significant shade of meaning because it implies an action rather than merely a sentiment.

25. Remember that foundations are nonprofit organizations. Overall, our broad definition of philanthropy has the benefit of easily encompassing both the more formal organizations in the field and the more informal grassroots groups. The groups that are probably the most difficult to fit into our specific definition of philanthropy as "voluntary action for the public good" are the mutual-benefit or member-serving nonprofits (described earlier). This is because those groups provide goods that are explicitly exclusive in some way, and therefore not fully public—economists often call these "club goods" as opposed to "public goods." But as we explain later, our concept of public good is more generalized than the economists' definition, and we don't require that the public good pursued by philanthropic action be a universally accessible good.

26. *Caritas* also meant "fondness" and "dearness" in the sense that something has special value or esteem.

27. Robert Gross argues that, historically speaking, these differing understandings of charity and philanthropy arose separately (and sequentially) as dual traditions in America. Coming first was charity, focused on compassionate service by individuals; joining it later was philanthropy, focused on broader social reform. See Robert A. Gross, "Giving in America: From Charity to Philanthropy," in *Charity, Philanthropy, and Civility in American History*, ed. Lawrence J. Friedman and Mark D. McGarvie (Cambridge: Cambridge University Press, 2003), 29–48.

28. Brian Vickers, ed., *Francis Bacon* (Oxford: Oxford University Press, 1996), 263.

29. On these "new vehicles" of giving in general, see John J. Havens, Mary A. O'Herlihy, and Paul G. Schervish, "Charitable Giving: How Much, by Whom, to What, and How?" in *The Nonprofit Sector*, ed. Powell and Steinberg, 560–62; and Virginia Hodgkinson et al., "Individual Giving and Volunteering," in *The State of Nonprofit America*, ed. Lester Salamon (Washington, D.C.: Brookings Institution Press, 2003), 413–14. On the rise in giving circles, see Angela M. Eikenberry, "Giving Circles: Growing Grassroots Philanthropy," *Nonprofit and Voluntary Sector Quarterly* 35, no. 3 (2006): 517–32. Some observers note how these new vehicles exacerbate an existing tension in philanthropic relations: the control that donors have relative to recipients. Some grantmakers are responding to this problem by seeking innovative ways to involve recipients in various aspects of the giving process. For one in-depth example of this, see Susan Ostrander, *Money for Change: Social Movement Philanthropy at Haymarket People's Fund* (Philadelphia: Temple University Press, 1995).

30. Virginia A. Hodgkinson and Murray S. Weitzman, *Giving and Volunteering in the United States 2001* (Washington, D.C.: Independent Sector, 2001). The correlation between volunteering and giving is a robust finding reported in many other studies as well. See Havens et al., "Charitable Giving," 550.

31. See Hodgkinson et al., "Individual Giving and Volunteering," 391; Havens et al., "Charitable Giving," 545–55; and Hodgkinson and Weitzman, *Giving and Volunteering*. A number of other factors, the most significant of which relate to income and wealth (as we suggested in chapter 1), have more complicated relationships with either the amount of giving, the likelihood that a household will give, or the patterns in that giving. See Havens et al., "Charitable Giving," for a detailed discussion of these relationships. These other factors include broader social, economic, political, and cultural features of communities and regions, such as the level of poverty and need, income levels and size of the income gap, state-level political variables, aspects of political culture, and so on. For a study of the effect of these factors on giving, see Wolfgang Bielefeld, Patrick Rooney, and Kathy Steinberg, "How Do Need, Capacity, Geography, and Politics Influence Giving?" in *Gifts of Time and Money: The Role of Charity in American Communities*, ed. Arthur C. Brooks (Lanham, Md.: Rowman and Littlefield, 2005), 127–57.

32. It would be interesting if they kept a similar record of the other good works they do—an annual accounting of voluntary service and helping, for instance.

33. The Independent Sector survey found that itemizers give 37 percent more in contributions than nonitemizers, and this greater amount of giving was true across income levels, so it was not just a result of the fact that itemizers as a whole tend to be wealthier. See *Deducting Generosity: The Effect of Charitable Tax Incentives on Giving* (Washington, D.C.: Independent Sector, 2003).

34. See Hodgkinson and Weitzman, *Giving and Volunteering*. Taken together with the finding that volunteers are more likely to give money, we can see how involvement of individuals in organizations, or more broadly in networks or "communities of participation," is a good way of summarizing many of the major factors that increase giving money. See Havens et al., "Charitable Giving," 545. Also see

Putnam, *Bowling Alone*, for an explanation of how participation in civic activities and membership in organizations is positively correlated with (among other things) voluntary giving.

35. See Diogenes Laertius, *Lives of Eminent Philosophers*, trans. R. D. Hicks (Cambridge: Harvard University Press, [1925] 1970).

36. Hodgkinson et al., "Individual Giving and Volunteering," 409.

37. See Laura Leete, "Work in the Nonprofit Sector," in *The Nonprofit Sector*, ed. Powell and Steinberg, 169–70; Hodgkinson et al., "Individual Giving and Volunteering," 409–10; and Hodgkinson and Weitzman, *Giving and Volunteering*. The finding that belonging to an organization increases volunteering echoes the findings reported earlier about the importance of participation and membership for giving of all sorts. Also, the finding about employed people volunteering more includes those employed only part-time—these people actually have the highest rate of volunteering, compared to full-time employed and unemployed.

38. Many uses of the term *voluntary association* restrict the term to small, grassroots, or less formalized groupings, but we prefer to use the term in a way that emphasizes the continuum (and similarities) of associations, from the small ones to the large ones.

39. See Kieran Healy, *Last Best Gifts: Altruism and the Market for Human Blood and Organs* (Chicago: University of Chicago Press, 2006).

40. Tocqueville, *Democracy in America*, 513.

41. Max Weber, "Politics as a Vocation," in *From Max Weber: Essays in Sociology*, trans. and ed. Hans Gerth and C. Wright Mills (New York: Oxford University Press [1921] 1946), 84.

42. Commission on Private Philanthropy and Public Needs (Filer Commission), *Giving in America: Toward a Stronger Voluntary Sector. Report of the Commission on Private Philanthropy and Public Needs* (Washington, D.C.: Commission on Private Philanthropy and Public Needs, 1975). For a comprehensive study of the Filer Commission, see Eleanor Brilliant, *Private Charity and Public Inquiry: A History of the Filer and Peterson Commissions* (Bloomington: Indiana University Press, 2000).

43. Donee Group, *Private Philanthropy: Vital & Innovative? or Passive & Irrelevant?* (Washington, D.C.: Donee Group, 1975). The work of the Donee Group continued via the National Committee on Responsive Philanthropy, which they formed in 1976 and which continues this work today.

44. Peter Dobkin Hall reviews the history of the invention of this idea of a unified sector, including the important role of the Filer Commission in that invention. But he is skeptical about the Commission's success in creating this unified sector conception in the face of the diverse interests, voices, and groups they were trying to encompass. He also reminds us that this diversity continued to be the major problem facing the umbrella group, Independent Sector, which was formed after the Filer Commission. See Peter Dobkin Hall, *Inventing the Nonprofit Sector, and Other Essays on Philanthropy, Voluntarism, and Nonprofit Organizations* (Baltimore: Johns Hopkins University Press, 1992), 77–80.

45. Compare this to the attempt by James Douglas to come up with defining features of the three sectors. For Douglas, the government sector is essentially characterized by authority, the market sector by exchange, and the third sector by "voluntary collective identification," by which he means uncoerced focus on pursuing

some collective interest. See James Douglas, *Why Charity?* (Beverly Hills: Sage, 1983), 28ff. Najam, "Understanding the Third Sector," 213, lists the basic coordinating mechanisms of the three sectors as authority/coercion, negotiated exchange, and shared values.

46. Max Weber, "Politics as a Vocation," in *From Max Weber: Essays in Sociology*, trans. and ed. Hans Gerth and C. Wright Mills (New York: Oxford University Press [1921] 1946), 78.

47. Eviatar Zerubavel, *The Fine Line: Making Distinctions in Everyday Life* (Chicago: University of Chicago Press, 1991).

48. Martin, *Virtuous Giving*, similarly defines "voluntary" philanthropy as that which is "intended and uncoerced" (8).

49. Kenneth E. Boulding, *A Preface to Grants Economics: The Economy of Love and Fear* (New York: Praeger, 1981). This is a revised edition; the book was originally published with just the subtitle here as its title, which we think was much more interesting.

50. On the increase in nonprofit advocacy groups, see Craig Jenkins, "Nonprofit Organizations and Political Advocacy," in *The Nonprofit Sector*, ed. Powell and Steinberg, 307–32; Jeffrey M. Berry and David F. Arons, *A Voice for Nonprofits* (Washington, D.C.: Brookings Institution Press, 2003); and Theda Skocpol, "Advocates without Members: The Recent Transformation of American Civic Life," in Theda Skocpol and Morris Fiorina, *Civic Engagement in American Democracy* (Washington, D.C.: Brookings Institution Press, 1999), 461–509.

51. See Brian O'Connell, "What Voluntary Activity Can and Cannot Do for America," *Public Administration Review* 49, no. 5 (September/October 1989): 486–91.

52. See Ira Chernus, *American Nonviolence: The History of an Idea* (Maryknoll, N.Y.: Orbis Books, 2004).

53. See Jean-Jacques Rousseau, *The Social Contract*, trans. Donald A. Cress (Indianapolis: Hackett, [1762] 1987). Modern-day "Communitarians" borrow this notion from Rousseau and warn against the focus on particular interests that they say will detract from the collective public good, from a focus on what we share. See Amitai Etzioni, *The Spirit of Community: Rights, Responsibilities, and the Communitarian Agenda* (New York: Crown, 1993).

54. James Madison, "Number 10," in *The Federalist Papers*, ed. Clinton Rossiter (New York: Penguin Books, [1788] 1961), 78.

55. Martin Marty, *The One and the Many: America's Struggle for the Common Good* (Cambridge: Harvard University Press, 1997), 133 (emphasis added). Paul Lichterman calls views of the public good like Madison's "seesaw models"—they see personal interests or individualism on one end of the seesaw and the public good or community concerns directly opposed at the other. See Paul Lichterman, *The Search for Political Community: American Activists Reinventing Commitment* (Cambridge: Cambridge University Press, 1996).

56. We discuss this "failure" argument further in the next chapter. In addition, some philanthropic groups, such as mutual-benefit associations, provide what economists call "club goods," which are nonrivalrous like pure public goods but are excludable based, for instance, on paying dues or official membership in a group. We include voluntary associations providing club goods in our definition, despite this technical distinction.

57. See Mancur Olson, *The Logic of Collective Action: Public Goods and the Theory of Groups* (New York: Schocken Books, [1965] 1971). There is also a problem known as the "tragedy of the commons" that is similar to the free-rider problem and poses similar problems for understanding how voluntary action for the public good can arise in a world of self-interested actors. This "tragedy" occurs because common pool resources, like free grazing grass on the village commons, will inevitably be depleted because self-interested individuals have no reason to limit their use. See Garrett Hardin, "The Tragedy of the Commons," *Science* 162 (December 13, 1968): 1243–48.

58. The criticisms of "dropping coins in the bucket" philanthropy, though offered infrequently, come from opposite ideological poles. One criticism says that such giving merely perpetuates the poverty of those being helped by the services it (barely) funds, whereas real solutions are to be found in self-help and mutual aid. Another criticism says that such giving deceives us into thinking that many small gifts can actually reduce poverty, whereas to reduce poverty we actually need money on a scale that only taxation and systematic government action can provide.

59. So, technically, actions that are intended to achieve the public good but actually lead to bad outcomes should be considered philanthropic by our definition. And we would probably consider an action philanthropic if it accidentally served the public good, as long as it wasn't action designed to serve a "public bad." But we prefer the focus to remain on intended purpose rather than simply consequences. Martin, in *Virtuous Giving*, makes similar arguments but with much more extensive ethical analysis of these points. See his discussion of the useful ambiguity of the idea of "public purpose" (11–12).

60. Tocqueville considered this combination and connection of self-interest and public good—what he termed "the doctrine of self-interest properly understood"—to be a common and useful more in American democratic culture. See Tocqueville, *Democracy in America*, 525–28.

61. For a nice summary of this point, see Dwight Burlingame, *Altruism and Philanthropy: Definitional Issues*, Essays on Philanthropy, no. 10 (Indianapolis: Center on Philanthropy at Indiana University, 1993).

62. Craig Calhoun, "The Public Good as a Social and Cultural Project," in *Private Action and the Public Good*, ed. Walter Powell and Elisabeth Clemens (New Haven: Yale University Press, 1998), 32. See also Jane Mansbridge, "On the Contested Nature of the Public Good," 3–19, in that same volume.

63. Robert Wuthnow makes this point in a summary of studies of the voluntary sector in societies outside the United States as well. See Wuthnow, ed., *Between States and Markets*.

3. Because Things Go Wrong

1. John Gall, *Systemantics: How Systems Work and Especially How They Fail* (New York: Random House, 1977).

2. Max Weber, *Economy and Society: An Outline of Interpretive Sociology*, ed. Guenther Roth and Claus Wittich, trans. Ephraim Fischoff et al. (Berkeley: University of California Press, 1978).

3. Adapted from Ralf Dahrendorf, *Life Chances: Approaches to Social and Political Theory* (Chicago: University of Chicago Press, 1979); see also Dahrendorf, *The Modern Social Conflict: An Essay on the Politics of Liberty* (New York: Weidenfeld and Nicolson, 1988).

4. Michael Walzer, *Spheres of Justice: A Defense of Pluralism and Equality* (New York: Basic Books, 1983).

5. Plato, *The Republic*, trans. Richard W. Sterling and William C. Scott (New York: W. W. Norton, 1985), 262.

6. James Madison, "Number 51," in *The Federalist Papers*, 322.

7. The scholarly debate about the prevalence, causes, and even existence of human altruism has seen many contributions from many disciplinary perspectives over many years. Our statements here show that we think there is compelling evidence from this scholarship to support the idea that altruism exists, is widespread across human societies, and cannot always be explained by other motives such as disguised self-interest or the evolutionary drive to pass on one's genes. For a summary of the evidence from evolutionary biology and psychology, see Elliot Sober and David Sloan Wilson, *Unto Others: The Evolution and Psychology of Unselfish Behavior* (Cambridge: Harvard University Press, 1998). For other social science evidence, see Kristen Renwick Monroe, *The Heart of Altruism: Perceptions of a Common Humanity* (Princeton: Princeton University Press, 1996), and Jane Mansbridge, ed., *Beyond Self-Interest* (Chicago: University of Chicago Press, 1989).

8. Cara Buckley, "Man Is Rescued by Stranger on Subway Tracks," *New York Times*, January 3, 2007.

9. William Bennett, *The Book of Virtues: A Treasury of Great Moral Stories* (New York: Simon and Schuster, 1993); Stephen Covey, *The Seven Habits of Highly Effective People: Restoring the Character Ethic* (New York: Simon and Schuster, 1989).

10. See Martin, *Virtuous Giving*. Martin also provides a helpful philosophical review of the fact that "mixed motives"—egoistic and altruistic both—typically engender philanthropic actions.

11. Aristotle, *Ethics*, in *The Basic Works of Aristotle*, ed. Richard McKeon (New York: Random House, [1941]).

12. See Robert L. Payton, "Philanthropy as Moral Discourse," in *America in Theory*, ed. Leslie Berlowitz et al. (New York: Oxford University Press, 1988).

13. Arthur O. Lovejoy, *Reflections on Human Nature* (Baltimore: Johns Hopkins University Press, 1961).

14. Mother Teresa, *A Simple Path* (New York: Ballantine Books, 1995).

15. John D. Rockefeller, *Random Reminiscences of Men and Events* (Tarrytown, N.Y.: Sleepy Hollow Press and Rockefeller Archive Center, [1908–9] 1984), 93, 98.

16. This ladder of different forms of charity is found in the section on "Gifts to the Poor" in Maimonides' commentary on code of Jewish law in the Mishneh Torah. See Isadore Twersky, *Introduction to the Code of Maimonides (Mishneh Torah)* (New Haven: Yale University Press, 1982).

17. See Muhammad Yunus, *Banker to the Poor: Micro-Lending and the Battle Against World Poverty* (New York: Public Affairs, [1999] 2003).

18. Georg Simmel, "The Web of Group-Affiliations," in *Conflict and the Web of Group-Affiliations*, trans. Reinhard Bendix (New York: Free Press, [1922] 1955),

125–95. The literal translation of the German phrase Simmel uses is "intersection of social circles."

19. This phrase was introduced in the classic article by Alvin Gouldner, "The Norm of Reciprocity: A Preliminary Statement," *American Sociological Review* 25, no. 2 (1960): 161–78. We will discuss reciprocity in more depth in chapter 4, when we describe the philanthropic principle of "serial reciprocity." This idea challenges some of Gouldner's basic assumptions and even extends the idea of reciprocity beyond the notion of generalized expectations within a closed group, as used here. See Michael Moody, "Serial Reciprocity: A Preliminary Statement," *Sociological Theory*, in press.

20. See Robert Putnam, *Bowling Alone: The Collapse and Revival of American Community* (New York: Simon and Schuster, 2000), for the most prominent argument about the positive social benefits of a generalized norm of reciprocity within networks that builds trust.

21. The best summary of Octavia Hill's approach comes in her own words. See Octavia Hill, *Homes of the London Poor*, 2nd ed. (London: Cass, [1875] 1970).

22. Gertrude Himmelfarb, *Poverty and Compassion: The Moral Imagination of the Late Victorians* (New York: Alfred A. Knopf, 1991), 214.

23. Helmut K. Anheier and Lester M. Salamon, "The Nonprofit Sector in Comparative Perspective," in *The Nonprofit Sector*, ed. Powell and Steinberg, 106. See also Lester Salamon and Helmut Anheier, "Social Origins of Civil Society: Explaining the Nonprofit Sector Cross-Nationally" *Voluntas* 9, no. 3 (1998): 213–48.

24. See Burton Weisbrod, *The Voluntary Nonprofit Sector* (Lexington, Mass.: Lexington Books, 1977); Burton Weisbrod, *The Nonprofit Economy* (Cambridge: Harvard University Press, 1988); James Douglas, *Why Charity?* (Beverly Hills: Sage, 1983). Henry Hansmann offers a further development of the failure theory of why nonprofits exist, focusing on "contract failure" or what has been called the "trust theory" to explain why, in cases of government failure, nonprofits would be preferred in some cases over for-profits. In this view, when there is imperfect information and/or a lack of trust, there will be a preference for nonprofits as the vehicle for providing public goods or services because they are bound by the nondistribution constraint. See Hansmann, "The Role of Nonprofit Enterprise." For reviews of these dominant economic theories, see Richard Steinberg, "Economic Theories of Nonprofit Organizations," in *The Nonprofit Sector*, ed. Powell and Steinberg, 117–39; and Helmut Anheier and Avner Ben-Ner, eds., *The Study of Nonprofit Enterprise: Theories and Approaches* (New York: Kluwer Academic and Plenum, 2003).

25. This shift toward more cross-sectoral governance was popularized in the United States most prominently by the "reinventing government" movement that influenced the Clinton-Gore administration in particular. See David Osborne and Ted Gaebler, *Reinventing Government* (Reading, Mass.: Addison-Wesley, 1992). Lester Salamon has been making the case for many years that government and the nonprofit sector have always been (though are becoming more so) interdependent "partners," a claim supported by the facts we presented earlier about the large chunk of nonprofit revenues that come from government funding. Salamon even incorporates a nice theoretical twist on the "failure" theories to explain these wide-

spread partnerships, reasoning that government-nonprofit partnerships emerge when the voluntary efforts of nonprofits are insufficient to provide a certain good; he calls this "voluntary failure." See Lester Salamon, *Partners in Public Service: Government-Nonprofit Relations in the Modern Welfare State* (Baltimore: Johns Hopkins University Press, 1995). Salamon's theory is useful for us because it acknowledges that in many cases voluntary action is the *preferred* mechanism for providing or seeking some public good; it is what people turn to first, not just when other mechanisms have failed.

26. In addition to the work cited earlier on the roles or functions of the nonprofit sector and philanthropy, there are others who offer what the economists call "supply-side" theories that fit with the understanding of nonprofits described in this section. For a well-known summary of the supply-side view, see Estelle James, "The Nonprofit Sector in Comparative Perspective," in *The Nonprofit Sector: A Research Handbook*, ed. Walter Powell (New Haven: Yale University Press, 1987), 397–415. For a seminal theory of nonprofit activity based on the idea of entrepreneurship, see Dennis Young, *If Not for Profit, for What?* (Lexington, Mass.: D. C. Heath, 1983); and see the previously cited work on "social entrepreneurship."

27. See Moody, "Serial Reciprocity," on the types of scenarios that call for a "serial reciprocity" response, including one in which giving to third parties is considered the appropriate, or even required, way to express gratitude for being the recipient of giving yourself. Sometimes, our benefactor even says "go and do likewise."

4. The World Can Be Made Better

1. See Paul Schervish, Platon E. Coutsoukis, and Ethan Lewis, *Gospels of Wealth: How the Rich Portray Their Lives* (Westport, Conn.: Praeger, 1994); Paul Schervish, "The Moral Biography of Wealth: Philosophical Reflections on the Foundation of Philanthropy," *Nonprofit and Voluntary Action Quarterly* 35, no. 3 (2006): 477–92; Robert Wuthnow, *Acts of Compassion* (Princeton: Princeton University Press, 1991); and Robert Wuthnow, *Learning to Care: Elementary Kindness in an Age of Indifference* (Oxford: Oxford University Press, 1995).

2. Frances Bacon, "Aphorisms Concerning the Interpretation of Nature and the Kingdom of Man," in *Novum Organum* (1620), xlix. See Lisa Hardine and Michael Silverthorne, eds., *Francis Bacon: The New Organon* (Cambridge: Cambridge University Press, 2000).

3. See Henry A. Rosso, *Rosso on Fund Raising: Lessons from a Master's Lifetime Experience* (San Francisco: Jossey-Bass, 1996). Rosso also refers to this as developing the case for an organization's fund-raising plan.

4. It is interesting to note the similarity here to what we teach public policy analysts about defining the problem that is meant to be addressed by the policy proposals they are analyzing. Eugene Bardach, for instance, argues that the first step in his "Eightfold Path" of policy analysis is to "define the problem" that requires a policy response. He suggests crafting a statement of the problem by thinking in terms of deficits or excess of something in society, perhaps using the word *too*—e.g., "there are too few nurses to staff public hospitals on the south side of Chicago," or "there are too many terrorists moving undetected on American soil." See Eugene Bardach,

A Practical Guide for Policy Analysis: The Eightfold Path to More Effective Problem Solving, 2nd ed. (Washington, D.C.: CQ Press, 2005). This reminds us that government and public policy are responsible also for achieving the public good and advancing what are often moral visions of the good society.

5. On the March of Dimes case, see David L. Sills, *The Volunteers: Means and Ends in a National Organization* (Glencoe, Ill.: Free Press, 1957).

6. See Debra C. Minkoff and Walter W. Powell, "Nonprofit Mission: Constancy, Responsiveness, or Deflection?" in *The Nonprofit Sector*, ed. Powell and Steinberg, 591–611. They explain why and how mission is more essential to nonprofit organizations than to other types—a point made by *all* theories of nonprofits—and why and how missions change. They also emphasize that nonprofit missions are oriented toward a vision of the public good.

7. See Robert L. Payton, "Philanthropy and the Good Samaritan," in *Philanthropy in America: A Comprehensive Historical Encyclopedia*, ed. Dwight F. Burlingame (Santa Barbara, CA: ABC-CLIO, Inc., 2004), 373–80. Portions of that article are included in edited form in this section.

8. Robert W. Funk, *Parables and Presence* (Philadelphia: Fortress, 1982), 29–34.

9. Wuthnow, *Acts of Compassion.*

10. See Chad Varah, ed., *The Samaritans in the '80s: To Befriend the Suicidal and Despairing* (London: Constable, 1980).

11. See A. M. Rosenthal, *Thirty-eight Witnesses: The Kitty Genovese Case* (Berkeley: University of California Press, [1964] 1999).

12. For a review of this research, see Bibb Latané and Steve Nida, "Ten Years of Research on Group Size and Helping," *Psychological Bulletin* 89 (1981): 308–24. See also Ervin Straub, "Transforming the Bystander: Altruism, Caring, and Social Responsibility," in *Genocide Watch*, ed. Helen Fein (New Haven: Yale University Press, 1992), 162–81.

13. John Darley and C. Daniel Batson, "From Jerusalem to Jericho," *Journal of Personality and Social Psychology* 27, no. 1 (1973): 100–108.

14. For a description of these laws, see Morton Hunt, *The Compassionate Beast* (New York: William Morrow, 1990).

15. See Samuel P. Oliner and Pearl Oliner, *The Altruistic Personality: Rescuers of Jews in Nazi Europe* (New York: Free Press, 1992).

16. This is the sort of explanation that evolutionary biologists and economists have offered to explain much of what is considered by others to be altruistic or cooperative behavior. "Altruism" is explained in terms of the (self-interested) anticipation of later reciprocity and/or the natural selection of people who help because then they are more likely to be helped themselves when they are in need. For a representative sum of one version of this explanation, see Martin Nowak and Karl Sigmund, "Evolution of Indirect Reciprocity," *Nature* 437, October 27, 2005, 1291–98. For a critique of these explanations, see Monroe, *The Heart of Altruism.*

17. Kenneth Boulding, *A Preface to Grants Economics: The Economy of Love and Fear* (New York: Praeger, [1973] 1981).

18. Hunt, *Compassionate Beast*, 80.

19. For more extensive examinations of the range of moral challenges—and potential pitfalls—of philanthropic actions, see David H. Smith, ed., *Good Intentions:*

Moral Obstacles and Opportunities (Bloomington: Indiana University Press, 2005), and Martin, *Virtuous Giving*.

20. Monroe, *The Heart of Altruism*, 197–98.

21. For an example of the provocative statements by communitarians that prompt this debate, see Amitai Etzioni, *The Monochrome Society* (Princeton: Princeton University Press, 2003).

22. *John Wesley's Sermons: An Anthology*, ed. Albert C. Outler and Richard P. Heitzenrater (Nashville: Abingdon, [1760] 1991).

23. Andrew Carnegie, *The Gospel of Wealth and Other Timely Essays*, ed. Edward C. Kirkland (Cambridge: Harvard University Press, [1889] 1962).

24. See John Higginbotham, *Cicero on Moral Obligation* (London: Faber and Faber, 1967).

25. Warren Buffett quoted in Thomas S. Mulligan and Maggie Farley, "A Fortune Based on Good Fortune," *Los Angeles Times*, June 27, 2006. It is interesting to note that Buffett, in his public statements, echoed the point from the previous section about giving money away before you die rather than passing it all on to your children.

26. See Herbert Spiegelberg, "Good Fortune Obligates: Albert Schweitzer's Second Ethical Principle," *Ethics* 85, no. 3 (1975): 227–34; Albert Schweitzer, *Out of My Life and Thought: An Autobiography*, trans. C. T. Campion (New York: Henry Holt, [1933] 1949).

27. Catherine Ryan Hyde, *Pay It Forward* (New York: Pocket Books, 2000).

28. Boulding, *A Preface to Grants Economics*. See Michael Moody, "Serial Reciprocity." See also Michael Moody. "Reciprocity," in *Philanthropy in America: A Comprehensive Historical Encyclopedia*, ed. Dwight F. Burlingame (Santa Barbara: ABC-CLIO, 2004), 409–11.

29. For a discussion of the philanthropic applications of stewardship, see Michael Moody and Robert L. Payton, "Stewardship," in *Philanthropy in America*, ed. Burlingame, 457–60.

30. John Calvin, *Institutes of the Christian Religion*, ed. John T. McNeill, trans. Ford Lewis Battles (Philadelphia: Westminster, 1960), 3:7:5:695.

31. Kenneth E. Goodpaster, "Ethical Imperatives and Corporate Leadership," in *Business Ethics: The State of the Art*, ed. R. Edward Freeman (Oxford: Oxford University Press, 1991), 89–110.

32. John Gall, *Systemantics: How Systems Work and Especially How They Fail* (New York: Random House, 1977). Gall's view echoes the famous argument of Philip Selznick that institutions often experience "goal displacement," especially when the goals are ambiguous. See Philip Selznick, *TVA and the Grass Roots* (Berkeley: University of California Press, [1949] 1984).

33. William James, *Pragmatism* (Cambridge: Harvard University Press, [1907] 1975), 137.

34. See Paul R. Ehrlich, *The Population Bomb* (New York: Ballantine Books, 1968); Julian L. Simon, *The Ultimate Resource* (Princeton: Princeton University Press, 1981).

35. *Diagnostic and Statistical Manual of Mental Disorders, Fourth Edition, DSM-IV* (Washington, D.C.: American Psychiatric Association, 1994).

5. The Social History of the Moral Imagination

1. For a wonderful collection of commentaries on the meaning and practice of philanthropy in different cultural and religious traditions around the globe, including some that have received little attention from scholars in this field, see Warren Ilchman, Stanley N. Katz, and Edward Queen, eds., *Philanthropy in the World's Traditions* (Bloomington: Indiana University Press, 1998). For a collection of reflections on the philosophical influences on philanthropy in the western tradition broadly, see J. B. Schneewind, *Giving: Western Ideas of Philanthropy* (Bloomington: Indiana University Press, 1996).

2. These primary influences are, as we said, not the only ones affecting the American tradition, by any means. The others (e.g., native American tribal practices, the range of eastern philosophies of compassion, etc.) have, in certain times and places and for certain actors, contributed significantly to the social history of philanthropy. We hope other scholars can pay more attention to these influences than we can here.

3. Clifford Geertz, *Local Knowledge: Further Essays in Interpretive Anthropology* (New York: Basic Books, 1983), chapter 2.

4. There is a great deal of quality scholarship on the history of philanthropy already available that is more comprehensive than we can be here. For recent work on the American tradition, see Lawrence Friedman and Mark McGarvie, eds., *Charity, Philanthropy, and Civility in American History* (Cambridge: Cambridge University Press, 2003); Peter Dobkin Hall, "A Historical Overview of Philanthropy, Voluntary Associations, and Nonprofit Organizations in the United States, 1600–2000," in *The Nonprofit Sector*, ed. Powell and Steinberg, 32–65; and Kathleen McCarthy, *American Creed: Philanthropy and the Rise of Civil Society, 1700–1865* (Chicago: University of Chicago Press, 2003). David Hammack, ed., *The Making of the Nonprofit Sector in the United States: A Reader* (Bloomington: Indiana University Press, 2000), compiles and expertly introduces many classic documents and writings on most of the themes and milestones in the history that we highlight here. For a fascinating review of the history of philanthropy in western civilization beyond the United States that is more detailed than ours, see Kevin Robbins, "The Nonprofit Sector in Historical Perspective: Traditions of Philanthropy in the West," in *The Nonprofit Sector*, ed. Powell and Steinberg, 13–31.

5. See Robert L. Payton, "Philanthropic Values," in *Philanthropic Giving: Studies in Varieties and Goals*, ed. Richard Magat (New York: Oxford University Press, 1989), 29–45. Portions of that article are included in edited form in some sections that follow.

6. As we said in chapter 3, some people say charity and compassion are more than a religious teaching. For them they are "instinctive." Compassion is in our bones, perhaps even in our genes.

7. The property base on which al-Ghazali indicates levies were to be assessed is livestock—camels, cattle, and sheep—whereas the Bible mentions fields and vineyards. In Judaism, the book of Peah in the Mishnah talks at some length about the defective clusters of grapes that are to be left to the poor. In time a portion of the field (one source says one-sixtieth) was to be allocated to the poor. The word *peah* means edge or border.

8. Cyril Glasse, *The Concise Encyclopedia of Islam* (New York: Harper and Row, 1989), 431.

9. "Tradition is a fence for Torah. Tithes are a fence for wealth. Vows are a fence for abstinence. A fence for wisdom is silence." Jacob Neusner, *The Mishnah: A New Translation* (New Haven: Yale University Press, 1988), 680.

10. Nabih Amin Faris, *The Mysteries of Almsgiving* (Beirut: Heidelberg Press, 1966), 5.

11. Merle Curti, "Philanthropy," in *Dictionary of the History of Ideas*, vol. 3 (New York: Charles Scribner's and Sons, 1973), 489.

12. St. Thomas Aquinas, "Charity," in *Summa Theologiae*, vol. 34, trans. R. J. Batten, O.P. (London: Eyre and Spottiswoode, 1975), 241

13. Walter Trattner, *From Poor Law to Welfare State: A History of Social Welfare in America* (New York: Free Press, 1974), 4.

14. Brian Tierney, *Medieval Poor Law: A Sketch of Canonical Theory and Its Application in England* (Berkeley: University of California Press, 1959), 69–70.

15. Trattner, *From Poor Law to Welfare State*, 6.

16. Paul Veyne, *Bread and Circuses: Historical Sociology and Political Pluralism*, trans. Brian Pearce (London: Penguin, 1990), 10. Veyne attributes the neologism "euergetism" to Andre Boulanger and Henri I. Marrou, who created it from wording found in decrees of the Hellenistic period that honored public-minded persons. The word that meant "benefaction" was *euergesia*.

17. Curti, "Philanthropy," 487.

18. Veyne, *Bread and Circuses*, 10.

19. John Higginbotham, *Cicero on Moral Obligation* (London: Faber and Faber, 1967), 54.

20. Trattner, *From Poor Law to Welfare State*, 6–7.

21. W. K. Jordan, *Philanthropy in England, 1480 1660* (New York: Russell Sage Foundation, 1959), 17–19.

22. Ibid., 18.

23. Ibid., 17–19.

24. Robert Bellah, *The Broken Covenant: American Civil Religion in Time of Trial* (New York: Seabury Press, 1975), 17–18.

25. John Winthrop, "A Modell of Christian Charity," in *The American Intellectual Tradition*, 2nd ed., vol. 1, ed. David A. Hollinger and Charles Capper (New York: Oxford University Press, 1993), 15.

26. Bellah, *Broken Covenant*, 20.

27. Tocqueville, *Democracy in America*, 513.

28. Both quotes from Robert H. Bremner, *American Philanthropy* (Chicago: University of Chicago Press, 1960), 47. Recent historical scholarship on philanthropy in early America can be found in the references cited in note 4.

29. Tierney, *Medieval Poor Law*, 59.

30. Jordan, *Philanthropy in England*, 84.

31. For a review of the development and principles of scientific philanthropy, see Judith Sealander, "Curing Evils at Their Source: The Arrival of Scientific Giving," in *Charity, Philanthropy, and Civility in American History*, ed. Friedman and McGarvie, 217–39.

32. Andrew Carnegie, *The Gospel of Wealth and Other Timely Essays*, ed. Edward C. Kirkland (Cambridge: Harvard University Press, [1889] 1962). Carnegie's essay was originally published in two parts in the *North American Review:* 148 (June 1889): 653–64; and 149 (December 1889): 682–698.

33. See Barry Karl and Stanley N. Katz, "The American Private Philanthropic Foundation and the Public Sphere, 1890–1930," *Minerva* 19 (1981): 236–70.

34. The total number of library buildings that Carnegie gave to the English-speaking world was 2,507 (*Collier's Encyclopedia*, vol. 5, 1995).

35. Charles S. Loch, *How to Help Cases of Distress* (London: Charity Organisation Society, 1895), v–ix.

36. Herbert Spencer, *The Study of Sociology* (London: Henry S. King, 1873), chapter 1.

37. In that same year, the Charity Organization Society launched a new publication whose name, *The Charities Review: A Journal of Practical Sociology*, reflected its editors' values and approach.

38. Toynbee Hall was named in honor of Arnold Toynbee (1852–83), an English social reformer who had a great influence on reform movements in England. His particular concerns were to obtain housing, libraries, and parks for the working-class poor in the Whitehall district of London, where Toynbee Hall was located.

39. Jane Addams, "The Subjective Necessity for Social Settlements," in Robert A. Woods, *Philanthropy and Social Progress*, ed. Robert A. Woods (College Park, Md.: McGrath, [1893] 1969), 2.

40. Robert A. Woods, "The University Settlement Idea," in *Philanthropy and Social Progress*, 68, 61–62. Many of the early "schools of philanthropy," in fact, were connected to new academic departments for the emerging discipline of sociology.

41. On this point, and for a review of current social science scholarship on social movements, see Sidney Tarrow, *Power in Movement*, 2nd ed. (Cambridge: Cambridge University Press, 1998).

42. See Michael Moody, "Caring for Creation: Environmental Advocacy by Mainline Protestant Organizations," in *The Quiet Hand of God: Faith-Based Activism and the Public Role of Mainline Protestantism*, ed. Robert Wuthnow and John Evans (Berkeley: University of California Press, 2002), 237–64.

43. Karl and Katz, "The American Private Philanthropic Foundation and the Public Sphere," 236–70.

6. Philanthropy, Democracy, and the Future

1. As we have noted in previous chapters, there has been considerable comparative research on philanthropic activities and the voluntary, nonprofit, civil society sectors in other countries, including many other democracies. For reviews using different sorts of comparative data, see Lester M. Salamon, S. Wojciech Sokolowski, et al., *Global Civil Society: Dimensions of the Nonprofit Sector*, vol. 2 (Bloomfield, Conn.: Kumarian Press, 2004), and Robert Wuthnow, ed., *Between States and Markets: The Voluntary Sector in Comparative Perspective* (Princeton: Princeton University Press, 1991). This research shows, in general, that while voluntary organizations and giving play a crucial role in maintaining a free, open, and democratic society in many

nations around the globe, the nature, size, and understanding of that role varies quite a bit across democracies. For example, certain aspects of the democratic society and its governance patterns will influence the role of philanthropy in that democracy. These can include the size and type of government financing for voluntary groups and the set of beliefs in the political culture that affect (among other things) public attitudes toward such financing, the legal and regulatory structures that determine the treatment of nongovernmental groups (e.g., tax-exemption laws) and the allowable place of nonprofit versus for-profit or governmental providers of key services like education or health care, the level of wealth and wealthy individuals in a country, and so on. Recall how these and other factors are emphasized by the "social origins" theory of nonprofits—summarized in chapter 3—which complements nicely our conceptual framework in this book. See Helmut K. Anheier and Lester M. Salamon, "The Nonprofit Sector in Comparative Perspective," in *The Nonprofit Sector*, ed. Powell and Steinberg, 89–114.

2. We described this rise in cross-sectoral governance in chapter 3 and explained how Lester Salamon has highlighted this essential "partnership" role of the nonprofit sector for many years. There are a number of well-studied challenges involved in this ongoing, critical, close relationship between government and philanthropic organizations that we cannot examine in depth here. For a summary of these issues, see Elizabeth T. Boris and C. Eugene Steuerle, *Nonprofits and Government: Collaboration and Conflict*, 2nd ed. (Washington, D.C.: Urban Institute Press, 2006).

3. Tocqueville, *Democracy in America*, 522, 517, 521. For a summary of recent work supporting Tocqueville's point that voluntary associations are crucial sites of political socialization and the potential threat to this role from nonprofit professionalization, see Clemens, "The Constitution of Citizens."

4. We should note, however, that while this is the standard view, some research suggests that certain kinds of involvements in local voluntary groups can lead to an avoidance of such political discussion, at least in the everyday public activities of the association. See Nina Eliasoph, *Avoiding Politics: How Americans Produce Apathy in Everyday Life* (Cambridge: Cambridge University Press, 1998).

5. See Craig Jenkins, "Nonprofit Organizations and Political Advocacy," in *The Nonprofit Sector*, ed. Powell and Steinberg, 307–32; Jeffrey M. Berry and David F. Arons, *A Voice for Nonprofits* (Washington, D.C.: Brookings Institution Press, 2003); and Elizabeth T. Boris and Jeff Krehely, "Civic Participation and Advocacy," in *The State of Nonprofit America*, ed. Lester M. Salamon (Washington, D.C.: Brookings Institution Press, 2002).

6. Jeffrey Berry, *The Interest Group Society*, 3rd ed. (New York: Longman, 1996).

7. Robert Putnam, *Bowling Alone* (New York: Simon and Schuster, 2000). For another view that finds the same trend but interprets its democratic implications differently, see Theda Skocpol and Morris Fiorina, eds., *Civic Engagement in American Democracy* (Washington, D.C.: Brookings Institution Press, 1999).

8. Putnam, *Bowling Alone*, also argues that voluntary associations serve the democratic purpose of creating trust. For him, trust is part of the "social capital" that is created by associational activity.

9. For a recent review of the data on this, see Russell J. Dalton, *Democratic Challenges, Democratic Choices: The Erosion of Political Support in Advanced Industrial Democracies* (New York: Oxford University Press, 2004).

10. James Madison, "Number 10," in *The Federalist Papers*, 78, 82.

11. Jason Kaufman studied the associations that have been so celebrated as important to America's "golden age of fraternity" in the years between the Civil War and World War I, but he found that they promoted ethnic exclusion, parochialism, and economic self-interests rather than the "common good." See Jason Kaufman, *For the Common Good? American Civic Life and the Golden Age of Fraternity* (New York: Oxford University Press, 2002). See also Clemens, "The Constitution of Citizens," 211–12. These critiques raise questions about the social capital argument made by Putnam in *Bowling Alone* and suggest we should be careful not to make blanket statements about the positive democratic benefits of associations.

12. See Robert L. Payton, "A Tradition in Jeopardy," in *Philanthropy and the Nonprofit Sector in a Changing America*, ed. Charles T. Clotfelter and Thomas Ehrlich (Bloomington: Indiana University Press, 2001), 481–98.

13. T. S. Eliot, "Tradition and the Individual Talent," in *Selected Prose of T. S. Eliot*, ed. Frank Kermode (San Diego: Harcourt Brace, [1933] 1975), 38.

14. See David H. Smith, *Entrusted: The Moral Responsibilities of Trusteeship* (Bloomington: Indiana University Press, 1995).

15. Clifford Geertz, *Local Knowledge: Further Essays in Interpretive Anthropology* (New York: Basic Books, 1983), chapter 1.

16. Jacques Barzun, *The House of Intellect* (New York: Harper Perennial Modern Classics, 2002).

17. Christopher Hitchens, *The Missionary Position: Mother Teresa in Theory and Practice* (London: Verso, 1995).

Suggestions for Further Reading

Below is a list of twenty-five books that we recommend for those readers who wish to pursue further the ideas and questions raised in this book. We included some books that cover a particular area of scholarship on philanthropy that is relevant to our view (e.g., philanthropy in history, in literature, in other cultures), many books that summarize and/or theorize the field in general like we do in this book, and some edited volumes containing up to-date reviews of research on this field. There are a couple classics in here, too, from Carnegie and Tocqueville that we believe are worth reading in the original.

Needless to say, this is not an exhaustive list. It is biased, of course, toward the issues in the field that we highlight most in this book. Nor is it the best. But it will serve as a guide to the next steps for a reader eager to explore this emerging field of inquiry or to encounter other ways of explaining philanthropy's meaning and mission.

Twenty-five Books about Philanthropy

Bremner, Robert H. *American Philanthropy*. Rev. ed. Chicago: University of Chicago Press, 1988.

Burlingame, Dwight F., ed. *Philanthropy in America: A Comprehensive Historical Encyclopedia*. Santa Barbara: ABC-CLIO, 2004.

Carnegie, Andrew. *The Gospel of Wealth and Other Timely Essays*. Edited by Edward C. Kirkland. Cambridge: Harvard University Press, [1889] 1962.

Clotfelter, Charles T., and Thomas Ehrlich, eds. *Philanthropy and the Nonprofit Sector in a Changing America*. Bloomington: Indiana University Press, 2001.

Douglas, James. *Why Charity? The Case for a Third Sector*. Beverly Hills: Sage, 1983.

Friedman, Lawrence J., and Mark D. McGarvie, eds. *Charity, Philanthropy, and Civility in American History*. Cambridge: Cambridge University Press, 2003.

Frumkin, Peter. *On Being Nonprofit: A Conceptual and Policy Primer*. Cambridge: Harvard University Press, 2002.

Hammack, David C., ed. *The Making of the Nonprofit Sector in the United States: A Reader*. Bloomington: Indiana University Press, 2000.

Ilchman, Warren F., Stanley N. Katz, and Edward L. Queen II, eds. *Philanthropy in the World's Traditions*. Bloomington: Indiana University Press, 1998.

Kass, Amy A., ed. *The Perfect Gift: The Philanthropic Imagination in Poetry and Prose*. Bloomington: Indiana University Press, 2002.

Lohmann, Roger A. *The Commons: New Perspectives on Nonprofit Organizations and Voluntary Action*. San Francisco: Jossey-Bass, 1992.

Martin, Mike W. *Virtuous Giving: Philanthropy, Voluntary Service, and Caring.* Bloomington: Indiana University Press, 1994.

O'Neill, Michael. *Nonprofit Nation: A New Look at the Third America.* San Francisco: Jossey-Bass, 2002.

Payton, Robert L. *Philanthropy: Voluntary Action for the Public Good.* New York: American Council on Education/Macmillan, 1988.

Powell, Walter W., and Elisabeth S. Clemens, eds. *Private Action and the Public Good.* New Haven: Yale University Press, 1998.

Powell, Walter W., and Richard Steinberg, eds. *The Nonprofit Sector: A Research Handbook.* 2nd ed. New Haven: Yale University Press, 2006.

Putnam, Robert D. *Bowling Alone: The Collapse and Revival of American Community.* New York: Simon and Schuster, 2000.

Salamon, Lester M. *America's Nonprofit Sector: A Primer.* 2nd ed. New York: Foundation Center, 1999.

———, ed. *The State of Nonprofit America.* Washington, D.C.: Brookings Institution Press, 2003.

Schneewind, J. B., ed. *Giving: Western Ideas of Philanthropy.* Bloomington: Indiana University Press, 1996.

Smith, David H., ed. *Good Intentions: Moral Obstacles and Opportunities.* Bloomington: Indiana University Press, 2005.

Tocqueville, Alexis de. *Democracy in America.* New York: HarperPerennial, [1840] 1988.

Van Til, Jon. *Growing Civil Society: From Nonprofit Sector to Third Space.* Bloomington: Indiana University Press, 2000.

Weisbrod, Burton A. *The Nonprofit Economy.* Cambridge: Harvard University Press, 1988.

Wuthnow, Robert. *Acts of Compassion: Caring for Others and Helping Ourselves.* Princeton: Princeton University Press, 1991.

Index

Robert L. Payton is Professor Emeritus of philanthropic studies and was formerly director of the Center on Philanthropy at Indiana University. Educated at the University of Chicago, Payton's long career included service as president of the Exxon Education Foundation, president of Hofstra University and of C. W. Post College, and ambassador to Cameroon under President Lyndon Johnson. Among Payton's many honors are seven honorary degrees. He has lectured and published widely about philanthropy and is the author of *Philanthropy: Voluntary Action for the Public Good.*

Michael P. Moody is Assistant Professor in the School of Policy, Planning, and Development at the University of Southern California. He is a cultural sociologist whose work focuses on the theory and practice of philanthropy and on the analysis of advocacy professionals, political culture, and public policy debates such as those about environmental issues. Moody has degrees from Indiana University, the University of Chicago, and Princeton University.